D1106159

Language, Education and Society
in a Changing World

Multilingual Matters

The Age Factor in Second Language Acquistion
    D. SINGLETON and Z. LENGYEL (eds)
Approaches to Second Language Acquisition
    R. TOWELL and R. HAWKINS
Child Language
    MICHELLE ALDRIDGE (ed.)
Curriculum Related Assessment: Cummins and Bilingual Children
    TONY CLINE and NORAH FREDERICKSON (eds)
Distance Education for Language Teachers
    RON HOWARD and IAN McGRATH (eds)
Foundations of Bilingual Education and Bilingualism
    COLIN BAKER
Inspiring Innovations in Language Teaching
    JUDITH HAMILTON
The Good Language Learner
    N. NAIMAN, M. FRÖHLICH, H.H. STERN and A. TODESCO
Language Diversity Surveys as Agents of Change
    JOE NICHOLAS
Languages in Contact and Conflict
    SUE WRIGHT (ed.)
Language Reclamation
    HUBISI NWENMELY
Mission Incomprehensible: The Linguistic Barrier to Effective
Police Co-operation in Europe
    ROY D. INGLETON
Multilingual Japan
    JOHN C. MAHER and KYOKO YASHIRO (eds)
Policy and Practices in Bilingual Education
    O. GARCÍA and C. BAKER (eds)
Quantifying Language
    PHIL SCHOLFIELD
Reflections on Language Learning
    L. BARBARA and M. SCOTT (eds)
Second Language Practice
    GEORGES DUQUETTE (ed.)
Validation in Language Testing
    A. CUMMING and R. BERWICK (eds)

Please contact us for the latest book information:
Multilingual Matters Ltd, Frankfurt Lodge, Clevedon Hall,
Victoria Road, Clevedon, Avon, England, BS21 7SJ.

Language, Education and Society in a Changing World

Edited by

Tina Hickey and Jenny Williams

IRAAL/MULTILINGUAL MATTERS LTD
Dublin • Clevedon • Philadelphia • Adelaide

For Tim and Caitríona
and Tony and Tommy

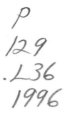

This publication and the conference from which it is drawn received financial support from the Commission of the European Community within the framework of the LINGUA programme (Action VA). The opinions expressed in this book are the sole responsibility of the authors themselves.

Library of Congress Cataloging in Publication Data

Language, Education and Society in a Changing World
Edited by Tina Hickey and Jenny Williams
Selection of papers from a conference hosted by the Irish Association for Applied Linguistics at the Marino Institute of Education in Dublin, June 1994.
1. Applied linguistics–Congresses. I. Hickey, Tina. II. Williams, Jenny.
III. Irish Association for Applied Linguistics
P129.L36   1996
418–dc20   95-23849

British Library Cataloguing in Publication Data

A CIP catalogue record for this book is available from the British Library.

ISBN 1-85359-315-X (hbk)

Irish Association for Applied Linguistics (IRAAL)
c/o ITE, 31 Fitzwilliam Place, Dublin 2, Ireland

Multilingual Matters Ltd
UK: Frankfurt Lodge, Clevedon Hall, Victoria Road, Clevedon, Avon BS21 7SJ.
USA: 1900 Frost Road, Suite 101, Bristol, PA 19007, USA.
Australia: P.O. Box 6025, 83 Gilles Street, Adelaide, SA 5000, Australia.

Typeset by Wayside Books, Clevedon.
Printed and bound in Great Britain by WBC Book Manufacturers Ltd.

97-27

Contents

SECOND LANGUAGE LEARNING/
SECOND LANGUAGE ACQUISITION

L1/L2 LITERACY

Preface

This collection draws on papers given at a conference in June 1994 hosted by the Irish Association for Applied Linguistics (IRAAL) with the theme *Language, Education and Society in a Changing World*. The conference, held in Marino Institute of Education, Dublin, attracted over one hundred papers from all five continents. The contributions in this volume are representative of the major issues discussed at the conference, and cover a wide geographical and theoretical range. The conference was organised under the auspices of AILA (Association Internationale de Linguistique Appliquée), and marked the thirtieth anniversary of its founding.

IRAAL is grateful to the LINGUA programme for the financial assistance and guidance it provided under Action VA. This support greatly facilitated both the organisation of the conference and the publication of this book, which makes the significant contribution of the conference to language teaching, research and planning available to a wider audience. The opinions expressed in the book are the sole responsibility of the authors themselves.

The editors wish to acknowledge the assistance of the IRAAL Conference Organising Committee, the Scientific Programme Committee and the Executive Committee. We are also grateful to Eoghan Mac Aogáin, the director of Institiúid Teangeolaíochta Éireann, and ITÉ staff, for their help. We would like to thank the contributors for their co-operation and we also wish to record our gratitude to Anne O'Neill for her invaluable assistance during the conference and in preparing this manuscript.

Introduction

TINA HICKEY and JENNY WILLIAMS

The papers in this volume are a selection from those presented at a conference whose theme was *Language, Education and Society in a Changing World*. This conference provided a forum for the discussion of some of the major issues facing language planners, policy makers, researchers and teachers, in a world where languages are becoming extinct at an alarming rate and are frequently a focus for dispute and conflict, where foreign language teaching and learning are confronted by new technological and practical demands, and where modern communication media require the development of new linguistic techniques. These factors, together with the continued slow economic and educational development in the third world, where access to a 'world language' is often promoted as an educational panacea, present applied linguistics with major philosophical as well as practical problems.

Mitchell addresses some of the issues relating to language and education and brings a refreshingly broad vision to a field which is too often viewed in a fragmentary way. She sees applied linguistics as the product of a liberal socio-political era, which must now review its role in the context of a politically less stable world. Ranging across mother-tongue teaching, foreign language education, language and learning across the curriculum, as well as language rights and language education policy, Mitchell argues for an integrative approach and outlines a strategy for applied linguistics into the twenty-first century. Ruane, responding to Mitchell, reflects on issues raised by Mitchell in relation to the current situation in language education in Ireland, and discusses the implications of Mitchell's approach.

Edwards considers the sociolinguistic implications of painful but inevitable social change, and argues that the question of identity (with language as one of its major markers), with its attendant socio-political unrest, constitutes a central issue for our times. He cautions applied linguists against simplistic formulations of current sociolinguistic problems, such as the view that 'authenticity' exists only in opposition to the 'mainstream'. He argues for the

1

inclusion in the debate about endangered minority languages an acknowledgement that the linguist is not always a disinterested observer, but can be
strongly committed to principles such as the maintenance of diversity. He
calls for greater efforts at developing a multidisciplinary approach to languages and language settings, in order to understand more fully the factors
influencing language maintenance and shift, and allow for greater breadth
of vision in the formulation of language policy. Ó Murchú, responding to
Edwards, considers the situation of the Irish language in the light of Edwards's
arguments. She looks to sociolinguistics to provide the tools of empowerment
for minority language policy makers and makes a plea for more collaborative research.

A number of papers consider the implications for *language policy* of
major social and political change. 1994 was a significant year for the Israeli–
Palestinian peace process and this situation of conflict also presents its unique
language planning requirements. Spolsky discusses language policy, past
and present, in the multilingual state of Israel, where for political, commercial,
cultural and heritage reasons a wide range of languages must be offered. He
stresses the need to build on the existing linguistic diversity and outlines
some of the major questions facing language policy makers in Israel. 1994
was also a significant year in the history of Ireland, with the declaration of
paramilitary ceasefires. Farren discusses recent language policy developments
in Northern Ireland, a society undergoing substantial change. Here segregated
schooling has produced two very different perspectives on education in general
and on language education in particular. He outlines recent changes in British
government education policy in Northern Ireland and considers the impact
of the cross-cultural themes of 'cultural heritage' and 'education for mutual
understanding' which have been implemented in all schools since 1989. Farren
compares and contrasts the effect of the new policy on the teaching of English
and Irish in a range of schools throughout Northern Ireland. He also discusses
the more positive policies towards the teaching of Irish resulting from political
pressures which seek parity of esteem for both cultural traditions.

Ó Laoire takes up the question of the Irish language in the context of the
Republic of Ireland. He reviews the efforts to revive Irish in the last two
hundred years, and draws instructive comparisons with the revitalisation of
Hebrew in Israel. By highlighting crucial dissimilarities between the successful
Hebrew and less successful Irish experiences, Ó Laoire makes proposals for
a more effective Irish language policy in the 1990s. Sarhimaa considers
language revitalisation in the context of the Republic of Karelia, part of the
former Soviet Union. She charts the language policies pursued by Soviet
and, for a brief period Finnish, governments between 1917 and the present
day. She discusses the results of these policies and reflects pessimistically on

the future of Karelian. Still within the former Soviet Union, Ter-Minasova outlines the legacy of teaching modern languages as though they were dead languages, in her discussion of the *planning of foreign language teaching* in the new political and social realities of today's Russia. She describes the challenges facing foreign language teachers as the result of the momentous changes of recent years. Despite the current difficulties, Ter-Minasova is confident that teachers will be able to build on the strengths of the past and adapt to the requirements of the future.

Mann addresses *language planning* issues in the post-colonial situation of Nigeria, and argues for the recognition of Anglo-Nigerian Pidgin (ANP) as an inter-ethnic *lingua franca*, and an appropriate means of empowering Nigerians. He bases his argument on an empirical study of attitudes towards ANP and its use, which provides evidence of a high level of acceptance of the language. Langan further explores the issue of empowerment through support for indigenous languages in Guatemala. She presents an ethnographic study of Mayan students, speakers of a range of Mayan languages, focusing on their role as agents of language change and maintenance. In her discussion of the Mayan situation she takes up the issue, raised by Edwards and Ó Murchú, of the linguist as participant rather than as disinterested observer.

Spoelders *et al.* return to the issue of *identity* in their study of *pronunciation in bilinguals*. They report on recent research which replicated in Belgium an Israeli study testing the hypothesis that bilinguals can only have fully native pronunciation in one language. The results obtained by Spoelders and the other members of the Ghent Bilingualism Research Group pose fundamental questions about the definition of a 'dominant' language and cast doubt on the widely accepted assumption that pronunciation is the ultimate marker of a person's linguistic identity. On the basis of this study, they recommend further research into syntactic and lexical markers of the linguistic ego. Backus examines a different type of *bilingualism*: that caused by recent population movements within Europe. Using the concept of *prototype,* he analyses the discourse of three generations of Turkish immigrants in The Netherlands, with particular reference to the type and frequency of code-switching. His analysis charts the emergence of a mixed lect in an immigrant community.

The notion of *prototypes* is taken up by Anderman, who relates recent work on prototypicality in psycholinguistics to *translation studies*. Anderman argues that insights from research in first and second language acquisition, for example in the area of the differences in verb typicality between languages, is of relevance for students and teachers of translation. Olohan and Zähner also discuss prototype theory in their attempt to develop a theoretical framework for translation studies which goes beyond the prescriptive and fragmentary approaches of the last few years. Rejecting the introspective method as theoretically unsound, they build on recent work in cognitive linguistics to delineate the parameters of a cognitive theory of translation. Focusing on another challenge for translation studies, O'Connell discusses the European-wide demand for media translation, with reference to her own experience in sub-titling. She touches on the technical aspects of translating for film and television, and draws out the implications of media translation for language policy and planning.

Gunnarsson deals with the issue of language planning with reference to Swedish and its relationship to a world language such as English. Within the framework of text analysis, she examines the *cultural and ideological dimensions of text patterns* and text production. On the basis of a corpus of medical texts she demonstrates the influence of English on Swedish scientific texts and raises questions about the future status of languages such as Swedish. Gibbon, too, analyses the cultural and ideological dimensions of texts, on the basis of a corpus of French, Belgian, Irish and English medical texts in the field of infertility treatment. Her contribution exposes the assumptions which underlie the syntactic and lexical choices made by the text producers.

A different aspect of *cultural awareness* is explored by Mac Mathúna in relation to language teaching. He describes the neglect of the cultural dimension in the teaching of Irish, and proposes the implementation of cultural awareness components in the Irish classroom. He views these as enriching *per se*, as well as being a means of sensitising pupils to the Irish culture around them in everyday life. Heffernan analyses the *cultural content* of French- and English-language history school-books in immersion and non-immersion classrooms in Canada. On the basis of a study of four groups of teachers and learners he draws conclusions about the effectiveness of different strategies of teaching culturally loaded material and considers the implications of his results for immersion education.

Among the papers dealing with second language learning, Cohen also discusses issues relating to *immersion*. With the aid of introspective reports, he explores the effect of linguistic interference on the performance of mathematical (i.e. non-linguistic) tasks. His results pose some fundamental questions about the nature and definition of immersion. Harris and Murtagh report on a different type of language learning situation in elementary school, with the results of their *classroom observation study* of the teaching of Irish in primary school. Using an adaptation of the Stirling system of lesson analysis, they analyse the nature of language interaction and use in the learning situation. Their conclusions draw out the implications of variation in lesson structure and content for second language achievement.

Computer Assisted Language Learning has attracted much interest in recent times. Buchholz and Düsterhöft discuss some of the developments in relation to databases, and assess their potential as a language teaching tool. They present a programme developed in Rostock for teaching English as a foreign language, which incorporates a number of linguistic and cultural features in a user-friendly way. Chambers discusses another recently burgeoning area, that of *Languages for Specific Purposes.* She takes as her starting point research in English for Specific Purposes and considers the relevance of the ESP experience for the much more recent developments in LSP. She assesses the relevance of the concept of discourse community, the importance of needs analysis and the role of cultural studies in each field. Her conclusions provide fruitful insights into the complex relationship between ESP and other Languages for Specific Purposes and highlight not only areas of significant difference but also areas for potential collaboration.

The L2 language learner arrives in the language class with a complex set of *motivations,* which recent research shows to be as much a result of successful learning as its cause. Ushioda's paper demonstrates just how diverse and variable these motivations are, using qualitative data from a group of learners. She points to changes over time in different aspects of motivation and takes a holistic approach to the learner by acknowledging the influence of competing interests and life events on the language learning process. Singleton also draws on data from the Trinity Modern Languages Research Project to analyse the way in which language learners store lexical items. He rejects both the separatist and integrationist model of bilingual *lexical organisation* and argues for a more flexible model of L1 and L2 lexical interaction.

First and second language reading skills have begun in recent years to receive more attention within applied linguistics, rather than being seen as peripheral disciplines, and the field is represented by three contributions in this collection. Tomlinson reports on the teaching of visualisation skills to second language readers, and outlines a number of methods of teaching such skills. He argues that visualisation improves L2 reading comprehension, by forcing learners to draw on their knowledge of the world and to make deductions from the preceding text. Masuhara *et al.* consider the relative merits of extensive reading as opposed to strategy training in L2 reading. Their results, based on a study of Japanese college students, indicate that both interventions improved reading performance, but the extensive reading group showed a greater improvement. They speculate about the factors influencing these results, and suggest that the success of strategy training may depend on learner variables such as developmental stage, learning style and their language learning experience. They suggest future research into the questions about why extensive reading works. Walker brings the discussion of language, education and society to a close by 'thinking crazy' about mother tongue literacy. In so doing he ranges across a number of issues raised by Mitchell and Edwards. He argues for mother-tongue education and literacy programmes which are generated by local communities, rather than by external aid agencies, and suggests the outlines of such an innovative approach.

The contributors to this volume present a number of the central challenges facing applied linguistics world-wide at the end of the twentieth century. Language is shown to be crucial to questions of identity, education, science, technology and culture. Applied linguistics emerges as an inter-discipline whose brief goes far beyond the narrow confines of academia, and embraces the major social and political issues of our time. This collection underlines the need for applied linguistics to avoid its traditionally compartmentalized and somewhat fragmentary approach and marshall the combined forces of its subdisciplines in order to meet the challenges of a changing world.

1 Language, Education and Applied Linguistics in a Changing World

ROSAMOND MITCHELL

Introduction

In this paper my aim is to bring an applied linguistics perspective to bear on a selection of educational issues concerning language, most of which are as old as organised schooling itself. In each case, we will scrutinise the contribution which applied linguistics has so far made to the development both of theory and of educational practice, and then go on to consider how applied linguists can most usefully contribute to further development, building on established strengths but also moving into relatively neglected areas.

Historically, mid-twentieth-century applied linguistics appears as the product of a relatively liberal era in education, in which progressivism vied with social reconstructionism as dominant philosophies. It can be seen as a largely scientific/rationalist project, with a reforming ethos in which greater knowledge and understanding of language and language learning would more or less unproblematically inform educational change and improvement. While a minority group within applied linguistics has questioned this view (e.g. Phillipson, 1992; Pennycook, 1994), many applied linguistics texts may be cited to illustrate it; for example, some clear examples are to be found in the recent AILA publication, *Language Teaching in the Twenty-first Century* (Matter, 1992).

However, as the century draws to a close, the optimism which informed earlier decades of applied linguistic activity must be questioned. In retrospect the relative political stability and bright prospects for economic development which characterised the post-World War II period seem much more a matter of temporary good fortune than we imagined. Our perceptions are now of a much more unsettled world, where the collapse of the Soviet Union and much of its sphere of influence has brought about no unproblematic transition to democracy and economic development through market forces, but instead economic dislocation, unemployment and the rise of ethnic and nationalist forces with associated regional conflicts. Parts of the world continue to make striking economic progress, including some sections of the ex-'third world', notably in the Pacific Rim. Here, the wonders of information technology, from CALL to computational linguistics to the Internet, seem to transform the possibilities for the scientific community, including applied linguistic activity. But other areas are characterised by increasing poverty, institutiona- lised debt and political instability. Within the developed world itself, notions of public service and the common good are weakened, with long term struc- tural unemployment creating an underclass increasingly uncoupled from the economic prosperity of the rest, ghettoised and with little realistic prospect for collective economic improvement. Applied linguists, like other specialists, have choices to make, as to how broadly we are willing to define our remit and our responsibilities in this changing world. Do we continue to practise our scientific-rationalist project on the life raft of the developed world, or do we sustain commitments to low-tech activity elsewhere, sensitive to a much more diverse range of sociocultural and political conditions?

Against this background view of our 'changing world', the educational areas which will briefly be considered are:

- Mother tongue and standard language education.
- Foreign language education.
- Language and learning across the curriculum.
- Language rights and language education policies.

Mother Tongue and Standard Language Education

Despite aspirations to be inclusive (as evidenced for example in the wide range covered by the commissions of AILA), it seems that applied linguistics as a discipline has established its identity primarily in respect of second/ foreign language education. For example, in the AILA Review volume mentioned earlier (Matter, 1992), just two out of the six papers pay some serious attention to issues of mother tongue/national language teaching (Trim, 1992; Gonzalez, 1992); the papers on language instruction (Single- ton, 1992), on assessment (de Jong, 1992) and on technology and language education (Jung, 1992), which might on the face of it have dealt with first language education, all assume an audience concerned with second/foreign languages. Scrutiny of such documents as, for example, the recent records of

AILA congresses, makes it clear that where applied linguists do occupy themselves with mother tongues, they tend to be interested mostly in the educational role and scope of 'minority' languages.

This is not to say, of course, that recognisably 'applied linguistic' activity does not take place with respect to national standard languages. The vast fields of L1 acquisition research, and of literacy research, largely have to do mostly with such languages. Yet, despite periodic efforts to incorporate literacy research within the scope of 'applied linguistics' (e.g. Grabe, 1992), researchers within these fields do not universally regard themselves as members of our applied linguistics community. Similarly, while positive connections have been made in some domains (genre studies, sociolinguistics, discourse analysis), the large and educationally influential communities of teachers of standard languages do not typically show up at applied linguistics conferences, read our journals, or seek our guidance more generally on matters of learning theory or pedagogy.

There are obvious historical reasons for this: contemporary standard language teaching derives from a wide variety of historical roots, by no means all linguistic in nature (see e.g. Michael, 1987 for English). However, a range of issues currently under contention within standard language education could clearly benefit from greater applied linguistic input. The effective teaching of 'oracy', now commonly part of the standard language curriculum (see e.g. Norman, 1992) requires applied linguistic insights into the nature of spoken language and its relationship with written standards. The renewed commitment to 'language awareness' or 'knowledge about language' in standard language education (Keith, 1990) will also benefit from applied linguistic perspectives regarding goals, developmental sequences and pedagogic approaches. If applied linguists show interest in the role of grammar instruction/consciousness-raising within the foreign language curriculum, they should recognise that a similar research agenda lies virtually untouched for standard language education.

There is indeed a history of attempted applied linguistic intervention in the standard language curriculum. In Britain, the 'Language in Use' project of the 1970s (Doughty, 1971) tried to promote a Hallidayan perspective on language study among English mother tongue teachers, but foundered on teachers' loyalty to literary and 'personal growth' traditions. The 'Language in the National Curriculum' project of the late 1980s (Carter, 1990; LINC, n.d.) again tried to promote a text-based perspective on systematic language study, but fell foul of the conservative cultural preoccupations of British government ministers. The genre-focused movement in Australian language education (see e.g. Cope & Kalantzis, 1993) seems the most successful current example of applied linguistics influence in standard language teaching. However, despite this mixed history, there are broader reasons why applied linguists should now seriously become engaged with the standard language teaching agenda, beyond the technical expertise they can offer on issues such as oracy or grammar teaching. Standard language teaching is necessarily entwined with social and cultural issues to do with national identities, and in a number of countries is currently an ideological battleground.

In the latest version of the British National Curriculum proposals, for example (SCAA, 1994), it is asserted that the top curriculum priority for English language is the explicit teaching of Standard English grammar and vocabulary to a population who, by implication, do not know it. These proposals have clearly lost all touch with linguistic reality. As Stubbs (1986), Trudgill & Chambers (1991), and other linguists have pointed out, the grammar of contemporary English in England is actually strikingly uniform, though working class speech is typically characterised by a small number of non-standard forms, which function as 'markers' in a classic sociolinguistic sense (Scherer & Giles, 1979). Similarly, the vocabulary of Standard English is simply not definable on linguistic grounds. The Standard/non-Standard distinction is an ideological rather than a scientific/linguistic construct (Widdowson, 1993), and it is very difficult to discern any workable pedagogic principles which could follow from it.

Applied linguists surely have a responsibility to contribute to debate in such contexts. Firstly, it is important that we equip our teacher colleagues with the fullest information on the actual nature of variation in contemporary standard languages, and its primarily sociolinguistic and generic bases, drawing for example on the recent valuable contributions of computational linguistics to genre studies (e.g. Biber, 1988) as well as on longer-established sociolinguistic traditions. Thus, we must actively engage in debate regarding the proper linguistic content of the teacher education curriculum for mother tongue/standard language teachers, as well as for foreign language teachers. But a disinterested provision of rational information will not alone be enough. In addition, we must dissect and make visible the 'language complaint' traditions which have historically been associated with standard languages (for English, see e.g. Milroy & Milroy, 1985; Crowley, 1991), and of which the current Standard English panic is one of the latest manifestations.

Foreign Language Education

In foreign language education, we turn to one of the central concerns of our discipline (Trim, 1992). We all recognise that applied linguistics has made sustained theoretical and practical contributions to FLs education, notably through the 'communicative language teaching' and 'language for specific purposes' movements, which have systematically promoted new ideas on the nature of language proficiency, design principles for FLs curricula, and classroom methodology. The ideas that language is best learned experientially, through meaning-oriented use, and to behaviourally defined ends, have been central, and have driven e.g. the immersion and content-based instructional programmes of North America (e.g. Snow, 1990; Crandall & Tucker, 1990), as well as bilingual schooling in Europe (Baetens Beardsmore, 1993), and many smaller-scale initiatives within the traditional teaching of FLs.

After 25 years or so of development however, the communicative language teaching movement is ready for self-evaluation and critique. Researchers who have tracked the North American immersion movement have moved on from the documentation and celebration of the undoubted learning achievements of immersion students, to examine critically the limitations to their achievement, and, in particular, the issue of fossilisation. In Canada, interventionist research programmes are under way, which seek to destabilise premature fossilisation through a renewed and re-conceived 'focus on form' (e.g. Spada & Lightbown, 1993; Lyster, 1994).

Those of us who are concerned with the teaching of FLs as individual curriculum subjects are also confronting the mixed implementation and results of communicative language teaching. Functional syllabuses, and methods involving group work, role play, etc. have in some contexts led to shallow phrasebook-style learning and continued pupil dependency on teachers who have largely deleted reflection and explanation from the classroom diet, while marginalising reading and FL literacy in favour of the rehearsal of transactional talk. In an in-depth study of the teaching of English in Malaysian secondary schools, Hamid (1995) has shown that a functional syllabus and communicative style methodological package can operate well in settings where pupils have supplementary contacts with English outside school. (Though even here, there were unsolved tensions between meaning-oriented pedagogy and perceived needs for exam practice to ensure high grades in an accuracy-focused school leaving exam.) But such a package has not by any means solved the problems of rural schools where pupils typically encounter English only in the classroom, and have an insufficient language base to cope with discussions, debates, problem-solving, etc.

Two somewhat different directions seem to offer themselves in current debates as solutions for these problems. One is to break the linguistic restraints of a functional syllabus itself and to move to an entirely 'task-based' model, which integrates both syllabus and methodology into a sequence of project-style activities (see e.g. Skehan, 1993; Crookes & Gass, 1993). The other trend builds on 'good language learner' and 'learning strategies' research (e.g. O'Malley & Chamot, 1990), and argues that an element of classroom time should be reserved for developing learners' reflective and analytic skills, so that they can take more conscious and self-aware control of the language learning context and process (as in Ellis & Sinclair, 1989). Theoretical discussions which promote 'input enhancement' through 'consciousness-raising', 'focus on form', etc. (Sharwood-Smith, 1993) are clearly connected with this trend.

Each of these possibilities has its potential pitfalls. The task-based model runs the obvious risk of falling into the fossilisation trap discernible in the immersion tradition. The 'learner autonomy/consciousness-raising' tradition runs the risk of reviving traditional structure-centred language learning, albeit in more learner-friendly styles, at the expense of hard-won experiential gains. To maintain a principled approach to development in FL education, it is vital that we stay in touch with the, at times, forbidding abstractions of second language acquisition research. It has been an historical fact about communicative language teaching that, while the concept of 'communicative competence' offered a shared view of the goal of FL teaching, no unified or well-developed learning theory underlay the movement, and teaching ideas were drawn from a wide range of traditions. Under favourable circumstances this openness and theory-neutrality has led to great flexibility and creativity, but *ad hocery* and conservatism have also been able to survive under the communicative language teaching banner. Over the past 15 years or so, however, great activity in the SLA field has resulted in a range of much better-worked-out theoretical orientations, which can inform (though not, of course, govern) our FL teaching practice. Thus, interlanguage studies and Universal Grammar theory offer many productive starting points for the development of principles for task-based learning, and for its evaluation; similarly, cognitive theories of SLA offer a rationale and critical perspective for more analytic approaches.

In the 'changing world' of the next few decades, however, there is a serious question as to how able and willing classroom teachers will be to innovate in a principled manner, in the light of maturing experience of communicative language teaching and developing theoretical insights into language learning. A de-professionalisation of teaching is detectable internationally to a degree, as the 'new right' attacks liberal education as a source of economic and cultural decline. Where intellectual traditions of 'reflective practice' are permitted to flourish (Wallace, 1991), the FL teacher can reasonably be expected to draw upon a mix of theoretical knowledge as well as upon sociocultural knowledge of the context within which she operates (Wright, 1992), in a creative manner, devising an appropriately tailored scheme of work and teaching methodology for the particular group of learners for whom she has responsibility. Where the craft of teaching is constrained by rigid behavioural competency specifications, the conservative dogma of 'good practice' unconstrained by problematising and enquiry is likely to prevail.

Language and Learning Across the Curriculum

Applied linguists have taken a long-standing active interest in relationships between language use, cognitive development and academic achievement. But, again, these interests have to a considerable extent been concerned with second language/multilingual contexts. Research on immersion education has monitored the consequences of schooling through a second/foreign language for academic achievement, with generally reassuring results (Swain & Lapkin, 1984). Research on bilingual education has monitored outcomes in terms of general academic achievement as well as language learning, and has also concerned itself with interactions between levels of bilingual proficiency and overall cognitive development (though with less clear-cut results: see e.g. reviews and discussion in Padilla et al., 1990a).

Historically however, much of this research was conducted within an 'evaluation' paradigm, somewhat one-sidedly preoccupied with the products or outcomes of different patterns of schooling, and it is increasingly recognised that we have neglected to explore the more detailed processes of interaction within bilingual or immersion classrooms; the explanatory power of much early immersion research was thus relatively weak. Even where immersion researchers have looked at classroom processes, they have tended to confine their concerns to the nature of the language learning opportunities on offer (e.g. Snow, 1990). But in studying the processes of immersion and/or bilingual education, we must surely not restrict ourselves to the language learning opportunities which these programmes provide, and pay serious attention also to the means whereby learners in such classrooms access academic content and develop their conceptual understandings.

In the limited number of cases where process studies of immersion have addressed issues of conceptual and academic development, they reveal a complex picture. For example, De Mejia (1994) has drawn a vivid picture of the first months of 'immersion' in English for kindergarten-aged pupils in Colombia. It seems that over the first months at least, the teachers in her study relied very substantially on ringing the changes through variety of activities, while the actual academic content of immersion classes comprised already-familiar material. This cognitively undemanding period was seen by the teachers as a necessary preliminary stage, before genuinely new academic content could be introduced directly through the target immersion language. Cohen (1994) is looking at immersion at a somewhat later stage, when 'new' content is supposedly being taught through the target language (in his case, Spanish). However, in a close study of children working individually on academic tasks (Mathematics), Cohen demonstrates continuing reliance on the first language (English) for reasoning and for calculations, despite use of Spanish by the teacher as the 'public' language for task explanation etc.

Descriptive research thus can reveal a variety of complications in the relationship between conceptual content and language medium in the dual-language context. Our colleagues in the general educational research tradition which seeks to unravel what it is that makes one school more 'effective' than another are in no doubt that the quality of classroom interaction is a vital ingredient in effective schooling. In a recent review, Gipps (1994: 30) summarises the conclusions of a series of major studies on the classroom behaviours of effective teachers, as suggesting:

> the importance of high levels of questioning and the need to engage in strategies which allow maximum levels of sustained interaction with all pupils . . . Too much teacher questioning is 'closed' and leads to low-level responses from the children. What raises the level of response is offering a longer response time. . . . or teacher input which is high in cognitive level itself – for example offering speculations, hypotheses and conjectures. . . .

Because of its large scale and quantitative nature, however, research in this 'school effectiveness' tradition relies on relatively crude and broad-brush observational measures to document classroom interaction. Typically, systematic time-sampling or 'sign' systems appropriate for survey and evaluation research are used (Croll, 1986). However, they are much less well adapted to the explanation of classroom interaction processes and precisely how different forms of classroom talk impact on learning, at an ongoing micro level.

Here, applied linguists surely have specialist expertise to offer our colleagues in general educational research. In fact, applied linguists have been trying to model classroom interaction in more comprehensive ways for many years, seeking rules and patterns which link successive utterances into larger conversational units. Unfortunately the most influential applied linguistic proposals of the 1970s for the modelling of classroom conversation, those of Sinclair & Coulthard (1975), were not connected with any systematic theory of the role of language in learning, and now seem an excessively formalist educational dead end. Many applied linguists have retreated to a selective functional analysis of classroom talk, counting occurrence frequencies for utterance types judged to realise educationally useful functions; examples are to be found in the many recent studies of the negotiation of meaning in the FL classroom (e.g. Long, 1983; Pica, 1987). However, the ultimate explanatory power of this research tradition, with respect to language learning, seems limited in similar ways to the general educational observation schemes which count 'higher order questions' etc.

Two other traditions for the study of interaction seem more promising for understanding the relationship between classroom talk and classroom learning. Firstly, ethnomethodology offers a more flexible way of examining the local organisation of talk, already being applied in the understanding of 'talk at work' and para-educational discourse such as doctor–patient talk (e.g. Drew & Heritage, 1992). Secondly, the Vygotskyan tradition within developmental psychology offers a theory which integrates linguistic and cognitive development, and with the concept of the 'Zone of Proximal Development', offers a powerful impetus for the detailed study of learner–teacher interaction over time (see review by Lantolf, 1994).

Like formalist discourse analysis, Vygotskyan ideas are not new to those concerned with language in education. Over 20 years ago, Vygotskyan thinking informed arguments for the introduction of group work and for the role of 'expressive' talk in conceptual development (Barnes *et al.*, 1969) – an important underpinning of the later 'oracy' movement (Norman, 1992). However, this early work was methodologically somewhat problematic and open to criticisms of over-interpretation. More recent work in a revived tradition which examines closely the development of classroom talk and the management of conceptual content over time (e.g. Edwards & Mercer, 1987; Maybin *et al.*, 1992; Mercer, 1994) is much less vulnerable to these criticisms, and offers exciting prospects for a role for applied linguistics at the heart of the study of learning across the curriculum.

Language Rights and Language Education Policies

The final issue to which we will turn our attention briefly is intertwined with all the others. It is possible to discern an international trend favouring the formalisation both of 'language rights', and of language-in-education policies. Phillipson & Skutnabb-Kangas (1993) have reviewed historical moves on the part of a range of international organisations to promulgate formal statements of the language rights of minorities; they point out that such policy statements are becoming more specific with respect to education. In addition to general statements opposing discrimination on grounds of language and supporting the rights of linguistic minorities to use their own language, which date back to the immediate post-war period, recent declarations by the UN (1992), and by the European Union (1992) make particular reference to the right to education in minority mother tongues. The European Commission is also keen to promote a policy of enhanced foreign language learning, though continuing national control of education systems keeps these embryo policies at the level largely of aspirations (Coulmas, 1991). Phillipson and Skutnabb-Kangas themselves argue a maximalist case for minority language rights, including the right of minority groups to a full education through the medium of the mother tongue, in addition to access to one or more official languages of their state. However, it is far from clear that this position attracts universal support, e.g. in many multilingual African states, where education through English or another language of wider communication is seen as a vital key to economic advancement (Haacke, 1994; Webb, 1994).

In addition to these international developments, an increasing will for the formalisation of language-in-education policy is apparent within a variety of nation states. In England, the introduction of a National Curriculum for schools has led to a series of decisions specifying the central place of 'Standard English' in the school language curriculum, the exclusion from the primary school curriculum of all other languages (including minority community languages), and the prescription of a short list of 'foreign languages' from which the newly-compulsory 'first foreign language' to be studied at secondary school level must be chosen (Mitchell, 1991; 1993; Stubbs, 1991). In the United States, the 1980s political movement to make English the 'official' language of the Union, though not yet successful at Federal level, carries obvious implications for language-in-education policy, e.g. the restriction of the use of languages other than English as media of instruction in bilingual/immersion programmes (Ruiz, 1994). In Australia on the other hand, the successive National Policy on Languages (1987) and Australian Language and Literacy Policy (1991), which despite their titles are largely concerned with language-in-education policy, aim to promote the learning of a range of languages other than English alongside the mastery of spoken and written English by all citizens (Eggington, 1994). Applied linguists and language professionals more generally have played a considerable role in the debates surrounding many of these national policy initiatives (notably in the US and Australia), informing debate and generally arguing on the side of linguistic pluralism. But the overall trend towards greater formalisation of language rights and language-in-education policies (and consequently potentially towards greater centralisation and political control of these matters) seems irreversible, and applied linguists around the world need to find an appropriate role in the process.

Conclusion

We thus identify a mixed agenda, as applied linguistics seeks to engage with language education issues in our changing world. Firstly we must pursue our research agenda, addressing the great issues of the relations between language and cognitive development, and of language learning itself, in the light of both new and rediscovered theoretical insights. Secondly we must defend and develop the professionalism of language teachers, so that curriculum and methodological innovation are both principled and broad-based. But to keep these agendas in being, in a changing world of economic imbalance and political instability, and to maintain our pluralist traditions of improvement and of equal opportunity in education, there is no doubt that we must also become more 'engaged' in policy debates than heretofore – whether over standard language teaching, over the choice of medium of instruction, or which foreign languages to teach to whom and when.

References

Baetens Beardsmore, H. (ed.) (1993) *European Models of Bilingual Education.* Clevedon: Multilingual Matters.

Barnes, D., Britton, J. and Rosen, H. (1969) *Language, the Learner and the School.* Harmondsworth: Penguin.

Biber, D. (1988) *Variation Across Speech and Writing.* Cambridge: Cambridge University Press.

Bourne, J. (ed.) (1994) *Thinking Through Primary Practice.* London: Routledge.

Carter, R. (ed.) (1990) *Knowledge About Language and the Curriculum.* London: Hodder & Stoughton.

Cohen, A. (1994) The extent of genuine language immersion in immersion programmes. Paper presented at AAAL Annual Conference, Baltimore, March 1994.

Cope, B. and Kalantzis, M. (1993) *The Powers of Literacy: A Genre Approach to Teaching Writing.* Brighton: Falmer.

Coulmas, F. (ed.) (1991) *A Language Policy for the European Community: Prospects and Quandaries.* Berlin: Mouton de Gruyter.

Crandall, J. and Tucker, G.R. (1990) Content-based instruction in second and foreign languages. In A. Padilla *et al.* (eds) *Foreign Language Education: Issues and Strategies* (pp. 187–200). Newbury Park: Sage.

Croll, P. (1986) *Systematic Classroom Observation.* Lewes: Falmer.

Crookes, A. and Gass, S.M. (1993) *Tasks and Language Learning: Integrating Theory and Practice.* Clevedon: Multilingual Matters.

Crowley, T. (1991) *Proper English? Readings in Language, History and Cultural Identity.* London: Routledge.

de Jong, J.H.A.L. (1992) Assessment of language proficiency in the perspective of the twenty-first century. In J.F. Matter (ed.) *Language Teaching in the Twenty-first Century: Problems and Prospects* (pp. 39–45). AILA Review no. 9.

de Mejia, A.-M. (1994) Bilingual teaching/learning events in early immersion classes. Unpublished PhD Thesis, University of Lancaster.

Doughty, P. *et al.* (1971) *Language in Use.* London: Edward Arnold.

Drew, P. and Heritage, J. (eds) (1992) *Talk at Work: Interaction in Institutional Settings.* Cambridge: Cambridge University Press.

Edwards, D. and Mercer, N. (1987) *Common Knowledge: The Development of Understanding in the Classroom.* London: Methuen.

Eggington, W. (1994) Language policy and planning in Australia. In W. Grabe (ed.) *Language Policy and Planning: Annual Review of Applied Linguistics 14* (pp. 137–55). Cambridge: Cambridge University Press.

Ellis, G. and Sinclair, B. (1989) *Learning to Learn English.* Cambridge: Cambridge University Press.

Gipps, C. (1994) What we know about effective primary teaching. In J. Bourne (ed.) *Thinking Through Primary Practice* (pp. 22–39). London: Routledge.

Gonzalez, A. (1992) Prospective issues and problems of language teaching in the third world. In J.F. Matter (ed.) *Language Teaching in the Twenty-first Century: Problems and Prospects* (pp. 55–62). AILA Review no. 9, Amsterdam: AILA.

Grabe, W. (ed.) (1994) *Language Policy and Planning: Annual Review of Applied Linguistics 14.* Cambridge: Cambridge University Press.

Grabe, W. *et al.* (eds) (1992) *Literacy: Annual Review of Applied Linguistics 12.* Cambridge: Cambridge University Press.

Haacke, W. (1994) Language policy and planning in Namibia. In W. Grabe (ed.) *Literacy: Annual Review of Applied Linguistics 12* (pp. 240–53). Cambridge: Cambridge University Press.

Hamid, R.A. (1995) The interconnections between English in Malaysian secondary schools and English language needs in the workplace. Unpublished Ph.D thesis, University of Southampton.

Jung, U.O.H. (1992) Technology and language education in the twenty-first century. In J.F. Matter (ed.) *Language Teaching in the Twenty-first Century: Problems and Prospects.* AILA Review no. 9 (pp. 21–38). Amsterdam: AILA.

Keith, G. (1990) Knowledge about language. In J. Harris and J. Wilkinson (eds) *In the Know: A Guide to English Language in the National Curriculum.* Cheltenham: Stanley Thornes.

Kennedy, C. (ed.) (1993) *IATEFL Annual Conference Report 1993.* Whitstable: IATEFL.

Lantolf, J.P. (1994) Sociocultural psycholinguistics: A brief historical overview. Paper presented at AAAL Annual Conference, Baltimore, March 1994.

LINC (n.d.) *Language in the National Curriculum: Materials for Professional Development.* Department of English Studies, University of Nottingham.

Long, M. (1983) Linguistic and conversational adjustments to non-native speakers. *Studies in Second Language Acquisition* 12/4, 177–94.

Lyster, R. (1994) The effect of functional-analytic teaching on aspects of French immersion students' sociolinguistic competence. *Applied Linguistics* 15/3.

Matter, J.F. (ed.) (1992) *Language Teaching in the Twenty-first Century: Problems and Prospects.* AILA Review no. 9. Amsterdam: AILA.

Maybin, J, Mercer, N, and Stierer, B. (1992) 'Scaffolding' learning in the classroom. In K. Norman (ed.) *Thinking Voices: The Work of the National Oracy Project.* London: Hodder & Stoughton.

Meara, P. and Ryan, A. (eds) (1991) *Language and Nation. British Studies in Applied Linguistics 6.* London: BAAL/CILT.

Mercer, N. (1994) Language in educational practice. In J. Bourne (ed.) *Thinking Through Primary Practice* (pp. 85–98). London: Routledge.

Michael, I. (1987) *The Teaching of English*. Cambridge: Cambridge University Press.

Milroy, J. and Milroy, L. (1985) *Authority in Language*. London: Routledge & Kegan Paul.

Mitchell, R. (1991) Multilingualism in British schools: future policy directions. In P. Meara and A. Ryan (eds) *Language and Nation. British Studies in Applied Linguistics 6*. London: BAAL/CILT.

— (1993) Diversity or uniformity? Multilingualism and the English teacher in the 1990s. In C. Kennedy (ed.) *IATEFL Annual Conference Report 1993* (pp. 9–16). Whitstable: IATEFL.

Norman, K. (ed.) (1992) *Thinking Voices: The Work of the National Oracy Project*. London: Hodder & Stoughton.

O'Malley, J.M. and Chamot, A.U. (1990) *Learning Strategies in Second Language Acquisition*. Cambridge: Cambridge University Press.

Padilla, A.M, Fairchild, H.H and Valadez, C.M. (eds) (1990a) *Bilingual Education: Issues and Strategies*. Newbury Park: Sage.

— (1990b) *Foreign Language Education: Issues and Strategies*. Newbury Park: Sage.

Pennycook, A. (1994) Incommensurable discourses. *Applied Linguistics* 15/2, 115–38.

Phillipson, R. (1992) *Linguistic Imperialism*. Oxford: Oxford University Press.

Phillipson, R. and Skutnabb-Kangas, T. (1993) Linguistic rights and wrongs. Paper presented at the 1993 AILA Congress, Amsterdam.

Pica, T. (1987) Interlanguage adjustments as an outcome of NS–NNS negotiated interaction. *Language Learning* 38, 45–73.

Ruiz, R. (1994) Language policy and planning in the US. In W. Grabe (ed.) *Language Policy and Planning: Annual Review of Applied Linguistics 14* (pp. 111–25). Cambridge: Cambridge University Press.

Scherer, K.R. and Giles, H. (eds) (1979) *Social Markers in Speech*. Cambridge: Cambridge University Press.

School Curriculum and Assessment Authority (SCAA) (1994) *English in the National Curriculum: Draft Proposals*. London: SCAA/ Central Office of Information.

Sharwood-Smith, M. (1993) Input enhancement in instructed SLA: Theoretical bases. *Studies in Second Language Acquisition* 15/2, 165–79.

Sinclair, J. McH. and Coulthard, M. (1975) *Towards an Analysis of Discourse*. Oxford: Oxford University Press.

Singleton, D. (1992) Second language instruction: The when and how. In J.F. Matter (ed.) *Language Teaching in the Twenty-first Century: Problems and Prospects* (pp. 46–54). AILA Review no. 9. Amsterdam: AILA.

Skehan, P. (1993) A framework for the implementation of task-based learning. In C. Kennedy (ed.) *IATEFL Annual Conference Report 1993* (pp. 17–25). Whitstable: IATEFL.

Snow, M.A. (1990) Instructional methodology in immersion foreign language education. In A.M. Padilla *et al.* (eds) *Bilingual Education: Issues and Strategies* (pp. 156–71). Newbury Park: Sage.

Spada, N. and Lightbown, P. (1993) Instruction and the development of questions in L2 classrooms. *Studies in Second Language Acquisition* 15/2, 205–24.

Stubbs, M. (1986) *Educational Linguistics*. Oxford: Blackwell.

— (1991) Educational language planning in England and Wales: Multicultural rhetoric and assimilationist assumptions. In F. Coulmas (ed.) *A Language Policy for the European Community: Prospects and Quandaries* (pp. 215–39). Berlin: Mouton de Gruyter.

Swain, M. and Lapkin, S. (1984) *Evaluating Bilingual Education: A Canadian Case Study*. Clevedon: Multilingual Matters.

Trim, J.L.M. (1992) Language teaching in the perspective of the predictable requirements of the twenty-first century. In J.F. Matter (ed.) *Language Teaching in the Twenty-first Century: Problems and Prospects* (pp. 7–20). AILA Review no. 9. Amsterdam: AILA.

Trudgill, P. and Chambers, J.K. (1991) Introduction: English dialect grammar. In J.K. Chambers and P. Trudgill (eds) *Dialects of English* (pp. 1–3). London: Longman.

Wallace, M. (1991) *Training Foreign Language Teachers: A Reflective Approach*. Cambridge: Cambridge University Press.

Webb, V. (1994) Language policy and planning in South Africa. In W. Grabe (ed.) *Language Policy and Planning: Annual Review of Applied Linguistics 14* (pp. 254–73). Cambridge: Cambridge University Press.

Widdowson, H. (1993) The ownership of English. In C. Kennedy (ed.) *IATEFL Annual Conference Report 1993* (pp. 5–9). Whitstable: IATEFL.

Wright, A. (1992) Language teaching and learning in classrooms. Unpublished PhD thesis, University of Lancaster.

2 Language, Education and Applied Linguistics in a Changing World: Response to Mitchell

MARY RUANE

Introduction

The challenges posed by change are such that language professionals could become defeatist. To avoid being overwhelmed, the response must be objective, positive and highly focused. This is the approach of Mitchell. After a detailed analysis of four themes, she concentrates on three practical implications: the need to pursue the research agenda, to defend the professionalism of teachers, and the need to become more involved in policy debates than heretofore. As my approach, too, must be selective, I will take these three themes and review them briefly. My perspectives are necessarily influenced by my own background in foreign language teaching, in teacher education and more recently in ELT.

Pursuing the Research Agenda

In the context of second and foreign language learning, the difficulty in pursuing the research agenda is knowing which direction this research should take if it is to be relevant. No one knows this better than Mitchell who has written extensively on the nature and role of research and how it should better serve language teachers. Despite the extensive work produced in this area in recent years – particularly in the field of classroom-based research – it is very clear that mixed opinions persist about the value and the direction of pedagogical research. The 1994 spring issue of the TESOL quarterly shows very clearly the uncertainty about the course of research and the degree of frustration among practitioners about its relevance.

There are many complex reasons for this present situation, but I will mention just two. As we know, there have been frequent paradigm shifts in methodology in recent years; recurring cycles of overstated dissatisfaction with an existing methodology followed by an exposition of the advantages of a replacement approach. Much research into language teaching methodology in recent years has been conducted very much within a 'method or instruction effectiveness' framework, and it is certainly this aspect that has most influenced teachers. It is only in recent years that the uncertain, intuitive basis for many of the findings have become apparent. Whilst in general, researchers are now more cautious about the claims they make, I believe that there is a legacy of distrust of research findings among language teachers which will take some time to overcome.

A second but related difficulty is dissatisfaction with the extent to which teachers' concerns receive attention from researchers. There is a perception by teachers that their real concerns are peripheral, and that, moreover, their potential input into research is not sufficiently valued. As Widdowson (1990) has said: 'Language teaching is often represented as a client activity and language teachers as consumers of findings that are retailed by research'. Others such as Pennycook (1989) have spoken about the disenfranchisement of teachers. This frustration of teachers can perhaps be exemplified by an experience that most language teacher educators have had at some time or another – that of listening to teacher reactions after a professional forum at which practices they themselves have used instinctively for many years are presented as original or innovative!

One way forward in this present situation is to give more attention to identifying research areas which teachers would like to see developed. By its nature, pedagogical research in institutions of higher education and elsewhere is driven by a variety of different motives, not all of them practitioner-related. Yet in genuinely trying to identify the research fields which teachers find most useful, researchers can perform an important service. There are still so many areas in which teachers have very urgent requirements which are not being met – mixed ability teaching, production of negotiated curricula, testing for special purposes, to mention just a few. The efforts of Pica (1994) and Brown (1992/3) are good models of an approach to defining research from the practitioner standpoint.

Paradigm shifts in language teaching could also be handled better if researchers proceeded, as Mackey (1965) has indicated, more by approximation than by sudden pendulum swing. While there is evidence of progress in this area, the risk of appearing reactionary and anti-progress is one that theoreticians, understandably, are slow to take. Thus, the new debate on task-based learning, for example, is not free of some of the old attitudes. One way of avoiding 'pendulum swings' would be to try and flag the difficulties of a method early on and assess the results before they are implemented or snapped up by publishers for their latest catalogues. In highlighting some of the difficulties and the deficiencies inherent in the latest panaceas to second language teaching, Mitchell provides a useful service.

There is also need to refigure the relationship between pedagogues and researchers to ensure more fruitful collaboration. For obvious reasons, researchers rarely have the means to see the implications of their theories or results translated into teaching materials which can then be used by practitioners. Yet giving teachers excellent classroom materials showing clear links to theory is one of the best possible ways of enhancing the teacher/ researcher relationship. Fortunately, there are some recent excellent examples of just such publications (Freeman & Cornwell, 1993; Underhill, 1994).

Professionalism

If research is one agenda item to be pursued, so too is the issue of language teacher professionalism. It has long been a matter for concern, but one can only concur with Mitchell when she asserts that it is under particular threat at present. I wish to comment on two aspects to this problem – status and career structure on the one hand, and opportunities for professional development on the other.

In the case of status and career structure, technology, so-called rationalisation, ideology, and over-supply have combined in various ways to weaken the standing of language teachers. As an example of such problems, let me cite two cases, the now well-documented position of ELT teachers and the position of teachers in the state sector. According to Swales (1993), 25 years' experience of observing ELT teachers shows no improvement in their professional standing; indeed the opposite may be the case. Despite the fact that English teaching is now more widespread than ever before, its progress into a mature and recognisable profession has been slow. The scale of the operation internationally has ensured that there is the panoply of a recognised profession in the form of publications and seminars and other structures. But it is a panoply covering up weaknesses in career structure and terms of condition of employment. Market forces, which continue to ensure a steady supply of teachers for whom ELT is still exceptionally attractive as a short-term para-career, ensure that this situation will not change.

Swales (1993) suggests that state sector teachers have a better fate. But this is not the full picture. Whilst it is true that teachers in state sector schools may at least aspire to job security – in the long term if not immediately – their sense of professional self-worth can be undermined in other ways. Public debates about quality and quantity in education, with attendant increases in reform efforts continue apace with schools expected to bear a heavy burden in trying to solve society's ills (Janitza, 1989; Clarke, 1994). The consequence of these reforms can be policy decisions which often override local concerns and which, when they happen in an unplanned way, can have a deleterious effects on the daily lives of teachers and students. A number of examples serve to make the point – problems arising from the wide-scale programmes to re-train teachers of Russian as teachers of English in the states of the former Soviet Union, the UK teacher shortage to meet the demands of the National Curriculum, the need to supply vast numbers of teachers to cater for the utterly unplanned expansion of German in this country (Sagarra, 1989). These are recent developments; we can expect many problems of a similar nature in the future.

The issue of professional education or development of teachers, whether at initial or in-service level, has received a great deal of emphasis in recent years. One could be forgiven for thinking that, with all this attention, significant progress has been made in the area. The reality, however, is that the scale of the expansion in language teaching in recent years and the diverse nature of this expansion are such that language teacher education cannot be expected to meet the demands made on it. And one senses a powerlessness on the part of many language teacher educators, as they stand on the side-lines and witness, at times, a downward spiral into conditions that would have been unthinkable a few years ago. New ways in language teacher education must be developed to cope with new demands. I will mention just two areas which I believe require further examination: preparing teachers to achieve greater autonomy in their professional lives and enhancing the role of the teacher as agent of change.

One of the great benefits of SLA research has been to move the focus in recent years from what is taught and how it is taught to how people learn (Ellis, 1986). This long overdue focus on helping the learner to learn has not brought with it sufficient emphasis on the needs of the teacher, both to provide for the independent learner and to take charge of her own professional development. In this context, I am reminded of a comment by Widdowson (1989: 25): 'Language learning (. . .) is too important a matter to be left to learners. I want then to argue for the primacy of teaching'. We cannot have learner-centredness unless we have effective teachers; in fact it takes better teachers to focus on learners. Yet the emphasis on autonomy for learners has not focused sufficiently on the implications for teachers of using autonomous approaches. A large number of works in recent years on learner autonomy (Dickinson, 1987; Little, 1991; Sheerin, 1989) have, of course, dealt with the role of the teacher but they have not made sufficiently explicit the physical, organisational and professional needs of teachers to meet learners' needs. Better links need to be made between the needs of learners and the requirements of teachers to meet these needs.

As well as teacher performance, a variety of elements impact on the effectiveness of language teachers in the classroom, including institutional, political and interpersonal conditions. According to some researchers (Clark, 1994), helping teachers gain perspective on these is as important as enhancing aspects of teacher behaviour. Traditionally, however, teacher development has not encouraged this perspective, and teachers do not always see it as their job to involve themselves in what they perceive to be wider concerns, i.e. the amount of time allocated to particular languages in the week, the number of languages offered, the order in which they are taught, teacher working conditions. Making teachers aware of the importance of such issues, making them aware of the possible connection between them and the final success of teaching can help teachers develop a decision-making role in language education (Corson, 1990). Modules on the role of teachers as agents of change need to be included in training programmes at both pre-service and in-service levels. Reference to this matter introduces the issue of language in education policy, to which I now turn briefly.

Language Policy and Planning

Mitchell sets out very clearly some of the reasons why applied linguists must get more involved in language policy debates than heretofore. One of the main reasons is that, with the utilisation of central planning concepts and methodologies, in language as in other areas of society, there is more and more central control of decision-making. In the linguistic sphere, decisions – with often significant impact on aspects of our lives – are increasingly being taken without an opportunity for widespread public debate or without the benefit of informed comment and analysis.

Potentially, there is a major role for the applied linguist in this area, that of contributing to informed public debate, specifically that of building bridges between the state, the practitioner, and the end-users, i.e. the general public, parents, students. Defining and managing this role, however, will be a demanding task. A particular challenge for the applied linguist will be that of finding the appropriate voice with which to convey relevant knowledge and information and with which to exercise influence. A capacity to work alongside the state apparatus will also be required, not to mention adeptness in the subtle art of compromise, when it becomes clear that in a particular area, too great a pursuit of the perfect may become the enemy of the good. Above all, the capacity to carry the support of the teaching profession will be critical, as a united front of teachers and researchers will be a powerful force to oppose change when it is not desirable or necessary.

One specific area where applied linguists could play an important role comes to mind. Language planning in second and foreign language learning with specific reference to the state educational system has emerged recently as an area of importance. R.D. Lambert wrote in 1989 that most of the problems that arise in language learning are not the result of poor classroom techniques – a topic to which the profession devotes most of its time – but to the ambiguities and inefficiencies of foreign language instruction, how the parts fit together. Since Lambert wrote this, more attention is now being given to charting the ways in which the many and different organisations engaged in language teaching add up to a *de facto* language system and to determining the extent to which that system meets national needs. Much more, however, needs to be done in this area of growing importance.

Fortunately, in the area of language in education policy, there are some inspiring models. Though it has its critics, Australia has led the English-speaking world in its ongoing performance in, and commitment to, a well-articulated, all-encompassing approach to language and language education policy-making (Clyne, 1991). The Netherlands has also had significant achievements in the area of language education policy, with the development of its National Action Programme (NAP) providing a set of measures to improve foreign language learning (Van Els & Van Hest, 1990). In both the Australian and the Dutch cases, applied linguists have played a key and much documented role in the development of their national policies.

Co-operation between practitioners, the state and applied linguists has also had a long and fruitful history in Ireland and I will end this review by providing some encouraging examples of this co-operation. The first is the important role played by linguists and applied linguists in the debate on the teaching of foreign languages in the primary school at a time when there was extensive public pressure to have it introduced into that sector of the educational system (Harris, 1991). Another example was the debate on the establishment of an interdisciplinary language awareness programme at school level in the Irish education system (Singleton, 1992). Finally, Irish applied linguists in a variety of institutions have collaborated on an ongoing basis with the state and with language teachers to play a significant role in the renewal of foreign language syllabuses at all levels of the second-level system.

Conclusion

The speaker concluded her address by outlining an agenda for the development of applied linguistics which I have used as the basis for this paper. The task of implementing these proposals, however, raises issues on a wider agenda over which we have little control, and about which we may have reason to feel pessimistic. As we begin to see the fall-out of recent expansion in language teaching, our early sense of optimism is now giving way to doubt and, in certain cases, even dismay. Growth and progress are not necessarily synonymous. A great deal of effort, co-operation and pragmatism will be needed if the agenda items outlined, and indeed others, are to be translated into effective programmes of applied linguistic and educational action.

References

Brown, J.D. (1992/3) What research questions interest TESOL members? (p. 20) *TESOL Matters*.

Clarke, M.A. (1994) The dysfunctions of the theory/practice discourse. *TESOL Quarterly* 28, 1, 9–19.

Clyne, M. (1991) Australia's language policies: Are we going backwards? *Australian Review of Applied Linguistics*, Series S, 8, 3–22.

Corson, D. (1990) *Language Policy Across the Curriculum*. Clevedon: Multilingual Matters.

Dickinson, L. (1987) *Self-Instruction in Language Learning*. Cambridge: Cambridge University Press.

Ellis, R. (1986) *Understanding Second Language Acquisition*. New York: Oxford University Press.

Freeman, D. and Cornwell, S. (1993) *New Ways in Teacher Education, New Ways in TESOL Series: Innovative Classroom Techniques*. Alexandria, Virginia: TESOL.

Harris, J. (1991) *Foreign Language Teaching in the Primary School*. Dublin: INTO.

Janitza, J. (1989) Rapport de la Commission de Réflexion sur l'Enseignement des Langues Etrangères. Paris: Ministère de l'Education Nationale.

Lambert, R.D. (1989) Issues in national language policy. In *Proceedings of the International Symposium on Language Learning and Teaching. Vol. 1: Stock-taking and perspectives* (pp. 99–101) Paris: L'Association pour les Etats Généraux des Langues.

Little, D.G. (1991) *Learner Autonomy*. Dublin: Authentik Language Learning Resources.

Mackey, W.F. (1965) *Language Teaching Analysis*. Bloomington: Indiana University Press.

Pennycook, A. (1989) The concept of method, interested knowledge, and the politics of language teaching. *TESOL Quarterly* 23, 4, 589–618.

Pica, T. (1994) Questions from the language classroom: Research perspectives. *TESOL Quarterly*, 28, 1, 51–73.

Sagarra, E. (1989) The German language in Ireland: A personal view of its recent history and its support system in the late 1980s. *Teangeolas/Journal of the Linguistics Institute of Ireland* 26, 12–9.

Sheerin, S. (1989) *Self-Access*. Oxford: Oxford University Press.

Singleton, D. (1992) Education towards language awareness in Ireland. *Language Awareness*, 1, 1, 47–57.
Swales, J. (1993) The English language and its teachers: thoughts past, present and future. *ELT Journal*, 47/4, 289–90.
Underhill, A. (ed.) (1994) *The Teacher Development Series*. Oxford: Heinemann.
van Els, T. and van Hest, E. (1990) Foreign language teaching policies and European unity: The Dutch National Action Plan. *Language Culture and Curriculum* 3, 3, 199–211.
Widdowson, H.G. (1989) Parameters in Language Teaching. In *Proceedings of the International Symposium on Language Learning and Teaching. Vol. 1: Stock-taking and perspectives*. Paris: L'Association pour les Etats Généraux des Langues.
— (1990) Discourses of inquiry and conditions of relevance. In J. Alatis (ed.) *Georgetown University Round Table on Languages and Linguistics 1990* (pp. 37–48). Washington, DC: Georgetown University Press.

3 Language and Society in a Changing World

JOHN EDWARDS

Introduction

For students of applied linguistics, sociolinguistics or the sociology of language, the interrelationships between language and society are of course central. While scholarly emphasis may vary (between, say, 'micro' and 'macro' perspectives), and while the range of disciplinary approaches is very broad (from laboratory experimentation to ethnography, from discourse analysis to questionnaire survey), the wish to illuminate social interaction through language, and vice versa, remains the driving force. It follows that, whenever either social or linguistic dynamics are especially volatile, the value of this illumination increases. We can conclude, consequently, that these are rich times for applied linguists and their colleagues in cognate disciplines. In this paper, I want to comment upon some aspects of this richness and, given both my own predilections and the general mandate assigned to me here, I hope I will be forgiven for stressing the larger canvas rather than the miniature.

Language and Social Change

Sociolinguistic volatility today can be best understood, in many settings, as a reflection of groups in transition. Transition is, almost by definition, painful – even when it is entered upon voluntarily; when it is forced, of course, the discomfort is augmented. However, viewed somewhat more closely, 'voluntary transition' seems oxymoronic. One of Newton's axioms of motion held that bodies remain at rest unless compelled to change, and there are surely social correlates of this. While we might easily agree that Russification under the Tsars represented an instance of involuntary upheaval, perhaps we should also concede that the massive emigrations from the old world to the new – with their profound sociolinguistic consequences – were not wholly voluntary.

On the other hand, not all the choices here have been of Hobson's variety. Beyond that – beyond the question of whether the Poles, the Germans, the Italians, the Greeks and all the others jumped or were pushed – there remains the fact that linguistic and cultural group 'markers' have historically been seen, in large measure, as negotiable commodities. In fact, for *all* groups, emigrant or not, this has been the way of the world – if that world has included any element of group contact, and any possibility of physical or psychological mobility. A social version of Newton's axiom, then, might have to make provision for the virtual inevitability of change.

The notion of some sociolinguistic cost-benefit analysis, which this explanation would seem to imply, can, I realise, often seem both strange and strained. I am arguing, however, for the essential *naturalness* of change, of transition and, conversely, the unlikeliness of stasis. Of course, there are groups which resist assimilative pressures more strongly than others but they do so at a cost of isolation higher than most have been, historically, willing to pay (the Amish in America come to mind). Furthermore, groups in transition, faced with the pressures attendant upon social contact, often make non-random choices. By this I mean that some group 'markers' succumb to pressure more quickly than others; thus, private manifestations of ethnicity linger longer than public ones, more symbolic attachments can remain almost indefinitely, and so on.

Now, it might be pointed out that this does not reflect group choice so much as it does the differing degree of external pressure which bears upon (say) public versus private markers. Nonetheless, with the examples of the 'isolated' Amish (on the one hand), and those many immigrants who, after a generation or so, ventured outside the ethnic enclaves which first sheltered them upon arrival (on the other), we can see that some room, at least, must be made for volition. To change focus for a minute, those Gaelic-speaking Scots among whom language shift became increasingly prevalent were, at the same time, capable of concerted resistance to other pressures (land 'reform', for example).

While one might argue that groups would be only too happy if they could materially advance themselves *and* retain, in some unbroken fashion, all their traditional cultural patterning, one must also admit that this has not generally proved possible (it is very important to bear in mind temporal considerations; I am taking a long-term view here). Whether one looks at the capitalist world or the erstwhile communist one, at contemporary times or historical ones, at small societies or empires, at immigrant minorities or indigenous groups – one sees an inexorability and similarity of pressures and these, quite simply, take their toll, exact changes, and throw populations into transitional states. To deny this is to deny an historical sweep which, at one time or another, has affected *all* groups.

Language and Identity

There is another element which I must add to this general prologue: the question of identity. When, in 1985, I published a book called *Language, Society and Identity*, the final word of the title was not nearly as widely used in the literature as it is now. Of course, there had existed for some time studies of ethnicity; in fact, these predate the formal inception of socio-linguistics and the sociology of language – generally associated with Hertzler's (1953) paper entitled *Toward a Sociology of Language*, his subsequent book (*The Sociology of Language*, published in 1965), and Bright's *Sociolinguistics* (1966: the proceedings of an American sociolinguistics conference). The acceleration of interest and research since then has been marked – and my contention is that this whole area is essentially about *identity*. But, within the last three or four years, identity *per se* has been highlighted to an unprecedented extent. To go back no further than the last two years: Calhoun has published a book on the politics of identity (1994); Hooson's volume on geography and identity has just appeared (1994); Rajchman has an edited collection entitled *The Identity in Question* (1994); Kroskrity's *Language, History and Identity* appeared last year (1993); Frese edited *Celebrations of Identity* in 1993; and so on. These, of course, are in addition to the many other works on the subject, which do not have *identity* in the title, and to the many articles and book chapters.

Why this growth of interest, a growth coming from both the humanities and the social sciences? The answer, surely, is not far to seek, and goes back to the transition and change I have already touched upon. We see, for example, opportunities for reasserting smothered nationalisms and ethnicities being grasped in eastern Europe and the former Soviet Union; we note the recent constitutional crises in Canada, most pointedly between the English and the French communities, but also involving demands for increased autonomy among aboriginal groups, and agitations for 'voice' among the 'allophones'; we observe American restiveness with multiculturalism (see the recent polemics of Schlesinger, 1992; Hughes, 1993; and the elegant 1992 essay by Taylor); and, more locally, we can consider a Europe in which the continuing momentum of continental federalism co-exists – sometimes uneasily – with demands and policies for increased recognition of minorities. In all of this we can discern the negotiation or renegotiation of identity. In fact, given that we could easily broaden the geographical perspective I have just illustrated, it is clear that concerns about diversity and discord, about collective and

individual rights and responsibilities, about pluralism and unity, are the
major socio-political themes of our times. As we struggle towards what has
been termed a 'new world order' we observe those inevitable dislocations
and discomforts that accompany political and cultural negotiation and change.
While these may not be of the same degree of violent upheaval in (say) Canada
and the USA as they are in (say) the former Soviet Union or ex-Yugoslavia,
the principles at issue are similar. This late-twentieth-century identity politics comprises the most pressing matters of our age, the most insistent of
'complaints'. Although the tensions can involve many specifics – language,
religion, sex, class, race, geography – it is the struggle for identity, for rooted-
ness, for 'groupness', which is at their heart.

Applied linguists and sociologists of language have an obvious role to play
in documenting and analysing changing states of identity; and, in so doing,
they might usefully recall Saussure's contrasting principles of *provincialism*
and *intercourse* (1980). On the one hand, Saussure argued, provincialism
(which he referred to as *l'esprit de clocher*) keeps a linguistic community
faithful to its own traditions – this, however, *'rend les hommes sédentaires'*.
On the other hand, members of the community are pulled by an opposing
force in the service of wider communication, for which Saussure used the
English term, *intercourse* (his editors observed: *'nous avons cru pouvoir
conserver cette pittoresque expression de l'auteur'*). This centripetal-centrifugal
opposition was seen by Saussure as of universal applicability – not just relating
to 'linguistic waves' and dialect variation, but to all human customs (*'n'importe
quelle habitude'*). Others have also attempted to capture this opposition; hence
the use of dichotomies such as 'roots and options', 'state and community',
'tribalism and globalism' and, of course, *Gemeinschaft* and *Gesellschaft* (see
Edwards, 1993).

Minority Languages in a Changing World

However we choose to label these opposing tendencies, it is clear that the
human urges which underpin them are of long standing. It is salutary to be
reminded of this when, faced with modern events – often of cataclysmic
proportions – we are sometimes tempted to believe that new and unimagined
forces are at work in the world. Within the framework of language and,
more specifically, within that of minority-language situations, there is a tendency in some quarters to reduce these matters to a struggle between the
small, the original, the 'authentic' (an invidious term) and some large, face-
less, impersonal, overarching globalism – a juggernaut beneath whose wheels
all individuality is immolated and crushed. However, the worshippers of
Krishna, we should remember, frequently threw themselves under the god's
car in an access of religious fervour. Equally, those minority-group members

who, to the horror of some, abandon some cultural markers and take on others (who engage, for example, in language shift) are not wholly robotic. Besides, the view that holds 'authenticity' to exist only in opposition to 'mainstream' life is very often both condescending and static. Further, when this mainstream is seen to comprise only crassly material advantages, a type of reductionism is at work. How curious it is that those apologists for minority-group maintenance who reject what they see as economic reductionism (on the part of so-called 'assimilationist' commentators on language and cultural shift) should, themselves, see in majority cultures only spiritually empty mammonism. How easily they seem to forget the advantages, the advances, the freedoms, the mobility which such cultures may offer. However, I mention this here, not because I wish to cast my lot either with the big battalions or with groups still in the shadow of Saussure's village bell-tower, but as a caution that applied linguistic analysis would do well to maintain the utmost sensitivity and to reject all tendencies to monolithic thinking.

It is natural (and perhaps praiseworthy) for educated minds to support the small, the weak and the downtrodden, but there are often gins and snares. Conor Cruise O'Brien (1973: 50) noted, 20 years ago, that we ought not to 'idealise minorities, or to forget that today's underdog may be tomorrow's power-crazed bully' and there are, surely, many historical and contemporary contexts which bear him out. We can easily observe some related difficulties, as well, and two instances come to mind in present-day Canada. Supporters of *Québécois* nationalism who maintain that the province's 'distinct-society' status has never been adequately acknowledged are unwilling to accord that same status to Canadian aboriginal populations and, more pointedly, to members of those groups within Quebec itself. And, in the midst of the recent Canadian constitutional wrangling, the broadly-based public support for increased aboriginal autonomy received a shock when aboriginal *women* pointed out that such autonomy might well signify, for them, a continuation (or even a heightening) of unwanted patriarchy.

For applied linguists, minority issues often centre upon the status of languages 'at risk' and, sometimes, upon their preservation and protection. Here, a recent exchange between Krauss and Ladefoged, in the pages of *Language*, is relevant. Krauss (1992: 7) presents data indicating that a large number of the world's languages is now seriously endangered: 'I consider it a plausible calculation that, at the rate things are going, the coming century will see either the death or the doom of 90% of mankind's languages'. What, he says (p. 7), 'are we linguists doing to prepare for this or to prevent this catastrophic destruction of the linguistic world?' If linguists do not act, Krauss (p. 8) observes, 'we should be cursed by future generations for Neronically fiddling while Rome burned'.

Endorsing the work that Krauss and his colleagues do, or wish to do, Ladefoged (1992: 809) notes that their views 'are contrary to those held by many responsible linguists'. Drawing upon his own work, Ladefoged points to the fact that not all groups believe that the preservation of their language is compatible with desired lifestyles. Many of the Toda, for example (speakers of a southern Indian Dravidian language),

> have accepted that, in their view, the cost [of becoming part of modern India] is giving up the use of their language in their daily life. Surely, this is a view to which they are entitled, and it would not be the action of a responsible linguist to persuade them to do otherwise. (Ladefoged, 1992: 810)

Ladefoged's solution? It involves a more traditional view of linguist-as-disinterested-scientist: 'the task of the linguist is to lay out the facts concerning a given linguistic situation' (1992: 811).

Linguists and Linguistics in a Changing World

This debate is likely to intensify in the future, and three aspects of it are, I think, of particular moment: (i) the *appropriateness* of active intervention on behalf of threatened varieties; (ii) the likelihood, assessment and definition of successful intervention; (iii) the implications for the language-identity relationship. I have written more fully elsewhere about the Krauss–Ladefoged exchange (of which Dorian, 1993, became a part) and about the general subject – the role of linguists in the face of language decline (Edwards, in press). For present purposes, let me simply say that I think it possible for linguists who are, themselves, strongly committed to the maintenance of diversity – and maybe uncommitted or neutral ones, too – to consider that one of the 'facts' to be presented to groups or governments is that very commitment. That is, one might argue that beleaguered language groups could profit from knowing that the issues which affect them so directly are seen as important by people other than in-group activists. This in itself would hardly remove the linguistic and social obstacles but, if any change in fortunes is at all possible, it must surely depend upon a solid grasp of historical and contemporary fact – and why not include here the ecologically-minded awareness which is increasingly evident in linguistics and the allied disciplines?

In much of the foregoing, I have been implicitly arguing for an increased awareness of, and sensitivity to, issues of sociolinguistic contact, negotiation and mobility. I also wish to re-emphasise a concern for a fuller embedding of language in context, and for greater cross-disciplinary study. If it is clear that applied linguistics has a part to play in the understanding of social life, it is equally obvious that that role has deepest meaning when it is fully integrated with those of the other players. I know this seems like a common truism but, as an editor of a language journal, I still see far too many single-case and monochromatic studies which add only to the height and not to the breadth of our data.

One useful corrective here might be some increased attention to classification and typology. While there exists a number of organisational schemes for languages and language settings, I have argued elsewhere that these have not been as comprehensive as they might. Still, the work that *has* been done here – by Haugen, Ferguson, Kloss, Stewart, Haarmann, Giles and others – has not, in my view, been systematically exploited, and my own efforts have attempted both to build upon and go beyond this earlier work (see Edwards 1990, 1991, 1992).

This is not the place to go into detail, but I should say here that the overall intent is to produce a framework of variables which could serve to illuminate contexts of maintenance and shift. One could imagine, as well, that such a scaffolding could be used to inform and guide relevant policies. If minority communities are described in a formalised or semi-formalised way, they can better understand their own situation (and how it compares to others), and can more accurately present themselves to others. Similarly, if particular responses are desired from a mainstream authority, the latter should be given the best and most candid information available; otherwise, inaccurate, inadequate or inappropriate interventions may result which do not proceed from a firm base and which will consequently have little likelihood of success.

More specifically, I believe that:

(a) a comprehensive, multidisciplinary analysis of ethnic-minority-language situations will be intrinsically useful context by context;
(b) emerging generalities may be found which will permit comparison and classification of different contexts under certain rubrics. We are aware, of course, that every context possesses unique features, but anyone who has ever attempted a contrastive analysis, or who has cited different examples to make a general point, has in effect argued that some features are constant or at least similar enough across contexts to lead to generalisation. Besides, the uniqueness of contexts lies in the patterning and weighting of elements, not in those elements themselves;
(c) information thus obtained may produce a useful socio-political picture of minority settings from the perspectives of both minority and majority communities;
(d) this in turn might enable predictions to be made about language maintenance and shift and, indeed, might even serve as an indicator of what is desirable, what is possible, and what is likely.

Conclusion

It is apparent that I have done little here to elucidate the nature of language and society in a changing world. I *have* indicated, I hope, some of the important features to which we might profitably direct our attention. For the most part, these are implicit in the very idea of 'a changing world' – language contact, policy and planning, sociolinguistic mobility, the struggles of 'smaller' and 'larger' languages, negotiated identities. None can be adequately understood in temporal, geographic or disciplinary isolation. While this does not mean that the applied linguist of today or tomorrow must be a polymath, it is clear, nevertheless, that the most useful and enduring contributions will come from those whose scholarly vision is broad. To say this is easy and, no doubt, repetitious. However, it could be argued that the many events of today which are of legitimate interest to applied linguistics (in its broadest sense), and the state of development of the discipline itself, combine to produce a singular opportunity. If this is seized, then both the discipline and the world it seeks to illuminate will benefit.

By way of illustration, let me again mention the current Canadian scene. Within the larger French–English dynamics, the other important elements in the sociopolitics of the 1990s are the 'allophones' and the aboriginal groups. The federal policies of official bilingualism and multiculturalism are under intense scrutiny. With a separatist party as the official opposition in Ottawa, and with a strong likelihood that the next provincial government in Quebec will also be separatist, it is not too fanciful to suggest that issues of language and culture could ultimately disunite the country. What could be of greater interest to scholars, and what better situation could arise to allow them to 'give back' some of their academic insights? In fact, books and articles over the past three or four years suggest that the linguists, political scientists, sociologists and others *are* contributing; for example, the best recent overview of the Canadian bilingual 'experiment' was presented by McRoberts (1990) in an eleven-part series in the *Globe & Mail* – Canada's leading newspaper.

No one wishes difficult social or linguistic problems to arise for the delight of academics. But if – or, rather, when – they *do* arise, we can hope that they will be dissected, explained and contextualised to the mutual benefit of academic knowledge and social policy.

References

Bright, W. (1966) *Sociolinguistics*. The Hague: Mouton.
Calhoun, C. (1994) *Social Theory and the Politics of Identity*. Oxford: Blackwell.
Cruise-O'Brien, C. (1973) On the rights of minorities. *Commentary* 55(6), 46–50.

Dorian, N. (1993) A response to Ladefoged's other view of endangered languages. *Language* 69, 575–9.

Edwards, J. (1985) *Language, Society and Identity*. Oxford: Blackwell.

— (1990) Notes for a minority-language typology: Procedures and justification. *Journal of Multilingual and Multicultural Development* 11, 137–51.

— (1991) Socio-educational issues concerning indigenous minority languages: Terminology and status. In J. Sikma and D. Gorter (eds) *European Lesser Used Languages in Primary Education* (pp. 207–26). Leeuwarden/Ljouwert: Fryske Akademy/Mercator.

— (1992) Sociopolitical aspects of language maintenance and loss: Towards a typology of minority language situations. In W. Fase, K. Jaspaert and S. Kroon (eds) *Maintenance and Loss of Minority Languages* (pp. 37–54). Amsterdam: John Benjamins.

— (1993) Parochialism versus wider communicative needs in the modern world. In J. Levitt, L. Ashley and K. Rogers (eds) *Language in Contemporary Society* (pp. 14–19). New York: American Society of Geolinguistics.

— (In press) What can (or should) linguists do in the face of language decline? *Proceedings of the Seventeenth Annual Meeting of the Atlantic Provinces Linguistic Association*.

Frese, P. (1993) *Celebrations of Identity*. Westport, Connecticut: Bergin & Garvey.

Hertzler, J. (1953) Toward a sociology of language. *Social Forces* 32, 109–19.

— (1965) *The Sociology of Language*. New York: Random House.

Hooson, D. (1994) *Geography and National Identity*. Oxford: Blackwell.

Hughes, R. (1993) *Culture of Complaint: The Fraying of America*. New York: Oxford University Press.

Krauss, M. (1992) The world's languages in crisis. *Language* 68, 4–10.

Kroskrity, P. (1993) *Language, History and Identity*. Tucson: University of Arizona Press.

Ladefoged, P. (1992) Another view of endangered languages. *Language* 68, 805–11.

McRoberts, K. (1990) Federalism and political community. *Globe & Mail* (Toronto): 19 March to 2 April.

Rajchman, J. (ed.) (1994) *The Identity in Question*. New York: Routledge.

de Saussure, F. (1980) *Cours de Linguistique Générale*. Paris: Payot.

Schlesinger, A. (1992) *The Disuniting of America: Reflections on a Multicultural Society*. New York: Norton.

Taylor, C. (1992) *Multiculturalism and 'The Politics of Recognition'*. Princeton, New Jersey: Princeton University Press.

4 Language and Society in a Changing World: Response to Edwards

HELEN Ó MURCHÚ

Introduction

Ba mhaith liom tosú as Gaeilge chun comhthéacs a chur láithreach lena mbeidh le rá agamsa. Mo bhuíochas, mar sin, le Cumann na Teangeolaíochta Feidhmí as an gcuireadh a thug siad dom bheith mar fhreagróir ar an Ollamh Edwards. I have begun in Irish, not as some kind of symbolic gesture (although these may have their own importance in the implementation of language planning as a signal of some sort of intent), but in order to declare from the outset where my particular biases lie. This, hopefully, will allow the reader to better interpret what I have to say.

Language Rights

When I became President of the European Bureau for Lesser Used Languages, one of the first tasks facing me was discussion of criteria for membership of the Bureau, including the problems of defining language and dialect. It became immediately obvious to me that social collectivities with particular characteristics were the real focus of our concern and that discussion of language variants divorced from the users of these variants might not be the most useful starting point. In addition, the socio-political context within which the Bureau operates lies largely in the area of *rights* and *anti-discrimination*, mentioned by Edwards. The existing philosophical framework for the delineation of these rights, however, whether within the UN, the Council of Europe or the European Parliament, encompasses only individual rights, or the rights of individuals belonging to specific groups. A philosophy of collective rights, with all its possible attendant political overtones, is lacking. Despite this, self-determination and autonomy of a kind appeared to be recognised at a level lower than the nation state with the acceptance in the 1992 Maastricht Treaty of the concept of subsidiarity and the new structure of the Committee of the Regions. Regional autonomy and community development need not necessarily coincide. But for lesser used language regions, the majority of which are situated in peripheral areas, it was clear that language survival and economic viability were closely entwined. For this reason, I requested the European Commission to ensure that aspects relating to the economy and to the newish development of cultural tourism were written into the latest tender for research on lesser used languages in Europe, now nearing completion (entitled Euromosaic).

The Need for Interdisciplinarity

All these factors would appear to indicate a need for a fresh approach within sociolinguistics to provide the kind of analyses needed both by the lesser used language speakers themselves and by those involved with them, or on their behalf, in language planning. Language policies for the European Union will undoubtedly receive added significance in the light of enlargement, a certain movement towards the extreme right, and increasing contact with multilingual Central and Eastern Europe. Identity may be layered and more than monolingually based. Community, region, nation, state and suprastate are more dynamically linked. The locus of power may be shifting and with it social relations may change. Participative, rather than solely representative, democracy must inevitably affect lesser used language communities' relations.

Interdisciplinary research carries its own problems. The extent to which linguistics and sociology have become properly integrated is open to discussion. Over a decade ago Glyn Williams (1980: 363) was arguing that 'good sociolinguistics is not possible outside of good sociology'. He argued convincingly that 'economic change is the driving force of social change' (1980: 364) and the 'conflict' between majority and minority (in whichever context) is primarily a struggle for control over resources. He criticised the statist approach and the static concepts of shift, maintenance, domain, diglossia, which prevail in sociolinguistic studies due to the reification of language and its separation from the social group that are its users. He contended (1988: 171) that there is a need

. . . to deconstruct the prevailing discourse which focuses upon the opposition between standard and dialect, between region or community and nation, between state and community, and begin rather from the (French) view that 'meaning is not fixed [but] a matter of struggle over which no group has a privileged view' (1988: 171). He wonders – rightly – why the term 'ethnic group' is rarely if ever used in relation to dominant groups in society, or why ethnic groups are generally discussed as if structurally uniform and their internal social differentiation ignored.

Language Planning: Bottom-up or Top-down?

Williams (1980: 365) asserts that the 'consensus approach denies the rôle of institutions in the perpetuation of discrimination' and shows how central to the struggle between minority and majority is the struggle for control of the agencies of cultural reproduction. *State*-controlled bilingual education, for example, 'limits the ability of the minority to reproduce its own culture except within the context of the dominant ideology' (*Euromosaic* study: private communication). The *bottom-up* phenomenon in Irish education has its counterpart all over Europe. Williams totally rejects the liberal/consensus argument that labels ethnic groups *underdeveloped*, for example, considering this merely a way of sustaining the state position that 'neutralizes a culture by its pejorativization' (*Euromosaic* study: private communication), by considering it in some way 'deviant'. (Who defines the *norm*?) State-controlled language planning he considers the resort of multilingual states in actually negating the demand for equality while appearing to accommodate their linguistic minorities. What is needed, in his opinion (1988: 178), are:

> . . . sociological perspectives . . . that speak from the place of the minority rather than the consensus perspective, that can speak only from the place of the state.

In a trenchant analysis of the rôle of *Bord na Gaeilge*, the state agency for Irish, Tovey (1988: 65–7) underlines the problems of activism versus technocracy. Is it possible to 'manage a revival effort'? If so, how? She argues (1988: 67) that the Bord has 'turned its back on the rôle of representative of the voluntary movement to the State, opting instead to represent the state to the language movement'. It would seem then that the social movement necessary could not 'occur under the auspices of *Bord na Gaeilge*'. The problem for the Bord is, as Tovey (1988: 67) admits, that:

> to redefine itself as an agency of a minority group, to recognise and attack existing linguistic power structures in Irish society, might free its capacities for innovative and decisive action but rob it of much of its rationale as an agency of the state.

I am personally aware of these tensions from my own experience as a former chairperson of the *Bord*. Most of the communities in the Bureau have such agencies; the majority began as a result of pressure from the bottom up. Many conduct social linguistic research. The questions being asked now concern the relationships between the language planning agency, the lesser used language community, and the state or implementing administrations. Where are the studies that might enlighten us?

The Research Agenda

The dilemma now seems to lie in the dearth of comparative research within an integrated theoretical framework that would provide more understanding of the interaction between the comparatively well researched areas of language planning within a statist perspective and the entirely under-researched social perspective. Fishman (1990: 11), for example, has referred in no uncertain terms to the absence in the literature of the literally millions of people involved in Reversing Language Shift (RLS), 'change-agents on behalf of persistence', a situation he finds 'ethically unjustified and intellectually as well as practically disappointing' (1990: 5).

Williams (1988: 174) agrees with de Vries (1987) that:

the interdisciplinary, international, comparative, institutionalised nature of the research venture into minority languages means that in order for all researchers to be discussing the same entity and context, there must be some form of theoretical, and consequently, conceptual unity.

He fails to see the analytical value or theoretical underpinning of most of the typology work available.

I have quoted at some length from Williams for several reasons. There are few alternative views available apart from the prevailing orthodoxy. Williams's more sociology-oriented approach does not appear to have been greatly exploited as yet. Husband & Khan (1982) do, however, argue from the same bases in their critique of the Giles *et al*. perspective on ethnolinguistic vitality as does Colin Williams (1994). The former (1982: 198–9) find 'the concept (of ethnolinguistic vitality) not only relative but dominant-centric . . . (with) also a monolingual monocultural bias'. They quite unequivocally state (1982: 201) that:

More fundamentally, in the absence of an explicitly articulated sociological framework we have no tools to analyse the inherent tension between those collectives whose members have different access to local resources.

It is crucial to the understanding of language and society in a changing world that we have the right analytical tools to examine how language groups are socially formed, how they operate, mobilise, change. One is then legitimately allowed to enquire whether researchers are, in fact, asking the right questions or are working from an integrated theoretical framework or whether such an agreed framework does exist. Is there 'something drastically wrong with the study of minority languages'? (G. Williams, 1988: 169). Are Giles *et al.* (1990) right in agreeing with Williams that the field of minority language studies 'has no integrative theme'? Is there a shift of focus needed? Such confrontations between differing theoretical frameworks could lead both to a new dynamism within sociolinguistics and an eventual agreed conceptual framework, that would allow better understanding in a comparative, and even perhaps predictive, context of the complex process at issue.

The rôle of linguists then in the context of minority languages could well be one of pioneering new perspectives within an integrated interdisciplinary approach to their own work. This, however, does not answer Edwards's question on how committed that rôle should be, how engaged with a desire to see these languages survive rather than die. Let me turn here to the matter of bias. Being committed or otherwise does not necessarily lessen the quality or negate the results of research. One is not necessarily *unbiased* by being *outside* the community under study. As I pointed out when asked to participate in the opening ceremony of the Fifth International Conference on Minority Languages (Cardiff, 1994), many researchers of minority languages cannot be neutral, since they are researching their own communities. However, such research should not be dismissed as 'emotive' or less than scholarly, since it is my contention that all research carries elements of bias. In fact, the very choice of what to study is a reflection of bias. Studies in the area of minority languages are no more or less biased than in any other. What is important is that we retain the ability to recognise bias, including our own.

If we accept Colin Williams's assertion (1991: 14) that 'questions of a language's relevance, legitimacy and survival are socially constructed, not naturally ordained', do we also accept with Skutnabb-Kangas, (1990: 78) that 'researchers participate in constructing and legitimating the new forms of racism, through the ways (they) construct and treat concepts like mother tongue, ethnicity and integration'? Do researchers – or indeed, can they or should they – 'help to construct and legitimate the message used for controlling – or to deconstruct and delegitimate them' (1990: 79)? She argues that when we view ethnicity and integration as socially constructed relations, rather than inherent or acquired characteristics, then we are forced to examine the power relationships between the parties in the definition process, instead of simply studying one side of the power equation, usually the dominated one. It might also be timely to ask, as Skutnabb-Kangas (1990: 98) does, 'who stands to benefit from (researchers') theoretical work in con-structing tools for (their) trade and from (their) empirical work in using these tools?'

It is in such considerations, perhaps, that lies the answer to Ladefoged's (1992) rather irritated reply to Krauss (1992) and others, in the same issue of *Language*, who see their rôle as one of conservation. It would appear that for Ladefoged this is not 'responsible' conduct, but is even 'paternalistic' and possibly 'self-serving'. Without an integrated sociolinguistic framework, without a deeper examination of the perspectives and concepts used by socio-linguists, without self-analysis by sociolinguists, without a clear answer to the question 'who benefits from professional sociolinguists' work?', such arguments as those that appeared in *Language* in 1992 are at a level that pre-cludes their being taken with the seriousness that the subject matter deserves. Edwards (1984: 268) has remarked elsewhere that 'all "small" languages exist in emotional contexts'. Perhaps it would be as true to say that *all* languages exist in emotional contexts. Certainly, one would be forgiven for holding such a view, (however unscientific), in the face of the French state's stance on behalf of French, for example.

Conclusions

Irrespective of the contexts in which languages exist, or the positions which are held either by linguists or states or lesser used language communities, sociolinguistics will undoubtedly continue. It might then be a more useful exercise to concentrate more on how that discipline might best develop, particularly since the services of linguists will be called upon in the changing world we are now witnessing. It is interesting that the views expressed by Giles *et al.* (1990: 51) were echoed at a conference on research priorities for lesser used languages, held on the Isle of Skye (Stradling, 1994), which stressed the need for linguists:

> to plan [their] own academic and interventionist policies . . . perhaps by establishing a working party briefed to negotiate ground rules, integra-tive academic themes and objectives, and practical policies to be reported back to a definable public assembly of [linguists].

Because of the large volume of work in this area accomplished over the years by Edwards, I address this plea to him, and to all researchers in the area. Crossdisciplinary studies within a more integrated theoretical frame-work are vitally necessary if we are to understand better the interaction of language and society in our world today.

Minority language communities, as other so-called minorities in society, are seeking empowerment. Power over their own institutions is one of the methods of that empowerment. There is now a growing impetus towards the establishment of research and academic networks across the lesser used language communities that would embark on collaborative research and could also provide training for researchers from the communities themselves – a growing autonomy, in fact. For too long, many of them feel that they have been exploited academically. Such a movement may perhaps provide the more holistic context that sociolinguistics apparently currently needs.

References

de Vries, J. (1987) Problems of measurement in the study of linguistic minorities. In G. Mac Eoin *et al*. (eds) *Third International Conferences on Minority Languages: General Papers* (pp. 23–31). Clevedon: Multilingual Matters.

Edwards, J. (1984). Irish: Planning and preservation. *Journal of Multilingual and Multicultural Development* 5, 3 & 4, 267–75.

Fishman, J.A. (1990) What is Reversing Language Shift (RLS) and how can it succeed? In D. Gorter *et al*. (eds) *Fourth International Conference on Minority Languages: General Papers* (pp. 5–36). Clevedon: Multilingual Matters.

Giles, H. *et al*. (1990) Minority language group status: A theoretical conspexus. In D. Gorter *et al*. (eds) *Fourth International Conference on Minority Languages: General Papers* (pp. 37–55). Clevedon: Multilingual Matters.

Husband, C. and Khan, J.S. (1982) The viability of ethnolinguistic vitality: Some doubts. *Journal of Multilingual & Multicultural Development* 3(3), 193–205.

Krauss, M. (1992) The world's languages in crisis. *Language* 68, 4–10.

Ladefoged, P. (1992) Another view of endangered languages. *Language* 68, 809–11.

Skutnabb-Kangas, T. (1990) Legitimating and delegitimating new forms of racism – the role of researchers. In D. Gorter *et al*. (eds) *Fourth International Conference on Minority Languages* (pp. 77–100). Clevedon: Multilingual Matters.

Stradling, R.N. (Rapporteur) (1994) Research Policy Group on Europe's Lesser Used Languages: Report on the Inaugural Conference. Léirsinn Research Centre, Isle of Skye. Unpublished report circulated to participants.

Tovey, H. (1988) The State and the Irish language: The role of Bord na Gaeilge. *International Journal of the Sociology of Language* 70, 53–68.

Williams, C.H. (ed.) (1988) *Language in Geographic Context*. Clevedon: Multilingual Matters.

— (1991) *Linguistic Minorities: Societies and Territory*. Clevedon: Multilingual Matters.

— (1994) *Called Unto Liberty! On Language and Nationalism*. Clevedon: Multilingual Matters.

Williams, G. (1980) Review of E. Allardt: Implications of the ethnic revival in modern industrial society. *Journal of Multilingual and Multicultural Development* 1, 363–70.

— (1982) In G. Braga and E. Monte Civeilli (eds) *Linguistic Problems and European Unity* (pp. 75–104). Milan: Franco Angeli.

— (1983) In B. Bain (ed.) *Sociogenesis of Language and Human Conduct* (pp. 497–517). New York: Praeger.

— (1988) Review of Third International Conference on Minority Languages. *Language, Culture and Curriculum* 1(2), 169–78.

5 Prolegomena to an Israeli Language Policy

BERNARD SPOLSKY

Introduction

Except when they are central to a major nationalist or ethnic movement, language policies, like Topsy, tend to grow without overmuch official intervention. Those writing constitutions for newly-independent states are often forced to define the role of the competing languages. More often, any existing language policy has evolved piecemeal, with a combination of law, regulation, and custom. From time to time, a concerted political effort is made to proclaim a new policy (such as the English Only movement in the United States, or the Australian National Language Policy), or a Ministry of Education sets out to redefine the school-related aspect of policy, as in the Dutch National Foreign Language Action programme. Practical language policy involves charting a feasible route from an existing sociolinguistic repertoire to what is desirable.

This paper deals with language teaching policy ('acquisition planning' in Cooper's term) for the Israeli educational system. It sketches the present national language profile and lists the key issues that need resolution if a workable policy is to be developed.

Schools

The Israeli Ministry of Education supervises 2500 schools, 2000 of them for Jews with Hebrew as the language of instruction and 500 for non-Jews with Arabic. There are also many schools outside the state system, serving ultra-orthodox Jews in Israel and Arabs in the Administered Areas and the children of diplomats. Some of the ultra-orthodox Jewish schools use Yiddish as the language of instruction. Church-related schools for Arab pupils generally teach the language of their sponsoring group – e.g. German at the Martin Luther School, French and English at the Collège des Frères, Spanish at the Pilar College – but since 1969, following the Jordanian educational reform, they no longer teach in the metropolitan languages.

Hebrew

The majority of the population of Israel use Hebrew as a first or second language. Revived as a normal spoken language in newly settled villages in Palestine between 1890 and 1910 as part of the ideologically driven Jewish return to Zion, it rapidly became widely used in the Jewish community. Recognised after the First World War by the British Mandatory Government as an official language alongside English and Arabic, it developed into the main public and private language of the Jewish community, serving as lingua franca among immigrants from many language backgrounds, and was continually propagated by a strong ideological campaign.

With the establishment of the State of Israel in 1948, Hebrew became the national language, and easily dominated the other official language, Arabic. Hebrew is spoken as a first or second language by most Israelis. Arabs who speak the Palestinian dialect of Arabic as their first language and whose schools teach Standard Educated Arabic, acquire Hebrew both formally in school and informally at work.

Hebrew is taught as the second language (the Ministry of Education stresses this term, in contrast to foreign) for Arabic speakers (although it is actually the third language for all of them), starting in the third grade, and continuing until the twelfth where it is a subject for the Bagrut (or secondary school leaving) examination.

Hebrew courses in intensive programmes (*ulpanim*) have been provided for the various waves of immigrants who have come to the State since its creation, more than doubling the population. Israel is still an immigrant country, with over half a million new arrivals in the last five years. Ideological and pragmatic conditions determine that the children of new immigrants are expected to learn Hebrew as soon as possible, and there is little or no provision for bilingual instruction.

Hebrew is the language of the Knesset (Parliament), of the law courts, of the government; the language of instruction in all except Arab schools and a few ultra-orthodox Jewish schools that continue to use Yiddish, the language of television and the main radio programmes, and the language of work and of the neighbourhoods.

With Hebrew, there are some policy issues to consider:

- What is the actual level of oracy and literacy achieved by various segments of the population?
- What are the most cost-effective methods of making sure that the various non-native speaking groups (minorities, immigrants, foreigners, Diaspora Jews, citizens of neighbouring countries) acquire an appropriate level of Hebrew oracy and literacy skills.
- How do corpus-planning efforts (purism, terminological development) mesh with these goals?

Arabic

Arabic is the second official language; there is a government radio station and the government television station broadcasts in Arabic two or three hours a day; it is the language of instruction in Arab and Druze schools; and it is taught in Jewish schools.

Non-Jewish speakers of Arabic, whether Moslem, Christian or Druze, have Arabic as their language of instruction. As is true throughout the Arabic-speaking world, they face the special problem in a diglossic situation of having to learn at school what is virtually a new language, Modern Standard Arabic (Amara, 1988).

In practice, the level of knowledge of Arabic by Jews is generally low (Spolsky & Cooper, 1991). The teaching and learning of Arabic in Jewish schools in Israel has been a problem for over six decades. (Spolsky, 1994) Much debate has focused on whether to teach spoken or Standard Arabic, or which variety to start at what level. During 1988, the Ministry of Education decided to make Arabic a compulsory subject in seventh to ninth grades. At the end of 1991, a new curriculum for teaching Arabic in Jewish schools was published. In it, priority is to be given to teaching Modern Standard Arabic, with spoken Arabic an optional subject in the fourth year. At present there are about 650 full-time positions for teachers of Arabic in Jewish schools, filled by about 1000 individuals, with varying levels of competence in spoken and standard Arabic; new teacher training programmes have been established and a strong effort is starting to be made to implement a previously nominal commitment to the teaching of Arabic. Its success is likely to be closely tied to political developments in the region; a state of peace would obviously be a major contribution. There are a number of questions to ask about Arabic:

- How effective are existing programmes for developing literacy in standard Arabic and oracy in vernacular and standard Arabic among native speakers and non-native speakers?

- What use can be made of existing knowledge of spoken Arabic among sectors of the Jewish population to build up the number of speakers?
- Given existing attitudes, what is the most cost-effective method of developing a cadre of Jewish Israelis with high levels of oracy and literacy skills in Arabic?

English

While not official, English is *de facto* the second language of speakers of both Hebrew and Arabic (Spolsky, 1996). It is the main language of external commerce and for tourism, and a required language for all Jewish and Arab schools, and for the universities (all of which teach in Hebrew). In spite of the widespread official and ideological policy support for Hebrew, English has continued to flourish and spread in all sectors of the Israeli population.

After Independence in 1948, the strength of ideology associated with the teaching of Hebrew, and the insistence on Hebrew as the lingua franca for the Jewish population, (becoming increasingly multilingual as it was doubled by immigration) naturally weakened the claims and place of English. It occupied a fairly tightly restricted niche functionally and demographically and in terms of proficiency. The rapid growth started some 20 years later, as a result of a changed demographic, political, and economic situation. Fishman, Cooper & Conrad (1977) documented the first years of these changes in what might be called the English warp in the Israeli sociolinguistic texture, and there is good evidence of the continued expansion that they predicted. The official curriculum recognised English as 'the principal means of international communication today . . . a World Language' and aimed to teach a practical communicative command of the language. Many schools now start teaching English well before the compulsory fifth grade. Thus, national educational policy supports English as the major language of wider communication for Israelis, and it is taught as a major subject at both elementary and secondary schools. This Israeli educational policy appears to be in response to demand rather than leading it.

There has been strong public pressure for more and earlier teaching of English. The Ministry has now reluctantly approved a new policy permitting (but not recommending) a start in the third grade. In the meantime, demand continues for beginning English instruction even earlier, in second or first grade. However inefficient this early teaching might prove to be (it is usually offered for no more than an hour a week), it both establishes the existence of a growing demand for knowledge of the language and, as this early acquisition takes effect, augurs a continuing expansion in the knowledge and use of English by Israelis.

In Jewish schools, about 40% of the teachers are native speakers of English, but in Arab schools all teachers are native speakers of Arabic. All teaching materials, including extensive television programmes, are written and published in Israel, with Israeli pupils in mind.

There are a number of questions whose answers will be needed for wise language policy decisions:

- What are the actual levels of English oracy and literacy skills developed by various sectors of the population? What contributions to this are made by formal school instruction (both state and private) and by non-school related exposure (TV, travel, work, etc.).
- At what point might the pull towards English constitute a threat to other languages? Might it threaten Hebrew?
- What is the cost-effectiveness of various school strategies (age of starting, distribution of hours, degree of intensity) to the various possible goals?

Other International Languages

Until the end of the First World War, French was the main foreign language of Jewish schools, and continued to be important in schools affiliated to the Alliance Israelite Universelle. Since the 1969 reform, it has dropped to the place of an optional additional foreign language and may be started only in seventh or tenth grade. About 30,000 pupils are reported to learn French in Jewish schools, and 1800 pupils took the Bagrut examination in it in 1988/9. Of the 300 teachers of French (295 of them female), nearly half are Francophone (born in France or members of North African immigrant families) and half are from Rumanian immigrant families.

A few other languages are taught as optional subjects at various schools. Italian, for example is taught in a school in Bat Yam and Spanish in Tel Aviv. German is taught experimentally at six schools, with assistance from the Goethe Institute. Other languages are recognised for examination by the Ministry of Education: Russian, Persian, Portuguese, Rumanian, Yiddish, French, German, Spanish as first or foreign language, Georgian, Italian and Turkish and also Polish, Norwegian, and Amharic. This policy of permitting special examinations enables pupils who are new immigrants or who have spent several years abroad (as children of Foreign Ministry staff or of other overseas missions) to be tested in a language they know well. There are a number of questions relevant to language policy planning for other international languages:

- Given the dominant roles of Hebrew, Arabic, and English, how many additional foreign languages is it reasonable to expect to offer in formal education settings? What additional languages should be included?
- How can provision be made for maintaining an appropriate cadre of people with high enough levels of oracy and literacy in the appropriate world and commerce languages to satisfy foreseeable needs? Which languages should be included?

Heritage Languages

A large portion of the Israeli population is bilingual or multilingual. A wide range of immigrant languages continues to be spoken at home: the various Arabic and Judeo-Arabic dialects spoken by immigrants from North Africa, Egypt, Syria, Iraq, Yemen, and other Arabic speaking countries; Yiddish among older immigrants from Eastern Europe and widely used among Ashkenazic ultra-orthodox Jews, a few of whom still refuse to use Modern Hebrew; Judeo-Spanish (Ladino) among Jews from Greece and the Levant; Judeo-Aramaic (Kurdit) among Jews from Iraq and Iran; most major European languages among immigrants from there and from Latin America; and English among immigrants from North America, South Africa, Great Britain, Australia, and New Zealand. In the last few years, there have been two major waves of immigration: 20,000 Jews from Ethiopia speaking Jewish varieties of Amharic and Tigrinya but also reading Giiz; and 500,000 from the disintegrating Soviet Union speaking mainly Russian but also other languages of the region. There are newspapers and radio programmes in many immigrant languages, which continue to be used within the home and the community. Younger immigrants (children going to school or younger adults serving in the Army) rapidly become Hebrew speakers.

From its period as the principal competitor for the claim for Hebrew as a Jewish national language, Yiddish continues to have an ambivalent status in Israel. Yiddish became a recognised school subject only in 1973, with growth only after 1984, when the Ministry appointed a half-time Chief Inspector, started to fund and control teaching hours, and organised teaching, and teacher training in general. Yiddish is now an optional subject in over 50 Jewish schools, at primary, intermediate, and upper levels. All 35 teachers of Yiddish are women, many of them close to or past retirement age. Pupils learning Yiddish in tenth to twelfth grade can take a Bagrut examination; in the summer of 1992, 32 pupils did so. While still small, the growth of the teaching of Yiddish must be considered to show revolutionary progress in the status of the language, and to reflect a changed willingness to accept a language previously under ideological attack.

There has been a beginning also of the teaching of another traditional Jewish language. Judezmo has been taught since 1989/90 at one school, the Amalia Religious School.

- What is the level of language maintenance in these heritage languages? What is the level of Reversing Language Shift activities?
- What support can be offered by the educational system to attempts to revive or maintain Jewish heritage languages?

Other Minority Languages

Other significant non-Jewish language communities use as their first language Armenian, Circassian, Assyrian, and Domari (a Gypsy language). Circassian, the language of a small non-Jewish minority, which has used the Cyrillic alphabet since the Russian Revolution, now has some role in part of the school system. Though their native language, it was until recently used by Israeli Circassians only at home. In 1971 it was introduced as a compulsory subject for Circassians in the sixth to eighth grades and textbooks were prepared. Armenian is taught in the Armenian school in Jerusalem.

Conclusions

Language teaching policy in Israel continues to be dominated by the ideological role and practical value of Hebrew. It is further driven by the existence of non-Hebrew speaking groups, such as the non-Jewish minorities and the 70,000 new immigrant children who entered school in September 1991. It responds strongly to the instrumental claims for English as a world language, and is starting to recognise the political values of Arabic, and to a lesser extent, of French. Any limited recognition of other languages is a reflection of the linguistic complexity of the population.

These language-related pressures, coming at a time when the State continues to struggle with major problems of defence, immigrant absorption, and economic development, means that the selection of priorities for language education has been very difficult. The highest priority has been accorded to ensuring that the whole population is capable of using Hebrew. A second major programme has been building effective teaching of English. More recently, a serious start has been made on the teaching of Arabic to Jews.

Time has also been found for limited recognition of some of the many other languages that might one day have a claim for a place in an elaborated language policy.

There are a number of signs that the present *ad hoc* policy needs some changes. One is the new phenomenon of a growing population of monolinguals, young Israelis who function effectively only in Hebrew and are hard put to learn instrumentally useful languages like English and Arabic or the languages of their own ethnic origins. Another is a school policy that tends to assume that English is a second language for everyone, including the large Arabic and immigrant minorities for whom it is at least the third. The drive to English is an unhealthy sign of growing linguistic insecurity – the failure to develop strong programmes for other international languages like French and Japanese and Spanish and Italian and Chinese will limit a more balanced international policy. The weakness of knowledge of Arabic means not just lack of communication with the Arabic speaking minorities, but also regional isolation. The undue ideological emphasis of new immigrant programmes weakens the needed focus on functional language skills.

One critical factor missing in language policy is the enormous potential value of minority, ethnic, and immigrant languages in providing (through encouragement of Reversing Language Shift activities) a valuable pool of fluent multilinguals providing access to large sectors of the world's population. A programme building on this linguistic raw material would be at once cost-effective and socially valuable.

Note

This paper began with research carried out by Michael Hallel in a course taught by Bernard Spolsky and was then developed by them into Hallel & Spolsky (1993). After extensive discussions of the need for language policy with Elana Shohamy, Spolsky wrote a first long version of this paper for presentation at a seminar held at the National Foreign Language Center at Johns Hopkins University on 10 March 1994. It was later revised to include ideas and passages from Shohamy (1994). This is a shortened version, written for the International Conference on Language, Education, and Society in a Changing World sponsored by the Irish Association for Applied Linguistics at the Marino Institute of Education, Dublin 23–25 June 1994.

References

Amara, M.H. (1988) Arabic diglossia: Conditions for learning the standard variety (in Arabic). *Aljadid* 12, 14–23.
Fishman, J.A., Cooper, R.L. and Conrad, A.W. (1977) *The Spread of English: The Sociology of English as an Additional Language*. Rowley, MA: Newbury House.

Hallel, M. and Spolsky, B. (1993) The teaching of additional languages in Israel. *Annual Review of Applied Linguistics* 13, 37–49.
Shohamy, E. (1994) Issues of language planning in Israel: Language and ideology. In R.D. Lambert (ed.) *Language Planning Around the World: Contexts and Systemic Change* (pp. 131–42). Washington, DC: The National Foreign Language Center.
Spolsky, B. and Cooper, R.L. (1991) *The Languages of Jerusalem.* Oxford: Clarendon Press.
Spolsky, B. (1994) Policy issues in testing and evaluation. *The Annals of the American Academy of Political and Social Science* 532, 226–37.
— (1994) The situation of Arabic in Israel. In Y. Suleiman (ed.) *Proceedings of the 1993 Edinburgh Symposium on Arabic Sociolinguistics.* Richmond: Curzon Press.
— (1996) English in Israel after Independence. In J.A. Fishman, A. Rubal-Lopez and A.W. Conrad (eds) *Post-Imperial English.* Berlin: Mouton.

6 Language Policy in a Divided Community

SEAN FARREN

Introduction

Since the foundation of Northern Ireland in 1921, school curricula, though in broad terms similar for the schools which served the two politico-religious communities (Catholic-Nationalist and Protestant-Unionist) in the region, were effectively mediated through quite distinct and almost exclusive cultural perspectives. In schools serving the Protestant-Unionist community what can best be described as a Northern Irish Britishness formed the basis to their perspective (Farren, in press). In essence, this entailed a stress on a Protestant approach to the British way of life and, with it, the deliberate avoidance of cultural expressions which seemed distinctively Irish, even where these would have pertained to the Protestant tradition in Ireland itself. In curricular terms, this also meant the avoidance, or deliberate exclusion from courses of study of many literary works associated with the Anglo-Irish tradition, the avoidance of a detailed study of Irish history and the exclusion of the Irish language and other expressions of the Gaelic-Irish heritage.

On the other hand, in schools serving the Catholic-Nationalist community, the perspective was, by definition, Catholic, but also Irish. In such schools not only was their Catholic ethos celebrated, but so also was its Irish context through an emphasis on the Anglo-Irish literary tradition, on the Irish language and on such other features of the Gaelic-Irish heritage as Gaelic games, music and song.

The exclusiveness of both perspectives has for long been recognised as at least reinforcing, if not exacerbating, socio-political division in Northern Ireland. For the past 20 years considerable energy has been expended in devising means whereby schools might assist both communities to escape the negative aspects of their respective cultural inheritance (Farren, 1991). The

Education Reform Order (Northern Ireland), 1989, reflected a quiet revolution in educational policy with respect to most areas of school curricula, not least the language curriculum. Among the most notable changes in this area have been the cultural dimension to the study of English and the status afforded the Irish language. In a number of respects the Education Reform Order marked the extent to which the efforts of the last 20 years have been successful in achieving some of their more important objectives.

This paper is intended as a contribution to the on-going evaluation of that achievement through a consideration of the changes affecting English and Irish in Northern Ireland.

Cultural Heritage and Education for Mutual Understanding

Under the Education Reform Order 'Programmes of Study' were devised for each subject. These programmes set out the main objectives and attainment targets for each of four age-related stages of schooling. Of particular significance to those charged with preparing the programmes of study for each school subject was a requirement to include a set of cross-curricular 'educational themes', one of which has a direct bearing on our discussion, namely the 'cultural heritage theme'. The theme is defined in the anthropological sense which states that culture and cultural heritage are

> . . . the artefacts, ideas and learned behaviour which make up people's ways of life. The term 'cultural heritage' should be taken to mean those elements of culture which are inherited. (Department of Education, NI, 1992: 8)

Its aims are to enable 'pupils know about, understand and evaluate: the common experiences of their cultural heritage; the diverse and distinctive aspects of their culture; the interdependence of cultures' (1992: 8). The scope of the theme is universal in the sense that it envisages the exploration of cultures from the most local to the most distant, in order that pupils should appreciate their diversity, distinctiveness and interdependence.

Complementing the 'cultural heritage' theme is that of 'education for mutual understanding' which is 'about fostering self-respect, respect for others and the improvement of relationships between people of differing cultural traditions' (Department of Education, NI, 1992: 5). The theme's objectives include that of developing 'knowledge and understanding of conflict in a variety of contexts and of approaches to its resolution by non-violent means' (1992: 5). Together, both themes have provided a clear imperative for curriculum planners to ensure that never again will pupils in either of

Northern Ireland's two main communities fail to address each other's origins or their relationships to one another.

Language, Cultural Heritage and Education for Mutual Understanding

Language, as a major repository of culture, is a primary means for meeting the aims of both themes, providing as it does potential access to an enormous diversity of cultural experiences, local, national and international. At curriculum planning level, the impact on English has been to widen and deepen the natural account which the subject takes of 'cultural heritage'. This is most notable

(a) in the requirement in the new *Programmes of Study* for English (Department of Education, Northern Ireland, 1990) to study works by local authors together with those of authors from other English-speaking communities across the world;
(b) in the requirement to study local varieties of English as a contribution to developing pupils' 'knowledge about language';
(c) in the requirement to explore through discussion, role play and extra-school contacts controversial issues relating to life in Northern Ireland and elsewhere.

As far as 'education for mutual understanding' is concerned, English allows for considerable overlap between it and 'cultural heritage', especially given the stress in English upon exploring relationships and issues, whether in a literary or real life context.

A second area of the curriculum upon which recent changes have impacted is the study of the Irish language, now undergoing significant change in terms of its educational and general social status. Since the early decades of this century when the language revival movement became ideologically part of the movement for political independence in Ireland, Irish had been almost exclusively a nationalist possession. As a result, much of the pre-existing sympathy for and interest in Irish amongst Unionists evaporated (Farren, 1985). In Northern Ireland the language was ghettoised within the Catholic-Nationalist community. Meanwhile, successive Northern Irish governments evolved a virtual policy of official neglect of, and contempt for, any move to encourage the teaching, or use of the language (Andrews, 1991).

Recent political pressures stressing parity of esteem for the cultural traditions of both communities in Northern Ireland have produced a significant change in official policy towards Irish. One product of these pressures, the

Anglo-Irish Agreement (1985: 1), refers to the need to recognise and respect 'the identities of the two communities in Northern Ireland'. Another important influence on official attitudes towards Irish in Northern Ireland has been the European Community's recognition of and support for 'lesser used languages'. As a result of such pressures, the language has begun to acquire an enhanced status, evident in education, as well as more generally through the acceptance of Irish as an important part of the cultural life of Northern Ireland. Consequently, for the first time since the establishment of Northern Ireland, positive policies are evolving within government aimed at affording recognition and respect for the use of Irish, as well as at promoting the learning of Irish and knowledge about the language. Irish is now slowly emerging from its exclusive association with the Catholic-Nationalist community and acquiring a degree of common ownership across the communal divide in Northern Ireland, thus, as Hawthorne (1989: 2) put it, advancing the language 'beyond the immediate tribal stereotypes'.

Within education this has resulted in a number of initiatives, in particular recognition and support for Irish-medium schools, of which there is now a small, but growing, number as well as more positive attitudes towards the teaching of Irish at primary and post-primary levels throughout the school system. These steps have been paralleled by the initiatives which are conferring a more positive status on Irish generally, together with support for promoting its use. Most notably, there has been the establishment of a small, government-funded agency, Iontaobhas Ultach/Ultach Trust, to promote interest in and knowledge about Irish across the communities, while broadcasts in Irish have begun to make an appearance in the programming of several radio and television channels. As yet, the use of Irish for official purposes is limited, but now at least letters written in Irish to government departments will be answered and not discarded, or returned to their senders, as used to be the practice.

The Ultach Trust aims '. . . to advance the Irish language traditions and cultural heritage, and to make the same more readily available to the people of Northern Ireland' (Iontaobhas Ultach/Ultach Trust, 1990–1: 6). Its establishment is probably the most significant political measure taken to provide support for the Irish language, not least because it has been able to attract to its board persons from the Protestant-Unionist community as well as from the Catholic-Nationalist community. The fact that such cross-community involvement has been achieved is an important breakthrough, though one which should not be exaggerated, because the challenge posed by continuing hostility to the language, and more so to what it connotes politically, remains formidable.

Taking developments in and outside education, it is possible to argue that significant changes have taken place over the past decade in official and other attitudes not only towards the Irish language, but also towards the wider Gaelic tradition, all achieved within a context which stresses relationships and contrasts between the different cultural traditions existing in Northern Ireland and, more generally, in Ireland as a whole.

The Effects of Change

Determining the effects of these initiatives is not easy since, by their very nature and their gradual implementation, considerable time will have to be allowed before an evaluation is possible. Even then, identifying direct causal links between these initiatives and any behavioural, or attitudinal changes will be difficult, if not impossible, to establish. Nonetheless, it is possible to point to some indicators as to possible effects and in this section of the paper a number will be referred to, beginning with evidence relating to the English curriculum.

English

As part of a wider investigation into aspects of the English curriculum at secondary level conducted by the author, 30 teachers in schools throughout Northern Ireland were interviewed in depth in 1993 on issues which included the cross-curriculum themes of 'cultural heritage' and 'education for mutual understanding'. The interviews were conducted in a sample of schools which included selective and non-selective entry schools, Catholic and Protestant, rural and urban schools. The interviews attempted to elicit teachers' understanding of both themes and how they incorporated them into their English curricula.

The responses reveal a remarkable consensus in favour of both themes. Most teachers expressed considerable sympathy with the aims underlying the inclusion of the themes within the programmes of study, with many claiming that English had always taken cognisance of 'cultural heritage' since it is inherent to the subject. Not a single teacher of the 30 interviewed expressed any reservations about the theme. Some were concerned that 'education for mutual understanding' was, as one teacher said, 'contrived' and another described it as 'social engineering' because it appeared to him/her as 'attempting to push people in Northern Ireland together – which is all very fine but is not the role of English teachers'. Paradoxically, this same teacher went on to say that '. . . education for mutual understanding cannot be ignored by English teachers since the novels, poems and writing in general have the theme built in'.

More precise responses included 'cultural heritage and education for mutual understanding go together. They cover such topics as self; relationships; respect; conflict; interdependence; cultural and linguistic relationships; mythologies; . . . a literature . . .'

'Cultural heritage' as a universally applicable concept is mentioned in many responses by teachers anxious not to see it exclusively confined to the region's indigenous cultures. As one put it, 'It is not good or productive to focus on the narrow . . . cultural heritage of Northern Ireland', while another argued that '. . . our cultural heritage is both local and worldwide'. Amongst the objectives acknowledged and accepted for both themes, teachers included 'tolerance', 'empathy', and 'understanding of other people'. One teacher imaginatively summed up the ultimate aim for both themes in the statement: 'if cultural heritage can be called the engagement, then education for mutual understanding is the marriage'.

Assimilating these themes into English teaching did not seem to pose many new challenges for most of the teachers questioned, though for some the need to broaden their knowledge of local literature and local dialects was acknowledged. Overall, therefore, their views suggest that the approaches adopted for 'cultural heritage' and 'education for mutual understanding' are regarded as satisfactory.

Irish

Determining the effects of the changes on Irish is even more difficult than for English. It is clear that a greater consciousness about Irish now exists across both communities together with a willingness to proclaim, on an individual basis, one's knowledge of the language. The latter point was most clearly made in responses to the question on Irish included in the 1991 population census – the inclusion of the question for the first time since 1911 being itself a signal of official acknowledgement of Irish. Responses to the question revealed that there are 142,000 persons with some knowledge of the language of whom 79,000 can speak, read and write Irish (*Northern Ireland Census*, 1991). Another quite general and, perhaps, surprising effect is the emergence within the Protestant-Unionist community of more favourable attitudes towards the Irish language and Irish culture as evidenced in the report, *Social Attitudes in Northern Ireland*, which revealed that more than 23% of Protestants interviewed 'favoured the teaching of Irish and Irish culture in schools' (Stringer & Robinson, 1991). Less scientific, but nonetheless indicative is the *Opsahl Report*'s finding that a considerable number of senior students in schools of both traditions requested that 'all schools should give pupils the option to study . . . the Irish language' (Pollak, 1993: 380).

There is, however, still evidence of considerable hostility within the Protestant-Unionist community towards Irish and towards what is perceived to be 'Irish culture' generally, not least because Irish culture is seen to be still closely associated with Catholicism and, by implication, Irish nationalism. According to the *Opsahl Report*, 'the single greatest factor causing Protestants to dissociate themselves from the Irish culture was considered . . . to be religion . . .' (Pollak, 1993: 381). This hostility probably explains why, despite some change in attitudes over the past few years, the Ultach Trust has recently reported that, in schools catering for the Protestant community, Irish is still rarely taught (Iontaobhas Ultach/Ultach Trust, 1991–3: 9).

In practical terms, therefore, at school level Irish continues to be mainly a Catholic-Nationalist subject, but even within this community the condition of the language is not as healthy as it could be. An important indicator of this condition is the declining number of pupils pursuing Irish courses (*Irish Times*, 1991). The Ultach Trust attributes the decline to pressures arising from the new Common Curriculum which it claims 'has imposed such a heavy compulsory timetable on schools that it is now difficult for all but the most dedicated and able to study more than one language to a meaningful level . . . this has created a damaging and unnecessary rivalry between the claims of modern languages' (Iontaobhas Ultach/Ultach Trust, 1991–3: 9).

While progress with respect to Irish-medium schools has been significant and perhaps even spectacular given the situation that existed previously, considerable challenges still remain. In September 1993 there were eight Irish-medium schools (seven primary and one second level) (Smith, 1994), together with a number of Irish-medium streams in other schools. In addition, there are approximately 15 Irish-medium pre-school groups operating throughout Northern Ireland. Among the objectives of the latter are the '[preparation of] the child for the demands of a normal Primary 1 curriculum in an Irish-medium school' (Mac Póilín, 1992: 40). In total this provision currently caters for about 750 young people between the ages of three and 16 (Iontaobhas Ultach, personal communication). These numbers are increasing, with several more schools at each level expected to open in the next year or so.

While the provision for Irish-medium education has been advanced, it still encounters serious problems, among which are official regulations not yet modified to respond flexibly to the particular needs of such schools. Regulations as to viability criteria, for example, which require an ultimate enrolment of 200 pupils in urban areas and 100 in rural areas, clearly pose major challenges for Irish-medium primary schools in a situation in which the average enrolment in primary schools generally is just over 100. While Irish-medium schools in large urban areas can have reasonable expectations of meeting the criteria, this is not the case in rural areas. Similar problems also exist for second-level schools, notwithstanding the fact that some relaxation of the criteria has been allowed in their case. In Mac Póilín's (1992) analysis, Irish-medium schools in Northern Ireland would appear to be at a considerable disadvantage, when compared with the conditions applying to the establishment of Gaelic-medium schools in Scotland and Gaelic units within English-medium schools. The disadvantage is even greater when the comparison is made with Welsh-medium education.

The greatest challenge, therefore, is to create such a demand for Irish-medium education as will oblige not just a relaxation of existing criteria but the adoption of specific criteria more in line with the needs of Irish-medium schools. This is a considerable challenge in á socio-political climate which regards education primarily in economic terms and, also, one which has a legacy of hostility towards the language. In such a climate, the task of convincing parents that their children would benefit from being educated in a language which is hardly used at all in business, industry, administration or in the professions, is a difficult one. Displacing the legacy of hostility and moving the language further from its ghetto existence is essentially a challenge for those who believe it to be central to the cultural heritage of the whole community in Northern Ireland.

Conclusion

Within the new climate of opinion affecting community relations policies in Northern Ireland, attitudes towards crucial features of cultural identity in Ireland have undergone rapid change. This is evident, in a positive sense, both at official level and, to some extent, at community level also, where it is ultimately intended to impact most. This paper has attempted to highlight aspects of this change as it has manifested itself in school curricula with respect to two subjects, English and Irish. The evidence reviewed for English suggests a positive picture in the sense that there has been widespread acceptance of programmes which require that attention be paid to the literary and linguistic heritage of both major cultural traditions in Northern Ireland.

As far as the Irish language is concerned the situation continues to be much more problematic. At school level, teaching the language itself and teaching through the language are still very much confined to the Catholic-Nationalist community; only in the freer context of adult education are large numbers from the Protestant-Unionist community to be found pursuing an interest in Irish. What is encouraging about Irish is the fact that the language is now no longer officially scorned and, as a result, not only are greater levels of support available for its promotion, but acceptance of the language as part of people's general heritage is now widespread across both communities. The time has probably come to strengthen this support with statutory guarantees such as would be provided in a special Languages Act for Northern Ireland.

References

Andrews, L.S. (1991) The Irish language in the educational system of Northern Ireland: Some political and cultural perspectives. In R.M.O. Pritchard (ed.) *Motivating the Majority – Modern Languages in Northern Ireland* (pp. 89–100). London: CILT, 6.

Department of Education, Northern Ireland (1990) *Programmes of Study and Attainment Targets in English.* Belfast: HMSO.

— (1992) *Educational Themes.* Belfast: HMSO.

Education Reform Order (Northern Ireland) (1989). Belfast: HMSO.

Farren, S. (1985) Protestant-Unionist reaction to education reform in Northern Ireland, 1923–1930. *History of Education* 14(3), 227–36.

— (1991) Culture, curriculum and educational policy in Northern Ireland. *Language Culture and Curriculum* 4 (1), 43–58.

— (in press) *The Politics of Irish Education 1920–1965.* Belfast: Queen's University Institute of Irish Studies.

Hawthorne, J. (1989) What is a 'cultural tradition'? Supplement to *Fortnight 327,* November, 2–3.

Iontaobhas Ultach, personal communication.

Iontaobhas Ultach/Ultach Trust (1991) *Tuairisc Bliantúil/Annual Report 1990–1991.*

— (1993) *An Dara Tuairisc/Second Report 1991–93.*

Ireland (1985) *Anglo-Irish Agreement.* Dublin: Stationery Office.

Irish Times (1991) Irish declines in North's schools. 12 February.

Mac Póilín, A. (1992) *Irish-Medium Education in Northern Ireland: A Preliminary Report.* Belfast: Ultach Trust.

Northern Ireland Census, 1991 (1992) (p. 159). Belfast: HMSO.

Pollak, A. (ed.) (1993) *A Citizen's Inquiry – The Opsahl Report on Northern Ireland.* Dublin: The Lilliput Press.

Smith, A. (1994) Education and intergroup relations. Unpublished paper to seminar, Centre for the Study of Conflict, University of Ulster, March.

Stringer, P. and Robinson, G. (1991) *Social Attitudes in Northern Ireland.* Belfast: Blackstaff Press.

7 Hebrew and Irish: Language Revival Revisited

MUIRIS Ó LAOIRE

Introduction

The debate on the revitalisation and extension of Irish, with its concomitant history of apparent failures, mobilised emotions and sustained discussion, has included in the past analogous references to the revival of Hebrew. It is interesting to note that such references appeared as early as 1924, when the editorial of the Irish language paper *Fáinne an Lae* considered the revitalisation of Hebrew as a paradigm for revivalists' efforts here (*Fáinne an Lae*, 19 January 1924). The 'miracle of modern Hebrew' (*ivrit*) has since then often been proposed as a prototype of language revival, with the subtle implication that efforts towards achieving revitalisation of Irish (*An Ghaeilge*) could at best imitate this linguistic transformation. More recently, however, the analogy of Hebrew has been dismissed as being over-simplified and largely untenable in the Irish context (Edwards, 1985; Hindley, 1990). This paper will concentrate on identifying some model for a comparison between the two revitalisation movements, while avoiding any over-simplified analogous references.

The revitalisation of Hebrew, which could be described in many respects as the fortuitous historical co-occurrence of many factors (Nahir, 1988), nonetheless would seem to have many partial parallels with other linguistic revivals (see, for example Blanc, 1968; Fellman, 1974). It is therefore hoped to extract some points of reference from the Hebrew revival situation regarding status planning for the home and school domain, which may be applicable to the situation regarding the promotion and extension of Irish today.

The research method employed here benefits largely from the approach and from the nature of the analyses developed by historians of language

63

revival, and from their contributions to sociolinguistics and language planning. This parallel study is relevant to the study of language planning in Ireland today in that it brings to the debate the important dimension of an external comparative critique, which safeguards against discussions which may be flawed by an over-introspective paralysis of analysis.

The Communicative Factor

A direct comparison between the two revival movements will reveal little by way of similarity and much by way of contrast. The main difference referred to by Edwards (1985) and by Spolsky & Cooper (1991) is that the attempted revival of Irish did not coincide with communicative need as happened in the context of multilingualism in Palestine at the beginning of the last century and in the early decades of this century. Peres (1964: 19), a contemporary source, writes as follows about the linguistically heterogeneous city of Jerusalem at the turn of the century:

> There was no common language in Jerusalem . . . The Sephardics spoke Judeo-Spanish . . . the Musta'Arabian spoke Palestinian Arabic, the Maghrebines (north African Jews) spoke Arabic . . . the Crimeans spoke Tatar and the Ashkenazim spoke different dialects of Yiddish.

This historical observation tends to indicate that a critical factor for the successful revival or restoration of a vernacular is what Nahir (1988) has termed 'the communicative factor' – a language of public interaction crucial for the organisation of, and survival of, society. Cooper (1989: 107) explains this as follows: 'The Jews needed a *lingua franca* to talk to one another, whereas the Irish did not'.

The fact that the communicative need was dominant in the case of Hebrew, especially during the early decades of this century, and that this factor was largely absent in the case of Irish, marks a salient difference between the two language revival movements. However, the communicative need was not as dominant and as crucial a factor when and where the Hebrew language was *first* renativised and revernacularised, namely on the agricultural settlements like Rishon-Le-Zion during the period of the first and second *aliyot* (mass emigration movement) between 1880 and 1920. It is worth bearing in mind that here in the agricultural settlements and small villages, unlike the multi-lingualism which prevailed in the cities, the linguistic situation was more homogeneous (Bar Adon, 1975; Nahir, 1987). The majority of the immigrants came from Eastern Europe and were Yiddish-speaking. Prior to their arrival, there is evidence to suggest that Arabic was used by up to thirty percent of the Jewish population. Hofman & Fisherman (1972) and Parfitt (1972) would maintain that Hebrew was being spoken by some communities in the cities. Yellin (1923: 26), a contemporary source, however, described the bizarre nature of the new communicative challenge to speak Hebrew as follows:

> People had been accustomed all their life to speak a language which was easy to them and then they were suddenly called upon to compel themselves to become accustomed to a language which they had never spoken and moreover which was not rich enough to express all they wanted to express.

It would appear that on the agricultural settlements the pressing need for a common language was absent. Yet, ironically, it was here that the processes of revernacularisation and renativisation first took place (Bar-Adon, 1977). It is these very processes of initial nativisation which may be worthy of further analysis with a view to their proposal as a paradigm for the current situation in Irish language planning.

The historical question relevant to the Irish situation is why and how Hebrew became vernacularised in the absence of any overriding communicative need. In this context, national and socio-political factors rather than communicative factors need to be examined.

National and Socio-Political Factors

The linguistic situation on the agricultural settlements and in the small villages in Palestine during the period 1880–1930 needs to be analysed in more detail in this context, in that it was here that Hebrew was first renativised and revitalised in the presence of certain socio-political factors.

Interestingly enough, it is this very socio-political background that affords a comparison with the Irish situation. Cooper (1989), adopting Stewart's (1968) list of language functions, finds a similarity between the Irish and Hebrew situation in the Group (g) function. This refers to the function of a linguistic system among the members of a single cultural or ethnic group. Linguistic and group membership are intrinsically linked and language is perceived therefore as the key component in the criteria for group membership definition.

This link between language and group membership was one of the central concerns of the *elites* who were to the forefront in the Irish language revival movement in the second half of the nineteenth century. Revivalists like De hÍde, Mac Néill and Ó Gramhnaigh in particular were exponents of cultural nationalism (Fishman, 1971), which stressed the intrinsic links between language and nationalism. Weinstein (1983) notes that these enthusiasts, espousing the Herderian belief in the existence of a separate language as a proof of nationhood, chose Irish as a symbol and as an instrument of efforts at political integration. The protection of the language, which was well and truly in demise in the *Gaeltacht* (geographically denoted regions where Gaelic/ Irish is the primary language) and virtually extinct outside of it, was verbalised and couched in defensive terms, advocating the rejection of assimilation (see, for example, De hÍde, 1894).

Similarly in the case of Hebrew, a European-derived and Herderian-influenced language and nationality philosophy also evolved, highlighting Hebrew monolingualism as a key to participation in group membership of the Jewish nation which Zionism was proposing. Ben Yehuda (1879) provides an exposition of this philosophy.

However, the socio-political factors using the same function (g) in both cases did not have similar effects, due to historical circumstances. In the Irish case, Fishman (1972) points out that loyalty to the socio-political ideologies of cultural nationalism was confined to the participation of *protoelites* of upper middle-class individuals and organisations. Cultural nationalism at the end of the nineteenth century, however, was a different type of nationalism from the type of nationalism which the Irish had espoused and had participated in, *en masse*, earlier in the nineteeth century. Comerford (1982) acknowledged that this type of nationalism had a strong, palpable socio-economic dimension, particularly with its prospects of agrarian reform. The cultural nationalism to which De hÍde and revivalists subscribed, on the other hand, was neither governed nor motivated by socio-economics and had little to offer the mass of the Irish population both inside and outside the *Gaeltacht* by way of financial gain. It is not surprising, therefore, that the language and culture agenda proposed by middle class language enthusiasts had little to engage the imagi-nation and needs of the masses.

One example of this class difference in response to cultural nationalism is the Gaelic League. This was very successful as a cultural movement, in that within a short period it had won wide support for its educational programme in particular. However, MacNamara (1971) shows that it failed to muster significant support among the working classes, with the main support for its 593 branches in 1904 coming almost exclusively from middle income groups. With the founding of the Free State in 1922, the thrust and nature of the ideology of language revival remained closely influenced by the cultural nationalism model, and proposals to revive the language on the basis of that model were largely alien to the culture and aspirations of the vast majority of the population. The national political factors were less successful in the case of Irish from then onwards, because economics competed with culture for the main ideology of the new state. Ó Doibhlin (n.d.) has commented, in fact, that it was the native government which dealt the greatest blow to the revival movement, by leaving it without its *raison d'être*. From then on, language planning in Ireland was confronted by socio-economic and personal judgements while holding on to its ideological base.

In Palestine's agricultural settlements from 1880–1920, on the other hand, the national-political factor engaged the imagination and support of the *halutzim* (pioneers) and played a significant role in the transition into Hebrew from dominant Yiddish. Here in small geographically isolated units, ideologies were easily nurtured among the early settlers, who saw themselves as pioneers and nation-builders. Fellman (1993) described these people as being mostly young, idealistic, educated and ideologically motivated. If we focus on the actual processes of language revitalisation here, we see that individual families made a choice to use Hebrew in the home domain. Eventually, Fishman (1991) points out, this choice effectively ensured the transmission of Hebrew to a new generation, thus achieving informal intergenerational oralcy. The actual shift which occurred tends to show, therefore, that ideological forces can work to overcome instrumental or pragmatic value systems, which historically were constraints in the Irish situation.

Interestingly enough, what happened in the urban centres in Palestine in the same period years mirrors what actually happened in the Irish situation. Here the process of revernacularisation was in the hands of protoelites like Ben Yehuda, who has often been called the father of modern Hebrew. However, while Ben Yehuda played a significant part in elaboration and codification, he held a peripheral position in code selection and in status planning. Rabin (1969) reminds us that Ben Yehuda was unable to create a popular movement, because 23 years after settling in Jerusalem, there were barely 10 Hebrew-speaking families there. The philosophy of language revival remained alien in many senses to the value system of the ordinary urban family of the era. Here, as in the Irish situation, the cultural nationalism which was the basis for Ben Yehuda's thesis touched the lives of only the few. Ideology in the urban centres in Palestine in the early years had not provided in any real sense a rationale to underpin motivation, just as it had not in the Irish situation.

The Schools as Agents of Revitalisation

We might well ask the important question at this stage as to *why* and *how* the critical steps were taken in the rural context of Palestine. The answer here is relevant to the Irish situation in that the schools on the agricultural settlements were seen as the prime agents of revival. It is true that the schools in Ireland were also the main focus for the revival and promotion of Irish outside the *Gaeltacht*. It might be instructional in the context of present day Irish language status planning, which has witnessed an extraordinary growth in all-Irish playschools and primary schools (with approximately 100 all-Irish primary and 22 post-primary schools) to briefly outline what happened in the promotion of Hebrew through the agency of the school and to compare it to what happened in the Irish situation.

In Palestine 1880–1930, the schools have often been credited with the revival of the language (Rabin, 1969; Bar-Adon, 1975; Fellman, 1979), in that they had more of an ideological focus. As already specified, the small geographically isolated units provided more fertile ground for the nurturance of ideologies among the early settlers, who saw themselves as pioneers and nation-builders. It was in this context that revernacularisation took place.

The question which needs to be explored in the Hebrew situation is how children and parents, once ideologically motivated, actually learned and acquired the language. Nahir (1987, 1988) has outlined a number of stages in the process and Spolsky (1991), drawing on a general theory for second language learning, explains the processes more fully. Firstly, schools conferred a high status and prestige on Hebrew, combining this with the inculcation of unfavourable attitudes to the mother tongue (especially Yiddish). Secondly, children acquired the linguistic model presumably in the classrooms of teachers who themselves were not fully fluent in the language.

The puzzle in the case of Hebrew centres on this question of how teachers were able to teach other subjects in a language which they themselves were just adopting under an act of will. In fact, most of these teachers would have had a solid, if passive, knowledge in Hebrew's Biblical or Talmudic varieties. There was also a rich literary tradition which had continued from the middle ages onwards, which witnessed a development in the language outside the specific domains of liturgy and prayer. By the mid-nineteenth century, Glinert (1987) notes, an interpretation of the law, the *Kitzur*, which included details on how the Torah affected every aspect of daily life, was published and had widespread circulation. It might be reasonably surmised that the type of Hebrew which the teachers taught and spoke was akin to the style and type of Hebrew found in these documents. All males would have been familiar with the style and with the vocabulary items of this type of Hebrew, so fathers were able to complement and reinforce teachers' efforts at home. Spolsky (1991) claims that this was an important component in the process, because successful language revitalisation may depend on previous knowledge of the language, which all parents and adults would have had in this case.

The next step, as outlined by Nahir (1988), is the most critical, and most difficult component in the formula to understand. Having acquired the linguistic model in school, children transferred the use of Hebrew to situations and domains outside the classroom. This stage is perhaps the most important for consideration in the Irish context. Here the motivating factors would tend to be linked significantly to socio-political factors. While it is reported that Hebrew school graduates who were already more or less fluent in the language stopped speaking Hebrew when they were away from school, especially at home (which summarises the Irish situation very well), there came a point however, when it did become socially desirable to speak Hebrew. Youth culture saw Hebrew as a vital component in its new identity, playing a part as it did in nation revival and nation building. Eventually, the use of Hebrew was behaviourally expected, and socially desirable and prestigious. The bridging between school and home was done by children in this first step at achieving informal intergenerational oralcy (children-to-adults-order) in reversing linguistic behaviour. The culmination of the process was where the newly born children of this generation received Hebrew as a mother tongue, by which the revival was eventually achieved.

A similar immersion approach (full or partial) was adopted in Irish primary and post-primary schools from 1922 onwards, although it was never fully realised. (Ó Riagáin (1988) notes that the highest percentage of schools adopting a full immersion approach reached 12% of the entire school cohort in 1940–41.) Although schools conferred a high status on the language, as schools did in the case of Hebrew, here children reacted negatively to it, in the absence of any mobilising ideological forces in the home. Evidence from the INTO (Irish National Teachers' Organisation) at the time would suggest that teachers themselves reacted unfavourably to the pressure brought to bear on them by compulsory Irish and the immersion approach (see Ó Muimhneacháin, 1974). Spolsky (1991), in positing the relevance of second language learning theory to understanding revitalisation, has stressed the importance of previous knowledge and exposure to the target language as essential ingredients in language revival. Both aspects were largely absent in the case of Irish in the home domain outside the *Gaeltacht*. While there was intensive teaching of the language, with full competence at the end of primary school being the declared aim (Dáil Debates, VIII, 414, 3 July 1924), the language was not used in the home or community. This is hardly surprising because, unlike the Hebrew case, families in general had become alienated from the cultural nationalism model on which the revivalist premises were based. It was the teachers who were imposing the language on children against their will in an ideological vacuum.

While Irish was and is a compulsory part of the curriculum, the Irish syllabus in primary and in post-primary schools has, until recently, had a narrow linguistic focus, with little or no reference to language use, to the history of the revival movement or to any ideology, other than gaining points for university entry. The Hebrew case would suggest that a concentration on pure linguistic forms in schools does not work. In Ireland, the isolation of the language and its relegation to the study of linguistic forms and literature has been most unhelpful and has traditionally been associated with negative attitudes to the language. While it is important that students are taught the language, the Hebrew situation may inform us that students, if they are to speak the language outside the domain of the school, must be imbued with a sense of purpose and with an awareness of language use. Current innovation in syllabus for Irish, in which I am involved, is beginning to take note of the importance of favourable attitudes and a sense of language use in second language learning in the context of a bilingualism.

Conclusion

I have set out in this paper to dispel the assumption that the revival of Irish can be directly compared to the revernacularisation of Hebrew. However, a parallel may emerge in studying the link between the home and the school as a step to achieving informal intergenerational oralcy within the current climate of bilingualism. This involves the verbalisation of socio-political factors which, for the case of Irish today, may involve a status planning which takes cognisance of the positive aspect of increasing participation in Irish immersion education programmes as an opportunity to raise an awareness of the prestigious role that the language could play in a youth culture. This paper points to the need for further research into the internal linguistic situation in the homes of children who attend all-Irish schools. The question needs to be examined as to why a family in Ireland today would make a conscious effort to change the language in the home to Irish. The Hebrew case challenges us to re-examine the ideology within which Irish is taught in schools. The Irish language revival movement has achieved much against all odds, but as we are now on the threshold of another revival we need to study the domain of youth culture in and outside school, so that the language, currently undergoing a positive revival among young people, might, within the context of a bilingualism, begin to play a larger part in their identity and culture.

References

Bar-Adon, A. (1975) *The Rise and Decline of a Dialect.* The Hague: Mouton.
— (1977) On the nativization of modern Hebrew and the role of children in the process. In P. Hopper (ed.) *Studies in Descriptive and Historical Linguistic* (pp. 487–98). Amsterdam: John Benjamin.

Ben-Yehuda, E. (1879) A weighty question, *Ha Shahar*. In E. Silberschlag (1980) *Eliezer Ben Yehuda: A Symposium in Oxford* (pp. 1–11). Oxford: The Oxford Centre for Postgraduate Studies.
Blanc, H. (1968) The Israeli Koine as an emergent national standard. In J. Fishman, C. Ferguson and F. Das Gupta (eds) *Language Problems of Developing Nations* (pp. 237–51). New York: Wiley.
Comerford, R.V. (1982) Míshuaimhneas agus náisiúnachas sa naoú haois déag. *Léachtaí Cholm Chille XIII* (pp. 151–65). Maigh Nuad: An Sagart.
Cooper, R. (1989) *Language Planning and Social Change*. Cambridge: Cambridge University Press.
De hÍde, D. (1894) The necessity for the de-Anglicisation of Ireland. In C. Duffy, G. Sigerson, D. Hyde (eds) *The Revival of Irish Literature*. London: T. Fisher Unwin. Reproduced in B. Ó Conaire (ed.) (1986) *Douglas Hyde: Language, Lore and Lyrics* (pp. 153–70). Dublin: Irish Academic Press.
Edwards J. (1985) *Language, Society and Identity*. London: Basil Blackwell.
Fellman, J. (1974) *The Revival of a Classical Tongue*. The Hague: Mouton.
— (1979) The teachers did it: A case history is the revival of a national language. In D. Feitelson (ed.) *Mother Tongue or Second Language* (pp. 48–56). Newark: International Reading Association.
— (1993) Some thoughts on the Hebrew revival. *Language Problems and Language Planning* Vol. 17, no. 1, Spring, 62–5.
Fishman, J. (1971) The impact of nationalism on language planning. In J. Rubin and B.H. Jernudd (eds) *Can Language be Planned? Sociolinguistic Theory and Practice for Developing Nations* (pp. 3–20). Honolulu: University of Hawaii.
— (1972) *Language and Nationalism: Two Integrative Essays*. Massachusetts: Newbury.
— (1991) *Reversing Language Shift*. Clevedon: Multilingual Matters.
Glinert, L (1987) Hebrew-Yiddish diglossia: Type and stereotype implications of the language of Ganzfried's Kitzur. *International Journal of the Sociology of Language* 67, 39–56.
Hindley, R. (1990) *The Death of the Irish Language*. London: Routledge.
Hofman, J. and Fisherman, H. (1972) Language shift and maintenance in Israel. In J. Fishman (ed.) *Advances in the Sociology of Language II* (pp. 342–64). The Hague: Mouton.
MacNamara, J. (1971) Successes and failure in the movement for the restoration of Irish. In J. Rubin and B.H. Jernudd (eds) *Can Language be Planned? Sociolinguistic Theory and Practise for Developing Nations* (pp. 65–94). Honolulu: University of Hawaii.
Nahir, M. (1987) L'aménagement de l'hébreu moderne. In J. Maurais (ed.) *Politique et Aménagement Linguistiques* (pp. 259–316). Quebec: Conseil de la langue française.
— (1988) Language planning and language acquisition: The great leap in the Hebrew revival. In C.B. Paulston (ed.) *International Handbook of Bilingualism and Bilingual Education* (pp. 275–95). New York: Greenwood Press.
Ó Doibhlin, B. (n.d.) Súil siar ar an athbheochan. In Ó Doibhlin, B. (ed.) *Aistí Critice agus Cultúir*. Baile Átha Cliath: FNT.
Ó Muimhneacháin, A. (1974) *Dóchas agus Duainéis*. Dublin: Mercier.
Ó Riagáin, P. (1988) Bilingualism in Ireland 1973–1983: An overview of national sociolinguistic surveys. *International Journal of the Sociology of Language* 70, 29–51.

Parfitt, T.V. (1972) The use of Hebrew in Palestine 1800–1882. *Journal of Semitic Studies* 42(2), Autumn, 25–39.

Peres, I. (1964) *One Hundred Years in Jerusalem* (Hebrew). Massachusetts: Rubin.

Rabin, C. (1969) The revival of the Hebrew language. *Ariel* 25, 25–39.

Spolsky, B. and Cooper R. (1991) *The Languages of Jerusalem*. Oxford: Oxford University Press.

Spolsky, B. (1991) Hebrew language vitalization within a general theory of second-language learning. In R. Cooper and B. Spolsky (eds) *The Influence of Language on Culture and Thought* (pp. 25–39). Berlin: Mouton de Gruyter.

Stewart, W. (1968) A sociolinguistic typology for describing national multilingualism. In J. Fishman (ed.) *Readings in the Sociology of Language* (pp. 531–45). The Hague: Mouton.

Weinstein, B. (1983) *The Civic Tongue: Political Consequences of Language Choices*. New York: Longman.

Yellin, D. (1923) Ben Yehuda and the revival of the Hebrew language. *Journal of the Palestine Exploration Society* 3, 26–108.

8 Language Planning and Sociolinguistic Trends in (Soviet) Karelia 1917–1994

ANNELI SARHIMAA

Introduction

Since the 1960s, language policy and language planning in the Soviet Union have been the subject of considerable investigation and numerous detailed studies have been published (e.g. Isaev, 1979; Kreindler *et al.*, 1982; Kirkwood *et al.*, 1989). They have been studied very intensively in such areas as Ukraine and Uzbekistan, which joined the Soviet Union after the Revolution, and the Baltic Republics, Estonia, Latvia, and Lithuania, which were annexed during the Second World War. Less attention has been paid to the policies implemented within the borders of the Russian Federation, and in many of the Autonomous Republics and National Districts the systematic study of these is still in its early stages. In this paper the focus will be on language planning and sociolinguistic trends in the Republic of Karelia (formerly the Karelian Autonomous Republic), which is located in the north-western corner of the Russian Federation. Originally, Karelia was inhabited by a few Finno-Ugric peoples, i.e. Lapps, Karelians, and Vepsians. Today it is a genuinely multinational republic, with a population made up of more than 60 nationalities. The largest ethnic group consists of Russians, who constitute about 74% of the entire population according to the 1989 census; Karelians constitute some 10%, and Vepsians a little less than one percent. The Lapps have withdrawn to the Kola peninsula. (Klement'ev, 1991: 59–60).

In what follows I shall approach language planning and sociolinguistic trends in Karelia from the point of view of one of the minority languages, Karelian. It has three main dialects: North Karelian, South Karelian, and Olonets Karelian. Together with its closest cognate languages, Vepsian, Ingrian, and

73

the eastern dialects of Finnish, Karelian forms the eastern branch of the Baltic-Finnic languages. According to the 1989 census, Karelian is spoken as a native language by some 41,000 speakers in the Republic of Karelia, and by some 20,000 speakers in the Tver', Tihvin and Valdai districts in Central Russia.

The aim of the paper is twofold:

(a) to provide a general description of language policies and language planning in Soviet Karelia in the period 1917–1993, and
(b) to relate the goals and procedures of the language policies to linguistic processes in Karelian, and the linguistic behaviour of its speakers.

I shall begin by giving a short outline of the history of language planning in Karelia.

An Outline of Language Policy and Language Planning in Karelia

At the time of the 1917 Revolution, Karelia was one of the 'hinterlands' of the Czarist empire. Altogether, there were about 630 Russian elementary schools (Churchill, 1970: 15) and the Finns had established quite a few Finnish schools in the northern and western districts (Nygård, 1978). (From 1809 to 1917, Finland was a part of the Russian Empire, with the status of an autonomous Grand Duchy.) Universal compulsory elementary schooling, however, was not introduced until 1930, and the literacy rate of the Karelians was low. According to the 1896 census (which was the last but one before the Revolution), only 10.4% of the Karelians were literate and the female literacy rate was as low as 3% (Pokrovskaja, 1978: 22–6, 88, quoted in Austin, 1992: 19). Consequently, one of the most urgent tasks faced by the new leaders was to increase literacy among the inhabitants of Karelia.

1917–1937: The first period of Standard Finnish

A vital first step in this direction was the choice of a language of administration and instruction. After the Revolution the minority nationals were encouraged to revive their extinct linguistic traditions. The smaller peoples, however, were recommended to unite around more developed languages (Crisp, 1989: 36–7). At first, this was what happened in Karelia: in 1920, the Peace of Tartu established Russian and Standard Finnish as the administrative languages of the newly formed Karelian Worker's Commune (from 1923 onwards: the Karelian Autonomous Republic) (Austin, 1992: 16).

What makes this choice rather odd is that in 1917 there were only about 1050 Finns living in Karelia. The reason most commonly given for this favouring of Finnish over Karelian is that there are significant differences between the Karelian dialects, which presumably made it difficult to decide which vernacular should be the basis for a literary standard (see, e.g. Markianova, 1993: 54–5). This may, however, simply be a case of being wise after the event. Russian linguists had never carried out any real research on Karelian (see Bubrih, 1929: 74), and the Communist leaders could not get any 'scientific' information about it. Consequently, it was very easy for Finnish-oriented politicians to convince them that Karelian was just another dialect of Finnish.

After the Finnish Civil war in 1918, there was an influx of Finnish communists into Soviet Karelia. These were followed by thousands of enthusiastic Finns from Canada, the USA and Finland who came to build socialism in Karelia. The Karelians being a rural people and the Finns more urban, with a higher level of education, in its early years Soviet Karelia was mainly administered by the expatriate Finns. The Finns considered it their socialist duty to bring the Karelians and their culture into the modern world. An important part of both tasks was to move the colloquial Karelian dialects closer to Standard Finnish (Austin, 1992: 16–20; Markianova, 1993: 55).

In the 1920s a very energetic *programme of finnicisation*, which was officially called *karelianisation*, was put into effect in Karelia. Finnish schools were established in areas where there had been no schools, and existing Russian schools were replaced by Finnish ones. In 1929 a Karelian Party resolution declared that the language of instruction for all Karelian children should be Finnish (Anttikoski, 1993: 40). A campaign for the eradication of illiteracy among the adult population was carried out in Finnish in the northern parts of Karelia, and in Russian in the southern districts. From 1926 to 1933 the literacy rate of the Karelians grew from 34.9% to 46.7% (Afanas'eva, 1989: 50; Anttikoski, 1993: 40, 42).

In the early 1930s a change of atmosphere began to take place in Soviet society. Simon (1982; quoted in Crisp, 1989: 40) explains this shift in terms of such factors as an increase in anti-nationalist policies, the rise of the Soviet patriotism, forced collectivisation, and the growth of industrialisation and migration, which changed the national composition of many regions. All this happened in Karelia, too. In addition, the political relationship between the Soviet Union and Finland deteriorated drastically and Finnish became increasingly associated with capitalist Finland and the so-called Greater-Finland nationalists, who wanted to incorporate Karelia into Finland (Markianova, 1993: 53–6).

In 1931 a prominent group of linguists working for the Soviet Academy of Sciences protested fiercely against the *finnicisation* which had been implemented in Karelia and Karelian language policies were extensively discussed, even in the pages of *Pravda* (Austin, 1992: 24; Anttikoski, 1993: 43–6). In two papers on Karelian nationality and language policies, D.V. Bubrih (1931, 1932), a well-known linguist and member of the Soviet Academy of Sciences, adduced a wealth of evidence to support the claim that Standard Finnish was incomprehensible to even educated Karelians. He also made a strong appeal for the right of the Karelian people to have a literary standard of their own, suggesting that this should be developed by making use of language-internal means of creating new vocabulary and by borrowing from the so-called 'international' languages, particularly Russian (Bubrih, 1931: 3–4, 5–8; 1932: 3–5, 34–8).

The leaders of the Karelian Republic rejected the idea of creating a new literary language for the Karelians (for details, see Anttikoski, 1993: 49–53). 1935, however, marked a turning point in language policies. Between 1935 and 1938 most of the expatriate Finns were removed from power and killed or sent to labour camps. Measures were taken to reduce the functional range of the 'fascist' Finnish language, to strengthen the position of Russian, and to introduce Karelian into all domains. In 1935 the District Committee of the Communist party decided to give the population of Karelia the freedom to choose the language of instruction for their children. In practice, however, the choice was restricted to Russian in most districts: from 1936 to 1937, instruction was given in Finnish only in the north-western parts of the republic. In 1937 Karelian was declared the third official language and very soon after this declaration a decisive resolution was adopted on the creation of a literary standard for Karelian using the Cyrillic alphabet (Afanas'eva, 1988: 27, 53; Austin, 1992: 16, 21–2; Anttikoski, 1993: 76–9, 84–9).

1938–1940: The period of Standard Karelian

On 1 January 1938, everything that was Finnish disappeared in Karelia. Russian was made a compulsory subject in all schools and Karelian, a language that was still in the making, was decreed the second official language alongside Russian. The leading role in creating a Karelian standard language and implementing these language planning policies was taken by D.V. Bubrih (Austin, 1992: 16, 23).

In 1937, just days before the new linguistic policies came into effect, Bubrih had published a Karelian grammar, written in the Cyrillic script and based on the northern dialects closest to Finnish. The following year, an attempt was made to create a grammar which would have a wider dialectal base and thus be more commonly applicable, and the 1937 grammar was supplanted by a totally new one. This grammar was heavily influenced by Russian and introduced a large number of Russian grammatical constructions and idioms into Karelian. The rich case system of Karelian was truncated by the reduction of the number of grammatical cases from 12 to nine, and the vocabulary was russified to a remarkable extent (Austin, 1992: 23–4; Markianova, 1993: 56).

Between 1938 and 1940 some 200 titles were published in Cyrillic Karelian, including translations and brochures, educational materials, readers and children's books, Party and other official documents. There was even a general literary journal, *Karelija*, and a newspaper called *Sovetskoi Karelija*. (For details, see Austin, 1992: 25–32, and for the numerous problems which arose, see Afanas'eva, 1988: 27–8.) Despite all these efforts, Standard Karelian was a complete disaster. In the first place, the selection of a dialectal base was so hurried and arbitrary that the language which was created did not represent any of the Karelian dialects properly. In the second place, the Cyrillic alphabet was poorly suited to the representation of the sounds of Karelian, the grammatical norms created were incomplete, there were no dictionaries or unified terminology, and the forced russification of the Standard Karelian vocabulary made it impossible for the Karelians to understand their new official language (Afanas'eva, 1988: 27; Austin, 1992: 25).

1940–1944: The restoration of Standard Finnish

The period of Standard Karelian lasted only until April 1940 when Finnish was restored as an official language alongside Russian and a new, more modest programme of *finnicisation* was initiated. During 1940 publishing in Finnish was restarted, and attempts were made to re-establish the network of Finnish-language schools. At the University of Petrozavodsk the foundations were laid for a Department of Finno-Ugric Language Studies; officially it was founded in 1947 (Anttikoski, 1993: 142–3; Virtaranta, 1990: 148). Finnish was also the official language during the Finnish occupation of Karelia which took place in the summer of 1941 and lasted until mid-1944. At its greatest extent, the occupied area covered most of Soviet Karelia west of Lake Onega. The ultimate goal of the Finnish military administration was to assimilate the Karelians into the cultural and political life of Finland. A programme of *dekarelianisation* was launched: Karelian was declared a dialect of Finnish again (see Hakulinen *et al.*, 1942: 11–2), and Finnish was introduced as the sole language of instruction in the occupied areas (Austin, 1992: 32).

The post-war period: The active promotion of Russian

After the war the position of Finnish in Karelia weakened. In 1950 there were some 160 Finnish schools, which were attended by only about 9% of Karelian and Finnish children. In 1954 Russian replaced Finnish as the language of instruction, although Finnish was taught as a compulsory subject to all Karelian and Finnish children until 1956. In 1956 the number of schools in which Finnish was taught was reduced to 27. Two years later, when the new education laws were introduced, all Karelian schools changed over to Russian only, and the Department of Finno-Ugric Language Studies at Petrozavodsk University was abolished (Lallukka, 1982: 82; Kreindler, 1982: 22, 1985: 355; Anttikoski, 1993: 144–5).

Despite this steady expansion in the teaching of Russian and systematic reduction of the functions of Finnish, Finnish had, and still has, the status of an administrative language in the Republic of Karelia. In the 1960s and 1970s the promotion of Russian accelerated all over the Soviet Union. As a result, non-Russian schools underwent several pedagogical changes, among them a growing emphasis on 'ethnopedagogy', which was a specific method of teaching not only the Russian language but also Russian values, aesthetics and even humour (Kreindler, 1985: 356–7). It was declared that a major aim of public education was to educate people to have a mastery of, and love for, the Russian language. Consequently, it was considered very important that, in addition to being formally taught in schools, Russian should be promoted through organised programmes of extracurricular activities (Kreindler, 1982: 21, 23).

By the mid-1960s political and economical contacts between the Soviet Union and Finland had normalised. There was a constant need for interpreters and teachers of Finnish, and in 1963 the Department of the Finnish was re-established at Petrozavodsk University. In 1968 Finnish was introduced into the curriculum of the Karelian schools as an optional foreign language (Anttikoski, 1993: 145). During the 1970s and 1980s there were no further systematic language planning programmes in Karelia. According to Anttikoski (1993: 146), this is mainly due to the extremely rapid russification of the non-Russian population, and to the fact that at present the restricted functional range of the minority languages does not give any reason for implementing systematic language policies.

Since 1988: The revival of Karelian?

Perestroyka and *glasnost* gave rise to a freer atmosphere, accompanied by official support for national minorities and their languages. In July 1990 the Karelian Republic declared its autonomy of Russia, and Karelian and Vepsian were recognised as administrative languages alongside Russian and Finnish. Serious attempts are now being made to create a new literary standard for Karelian, this time using the Latin script. Moreover, it is no longer Finns or Russians who are actively defending their national and linguistic rights but the Karelians themselves. At present, a very important role is being played by the recently founded associations, *Karjalan Rahvahan Liitto* ('The Association of the Karelian people') and *Tverin karjalaisten liitto* ('The

Association of the Tver' Karelians'), which are dedicated to the preservation of the Karelian language, culture and religion.

The last few years have seen the publication of several primers and readers based on the different dialects of Karelian. The Bible is currently being translated into Karelian, and a few authors have began to use their native language in their writing (see Pyöli, 1993: 63–4). Since 1990 there has even been a weekly-paper called *Oma mua*, 'Our Own Land'. Karelian is being taught as a school subject, and in Petrozavodsk and some other places, it is used alongside Russian as a language of instruction in the kindergartens. *A Dictionary of the Olonets Karelian Dialects* by Grigorij Makarov was published in 1990, and the publication of *A Dictionary of the Tver' Karelian Dialects* by Aleksandra Punzhina has been announced. In 1991 a Department of Karelian and Vepsian was established at the University of Petrozavodsk (Virtaranta, 1990: 225–9; Markianova, 1993: 57). Karelian TV and Radio broadcasts programmes in Karelian for about half an hour a day.

Sociolinguistic Trends

Recent years have seen a growing interest in the study of the socio-demographic and linguistic effects that systematic language planning has had in Russia. In the Republic of Karelia the emphasis until recently has been on the national political aspects of the question (e.g. Afanas'eva, 1989; Uimonen, 1989), whereas the study of linguistic aspects of the matter is still in its infancy. In his 1992 paper '*Soviet Karelian – a language that failed*', Austin widens the discussion of the history of language planning by examining the linguistic reflections it had in the pedagogical literature of the 1920s and 1930s. In his 1993 thesis, Anttikoski attempts to relate the procedures of the systematic '*sovietisation*' of the minority languages to the development of the variety of '*Soviet Finnish*' that was used in the 1930s.

Both Austin and Anttikoski concentrate on the standardised written forms of Karelian and Soviet Finnish, but the language planning measures also had a considerable effect on the fates of the non-standard varieties, too. The non-literary languages were never really the target of deliberate '*sovietisation*' campaigns, and thus the language *corpus*-planning which, especially in the 1930s and 1940s was accompanied by the systematic russification of the minority languages, played practically no role in their development. On the other hand, the sociolinguistic effects of language *status*-planning measures were considerable.

As far as Karelian is concerned, everything seems to have gone wrong from the very beginning: almost every aspect of the current situation seems directly or indirectly to stem from the decision in 1920 to make Finnish the literary standard for the Karelians. On the one hand, it curtailed the further development of Karelian and made it a clearly subordinate language; on the other, instead of pushing the Karelians towards using Finnish, as was intended, it actually impelled them in the opposite direction, towards Karelian/Russian bilingualism. Altogether the language policies implemented in Karelia led to a very rapid decline of Karelian.

The linguistic behaviour of the Karelians

Since it lacked a literary standard, it was not possible for Karelian to develop into a 'modern' language. From the very beginning of the Soviet period, it became primarily a domestic code, which was mainly used in informal settings. An ethnosociological study carried out in 1969 indicated that in the late 1960s more than 45% of Karelians aged under 20, and about 57% of those over 50, spoke only Karelian at home. At the same time, Karelian was used at work by less than 9% of the younger, and by some 26% of the older generations (Klement'ev, 1971: 40). It is obvious, however, that even 25 years ago, Russian was gaining ground as the means of communication in most informal domains, too: for example, while more than 12% of Karelians over 50 declared that they spoke Karelian with their children, fewer than 2% of those aged 30 to 39 did so and none of those under 30 (Klement'ev, 1974: 34, 1991: 51).

One important factor in this process was the nationality policies implemented during Stalin's regime, which led to radical changes in the ethnic composition of both the population of Karelia and the families of the Karelians. In the course of the forced collectivisation, a considerable number of Karelian men were either killed or sent to Siberia and many of those who survived the purges met their fate later on the battle-front. Since there were fewer Karelian men left in the villages, the girls married Russians or other non-Karelians. During the war whole Karelian villages were evacuated to Russia proper, which accelerated the ethnic mixing of Karelians with other nationalities.

Later, mixed marriages became even more common, due partly to the heavy immigration into Karelia of non-Karelian populations from other parts of the Soviet Union, and partly to the migration of Karelians into multiethnic cities. In the 1970s, for example, three-quarters of the marriages of urban Karelians, and about a half of the marriages of rural Karelians were mixed, and in about 70% of them one of the spouses was Russian. The children of mixed families are generally registered as Russian, and almost all the families speak only Russian at home (Birin, 1991: 150–3). Yet another reason for the spread of Russian into informal domains is that in the early 1930s, and again in the 1940s and 1950s, the speaking of Karelian was officially discouraged.

For example, children were forbidden to use Karelian during school-breaks and Karelian parents were advised to speak Russian to their children rather than Karelian. In many cases obedience to such orders led to an interruption in the transmission of the Karelian language to the next generation.

A third factor in the linguistic and national assimilation of the Karelians was that since it constituted a distinctively domestic code, Karelian became stigmatised even among the Karelians themselves (see, e.g. Birin, 1991: 153; Klement'ev, 1991: 55). The ethnosociological study mentioned above shows that young, educated Karelians in particular prefer Russian to Karelian in all domains, even if they are more or less balanced bilinguals (Klement'ev, 1971: 41–4; 1974: 30–3). The tendency to favour Russian in informal settings has, of course, been linked with other factors and most especially with industrialisation and urbanisation, which involved the mass migration of non-Karelian populations from the other parts of the Soviet Union (for details, see Lallukka, 1990: 5; Klement'ev, 1991: 46–8, 60–1). This widening of the ethnic base of the population has made Russian increasingly important as the language of communication between the different national groups, while the functional range of all the minority languages has been unremittingly contracting.

The rapid decline of Karelian is best illustrated by the census results. In 1926 the total Karelian population was approximately 100,000, of whom about 96% had Karelian as their mother tongue. Thirty years later, in 1959, after all the types of language planning described above, the total number of Karelians was around 85,000, and some 81% declared Karelian to be their native language. Today, after another period of 30 years during which there have been no systematic language planning programmes in Karelia, but urbanisation and industrialisation have changed the society drastically, the Karelian population numbers still about 79,000, but only some 52% of them consider Karelian to be their native language. Furthermore, the results of the 1989 census indicate that at present Karelian is clearly the language of the old people: the use of Karelian as a mother tongue is most common (81%) among the cohorts of those born more than 50 years ago, i.e. before the 1940s, whereas among Karelians under 30 years of age, native speakers of Karelian constitute some 11% to 32% of the total of the cohorts (Klement'ev, 1974: 29, 1991: 155).

The 1970 census was the first in which an attempt was made to determine the number of the Karelian/Russian bilinguals. It indicates that more than 95% of the Karelians had at least basic Russian (Lallukka, 1982: 64), but Karelian/Russian bilingualism must have been fairly common among the Karelians throughout the whole twentieth century. One indication of this is that the Karelians have tended to be literate in Russian. Forced to choose between Finnish and Russian in the 1920s and 1930s, the vast majority of Karelians opted for Russian as their language of education. In 1926 more than 76% of literate Karelians were literate only in Russian, while some 14% were literate only in Finnish, the rest being literate in both languages. Even in 1933, during the intensive '*finnicisation*' campaign, the literacy rate in Russian (51%) was noticeably higher than that in Finnish (26%) (Afanas'eva, 1989: 43).

The current 'habitus' of Karelian

Bilingualism has triggered several interesting linguistic processes in Karelian. First and foremost, as Pyöli (1993) has shown, are the considerable number of words of Russian origin in spontaneous speech, even in that of the Olonets Karelians, who have best preserved their native tongue. Sarhimaa's studies of Russian interference in Karelian syntax indicate that lexical inter-ference from Russian is accompanied by a host of grammatical and semantic items transferred from Russian by bilingual speakers (e.g. Sarhimaa, 1989, 1992; see also Filppula & Sarhimaa, 1994: 112–3). In addition to the so-called 'integrated loans', i.e. lexical and grammatical features that have become established in Karelian so that they are no longer recognised as 'foreign', intensive interference from Russian is revealed in countless cases of code-mixing arising from the ability of bilingual speakers to use any random word of one language while speaking another. It is also very common for Karelians to mix into their basically Karelian speech whole sentences, phrases and speech extracts consisting of several consecutive Russian words and, of course, they are able to switch codes from Karelian to Russian, and vice versa, at any point in the conversation.

One consequence of constant borrowing, 'instant loans', code-mixing and code-switching, is that the genuine shape of Karelian is clearly fading, even in the minds of its native speakers: very few Karelians that I have met during my field-work were able to find pure Karelian equivalents of Russian words or Russian-influenced constructions without considerable difficulty. In its present form Karelian shares a host of the features that are typical of so-called 'mixed languages':

(a) it has undergone, or is currently undergoing, several changes caused by the admixture of foreign structural features and lexicon;
(b) a considerable proportion of the features exhibited by Karelian speech come not from one specific source language but two; and
(c) the nature of language transmission is not 'normal', in the sense that even in cases when Karelian is still transmitted from the parents to the children, the linguistic input of the older generation is apparently no longer a complete language with all its lexical and grammatical properties,

but a more or less broken variety, a mixture of Karelian and Russian words and grammatical features.

(For detailed discussion of language mixture, see Thomason & Kaufman, 1988; Thomason, forthcoming.)

Conclusion

According to Fishman (1982), there are two opposed approaches to world languages: the 'Eastern' tradition which accepts the diversity of mankind and its tongues as natural and even desirable, and the 'Western' tradition that aims at the creation of a single system of values, culture, beliefs and language. In her 1985 paper Kreindler suggested that the Soviet Union inherited both traditions: during the early years of the communist power, it was the Eastern tradition that dominated, whereas developments from the 1930s onwards can be seen as a steady strengthening of the western tradition (Kreindler, 1985: 345, 347–53). More recently, there seems to have been a revival of the Eastern tradition in Russia. The big question is, however, is there a real future for such minority languages as Karelian?

Pyöli, who is currently studying Karelian from a language-sociologically oriented point of view, is rather optimistic about the prospects for Karelian: having analysed certain social and linguistic factors involved in the development of present-day Karelian, she concludes that Karelian may well be revived. However, it is more common for researchers in this field to hold quite the opposite view, and this is how I feel, too: the prospects for Karelian are not very promising. It is hardly realistic to believe that a language can remain vital when it is spoken mostly by elderly rural people and is no longer transmitted from one generation to the next in a 'natural' way, as the difficulties in reviving Irish, for example, suggests. Moreover, given that the total number of Karelians is not much more than that of a small city, that only half of them consider Karelian as their native language, that they live scattered all over the Karelian Republic, and that they speak three different dialects, which are already half way to linguistic destruction, it is more than likely that Karelian will fairly soon die out.

Nevertheless, whatever happens to Karelian in the long run, the new literary language and the work of the enthusiasts may be able to slow down the process of assimilation for a while. And what may be regarded as even more valuable, especially for the old people, is that after the long period of linguistic, national and cultural rejection they can be proud of being what they really are deep in their hearts: Karelians.

References

Afanas'eva, A.I. (1988) Karjalan kieliongelmat. *Sosialismin teoria ja käytäntö* 37, 26–8.

Afanas'eva, A.I. (1989) *Kul'turnye preobrazovanija v Sovetskoj Karelii 1928–1940.* Petrozavodsk: Karelija.

Anttikoski, E. (1993) Sovettisuomi? Kielenohjailua Neuvosto-Karjalassa. Manuscript, Department of Russian, University of Joensuu, Finland.

Austin, P. (1992) Soviet Karelian: The language that failed. *Slavic Review* 1, 16–35.

Birin, V. (1991) Karjalan ASNT:ssa asuvien karjalaisten demografinen tila 1950– 1970-luvuilla. *Carelia* 11, 146–53.

Bubrih, D.V. (1929) Neobhodim revoljucionnyj poein. *Prosveščenie nacional'nostej* 1, 73–4.

— (1931) *Kakoj jazyk – tverskim karelam?* Leningrad: LOIKFUN.

— (1932) *Karely i karel'skij jazyk.* Moskva: Izdatel'stvo Mosoblispolkoma.

— Churchill, S. (1970) *Itä-Karjalan kohtalo 1917–1922. Itä-Karjalan itsehallintokysymys Suomen ja Neuvosto-Venäjän välisissä suhteissa 1917–1922.* Porvoo/ Helsinki: WSOY.

Crisp, S. (1989) Soviet language planning 1917–53. In M. Kirkwood (ed.) *Language Planning in the Soviet Union* (pp. 23–45). Houndmills/London: The Macmillan Press Ltd.

Filppula, M. and Sarhimaa, A. (1994) Cross-linguistic syntactic parallels and contact-induced change. In Maria Vilkuna and Susanna Shore (eds) *SKY-94. 1994 Yearbook of the Linguistic Association of Finland* (pp. 89–134). Helsinki: Hakapaino Oy.

Fishman, J. (1982) Whorfianism of the third kind: Ethnolinguistic diversity as a world wide societal asset. *Language in Society* 1, 1–14.

Hakulinen, L. *et al.* (1942) *Itä-Karjalan murreopas.* Helsinki: Otava.

Isaev, M. (1979) *Jazykovoe stroitel'stvo v SSSR.* Moskva: Nauka.

Kirkwood, M. (ed.) (1989) *Language Planning in the Soviet Union.* Houndmills/ London: The Macmillan Press Ltd.

Kirkwood, M. (1989) Language planning: Some methodological preliminaries. In M. Kirkwood (ed.) *Language Planning in the Soviet Union* (pp. 1–21). Houndmills/ London: The Macmillan Press Ltd.

Klement'ev, E.I. (1971) Jazykovye processy v Karelii (po materialam konkretno-sociologieeskogo issledovanija karel'skogo sel'skogo naselenija). *Sovetskaja etnografija* 6, 26–36.

— (1974) Razvitie jazykovyh processov v Karelii (po materialam konkretno socio-logieeskogo issledovanija karel'skogo gorodskogo naselenija). *Sovetskaja etno-grafija* 4, 38–44.

— (1991) Karely. *Etnografieeskij oeerk.* Petrozavodsk: Karelija.

Kreindler, I. (1982) The changing status of Russian in the Soviet Union. *International Journal of the Sociology of Language* 33, 7–39.

Kreindler, I. *et al.* (1982) The changing status of Russian in the Soviet Union. *International Journal of the Sociology of Language* 33 (Special issue).

Kreindler, I. (ed.) (1985) *Sociolinguistic Perspectives on Soviet National Languages: Their Past, Present, and Future.* Berlin/New York/Amsterdam: Mouton de Gruyter.

Kreindler, I.T. (1985) The non-Russian languages and the challenge of Russian: The Eastern versus the Western tradition. In I. Kreindler (ed.) *Sociolinguistic Perspectives on Soviet National Languages: Their Past, Present, and Future* (pp. 345–67). Berlin/New York/Amsterdam: Mouton de Gruyter.

Lallukka, S. (1982) *Suomalais-ugrilaiset kansat Neuvostoliiton uusimpien väestön-laskentojen valossa*. Helsinki: Neuvostoliittoinstituutti.
— (1990) Karjalaisasutuksen eroosio Neuvosto-Karjalassa. *Suomen antropologi* 3, 3–14.
Markianova, L. (1993) Karjalan tasavallan kielitilanne. *Uralilaiset kielet tänään* (pp. 52–8). Kuopio: Snellman-instituutti.
Nygård, Toivo (1978) *Suur-Suomi vai lähiheimolaisten auttaminen?* Helsinki: Otava.
Pokrovskaja, I.P. (1978) *Naselenie Karelii*. Petrozavodsk: Karelija.
Pyöli, R. (1993) Karjalaiset kielenvaihtotilanteessa. Venäjän aiheuttamat sanaston muutosprosessit aunuksenkarjalassa. Manuscript, Department of Russian, University of Joensuu, Finland.
Sarhimaa, A. (1989) *Arheriale tegihežchuiged*. Nabljudenija nad vlijaniem russkogo jazyka na vostoenye pribaltijsko-finskie jazyki. – *Studia Slavica Finlandensia, Tomus* VI, 121–8. Helsinki: Neuvostoliittoinstituutti.
— (1992) Infinitiivirakenne nesessiivisyyden ilmaisukeinona karjala-aunuksessa. [The infinitive as a necessive marker in Karelian] – *Virittäjä* 4, 23–44. English abstract. Helsinki.
Simon, G. (1982) Nationsbildung und 'Revolution von oben'. Zur neuen sowjetischen Nationalitätenpolitik der dreissiger Jahre. *Geschichte und Gesellschaft* 2: 233–57.
Thomason, S.G. and Kaufman, T. (1988) *Language Contact, Creolization, and Genetic Linguistics*. Berkeley/Los Angeles: University of California Press.
Thomason, S.G. (forthcoming) Language mixture: Ordinary processes, extraordinary results. In C. Silva-Corvalan (ed.) *Proceedings of the First Conference on Spanish in Contact with Other Languages*. Georgetown University Press.
Uimonen, J. (1989) Neuvosto-Karjalan karjalankielisen kirjallisuuden kielitausta vuosina 1920–1936. *Punalippu* 4, 128–41.
Virtaranta, P. (1990) *Kulttuurikuvia Karjalasta: ihmisiä ja elämänkohtaloita rajan-takaisessa Karjalassa*. Espoo: Weilin+Göös.

9 Foreign Language Teaching in a Changing Russia

SVETLANA TER-MINASOVA

Introduction

A love of foreign languages and, consequently, a deep interest in other peoples' cultures and modes of life have always been so typical and characteristic of Russian social life that it might be considered an inherent feature of the Russian national character. At different stages of this country's history, different European languages have been the focus of public attention: German in the eighteenth century, French in the nineteenth century, German before World War II, and since the war, English has been overwhelmingly predominant.

In the Soviet Union foreign languages were studied even when such study was not socially respectable, prestigious and materially rewarding, as it is now. We did it in the darkest periods of our history, when we were completely cut off from the rest of the world, when it was politically unpopular, suspect and dangerous, since it inevitably implied 'mixing with foreigners', who were officially called 'potential enemies'. In spite of all that, people in Russia kept studying English even though they had to risk their reputation, careers, sometimes freedom and even life.

For decades, under such circumstances, generations of teachers who never set their eyes – or ears – on a native speaker of a foreign language, taught generations of students without any equipment, without authentic foreign language teaching (FLT) materials. They developed chalkboard theories and poor-but-honest, necessity-is-the-mother-of-invention techniques, and did it brilliantly.

Consequently, the Russian school of FLT has accumulated valuable experience in doing its job under all kinds of possible and impossible conditions, including states of emergency. Russian scholars have developed original and pragmatically-oriented linguistic theories because FLT has always been a topical and urgent concern of Russian linguistics and pedagogics. The interest is deep-rooted and stems from various social, historical and cultural reasons. One more important social reason is that the USSR was a multilingual state with Russian as lingua franca, and Soviet linguists were committed to the cultivation of a standard Russian language, to the teaching of Russian as a foreign language on a very large scale, and to prodigious lexicographic activity.

Before *perestroika*, before the sudden, drastic and dramatic changes in Russian social life, modern European languages were taught as dead languages. There are at least two explanations for this strange but habitual state of affairs. One is shared with us by most European countries and that is the tradition of classical and philological education, at both secondary and higher levels, based on studies of classical languages, principally Latin. Powell (1992), for example, points out that the British educational system was dominated by classical studies up to the 1970s. Following in this tradition, the goals and techniques of dead language studies were applied to living ones. The goal was to read classical authors, and the methods were concentrated on grammar and structure studies. This is exactly how my generation was taught English.

The second reason was political, ideological and, therefore, uniquely Russian. Because Russia was entirely isolated from the rest of the world, for about seventy years modern European languages were *actually* dead to learners, in that the world of their users did not, as such, exist. No communication was possible, so the only skill necessary was reading, and the most suitable and safe texts were Dickens and Thackeray. Modern English literature was represented by John Galsworthy.

Traditions

The traditions in FLT we inherited from previous generations can be summed up in three words: depth, thoroughness and perfectionism. The motto of Soviet times proclaimed: 'Soviet means the excellent'. Soviet FLT set itself the same goal: to give a perfect knowledge of the language under study. As the teaching was confined to reading classical authors for philologists and FL teachers and special texts for everybody else, (i.e. for students of other subjects), the idea of perfectionism resulted in a wide, deep and thorough overall study of grammar and vocabulary, regardless of the practical needs of students or the actual tasks of the course. These tasks were never defined but were taken for granted, since Soviet means perfect knowledge of everything.

Because FLT was deliberately anti-pragmatic, it went very well with the ideological basis of Soviet times, which viewed pragmatism as a capitalist feature, which, like individualism, was inherently bad. According to this ideology, acting idealistically, learning everything in full splendour and seeking to be perfect in all respects was what was considered good. This idea was actually quite sound, but of course it was impossible to realise. The nation-wide practice of trying to teach everything resulted most frequently (in ordinary schools and in all the innumerable specialised higher education institutions) in learning nothing. It worked only with students specialising in foreign languages.

Mass production foreign language teaching

Modern languages (first and foremost English) have always been compulsory on the curriculum of secondary schools. In higher education, too, students in all disciplines have foreign languages on the curriculum as an obligatory subject for three to four years out of the average five years of the full course. Thus, all of our students, regardless of their subject of study, must learn a foreign language as a part of their syllabus. In other words, they may go on with their chemistry, economics or electrical engineering only if they pass an examination in English. This means that we have to count our students in millions. It is no longer the piece-work of FL teaching to the elite children of the Russian aristocracy, but is, instead, mass production. It requires special mass production techniques and mass-production-oriented language teaching materials.

A by-product of this trend is that FLT was teacher-oriented, and the needs or problems of the individual student were neglected. In fact, as already mentioned, the neglect of the individual was a pivot of our ideology. This resulted in a rigid, severe and distant kind of teacher–student relationship which is especially dangerous for FLT. Indeed, foreign language learning, like no other subject, requires a special psychological approach, and an atmosphere of relaxation and trust. Since learning a foreign language, and through it a strange world view, strange mentality etc., is a difficult psychological barrier for many learners, anything that helps to overcome it is vitally important. Nothing helps more than an approachable, attentive, thoughtful teacher. However, the mass production situation of teaching a foreign language as an obligatory subject is not exactly conducive to establishing the necessary atmosphere of trust and friendship or to paying special attention to the problems of the individual.

Theoretical grounding

Another typical feature of FLT in Russia is that it has always been well grounded theoretically. There has always been a firm belief that a really efficient solution to the problems of FLT must be sought with the help of linguistics, that the practice of FLT must be based on theoretical studies of language, and that theory and practice must go hand in hand, as it will be good for both of them. FLT in Russia has been especially strong in such fields as vocabulary teaching, socio-linguistic and linguo-cultural studies, lexicology, lexicography, phraseology, collocation, word-combination – i.e. in all those spheres of knowledge which are centred on the study of the word's meaning.

A negative by-product of this very positive feature of FLT in Russia is the overloading of our grammar books and textbooks with terms. Indeed, the authors of Russian ELT materials use far more terminology than their western colleagues. Such common and simple terms for us as Indefinite Tenses, Oblique, Suppositional Moods, Compound Nominal Predicates, etc. often sound impenetrable to our colleagues from other countries. Even our grammar books for children are written in the same dry, rigorous, pseudo-scientific style and have the same large number of terms as books for adults. The problem with our terms is additionally complicated by the fact that they are uniquely and traditionally Russian and differ from the standard terminology accepted everywhere else.

Changes

A most striking change this country is now experiencing is, among other thrilling novelties, an unprecedented and ever-increasing demand for foreign language learning – overwhelmingly English. It seems now that all the newly-acquired possibilities, freedoms, and forbidden fruits of different kinds are irritatingly unreachable for a trifling reason: the language barrier. In addition to the ordinary student seeking to learn through the state system, there is now a surprisingly large and ever-growing number of rich people with a lot of hard currency, who are quite prepared to spend this money on English language learning for themselves, their children and their employees. Consequently, angry legions of potential students of foreign languages are storming universities, language schools, co-operatives and private teachers, desperately demanding immediate results in foreign language learning. A good teacher in this context is a 'quick' teacher, that is, one who gives quick results.

The demand far exceeds the supply, and FL teachers in this country are now the focus of public attention. Never before have they been so important, so highly paid (privately, of course), so 'wanted' by society, on the one hand, and so helpless or vulnerable on the other, because they cannot fully satisfy this ever-increasing cry for help.

'Dead' languages have suddenly turned into 'living' ones. Consequently, the communicative approach to FLT is at the centre of both teachers' and students' attention. The tasks of FLT have changed and the skills required are new, too. Speaking, listening, comprehension and writing are now in great demand.

Another new feature of FLT in Russia is the shift of interest from classical philology to what is called in many European countries 'new' or *neo-philology*, or applied linguistics oriented towards the functional aspects of language, the role it plays in the social life of the speech community, and how it serves to satisfy the economic, scientific and technological needs of the society. This is now causing fundamental changes in Foreign Teacher Training policy. The main pragmatic idea is to bridge the gap between the education and future jobs of the students, i.e. the applied dimension. For classical philological education the learning and teaching of a foreign language is a goal in itself, with the language as the object of studies. Classical philologists are the elite or chosen few, who study languages and literature in full splendour with equal attention to all the aspects of the history and the theory of languages. Neo-philologists or applied linguists regard language as a tool for achieving some other goal, a tool of someone else's trade, and training the armies of ESP teachers must, in principle, be different from training the chosen few. Thus, we must learn to be pragmatic, to learn to choose from the vast *knowledge about* the language those bits of information which are indispensable for the *use* of the language. This is where the difference lies between the philological faculty and the faculty of foreign languages.

A foreign language is now taught not so much in combination with classical literature (which is not always appropriate, to put it mildly, for the actual use of a language) but rather in combination with such subjects as economics, politics, business, sciences, computer science, etc. It is taught against the wide background of the information about the world where the language is used as mother tongue, in our case, the English-speaking world. And last but not least, the so-called 'applied' values of English as a foreign language have come to the fore: those features and values which can be applied to and used in science, commerce, industry, which will be of cultural, scientific and economic significance to the country and society, and which will help to further international relations, scientific and technological progress, trade, tourism, etc.

In brief, we are learning to be less idealistic and more pragmatic, less academic and more realistic. At the same time, our task is not to go to the other extreme but to combine both features. Dialectically, it should ensure progress and development in the right direction.

Problems and Conclusions

It is the problems facing the teaching of foreign languages in Russia which are most salient at this time, and it is more appropriate here to summarise them than to attempt to posit premature conclusions.

(1) *Demand exceeds supply.* In this country, despite the considerable efforts by dedicated people, the demand for FLT far exceeds the supply. Many Russians need to speak, understand, read and write English, in order to contribute to the further development of Russia. Very many more want to do so. The number and quality of EL teachers are not sufficient.

(2) *Need for further training.* Many Russian teachers of foreign languages need further training both in languages and in teaching methods, in acquiring a new approach to ELT under the new circumstances.

(3) *Internal brain drain.* There is an internal brain drain currently. Teachers of foreign languages leave schools and universities for banks, travel agencies, foreign firms, etc. – simply because they are paid many times more there.

(4) *Lack of FLT materials.* The most critical problem centres on the lack of FLT materials. Most of the previous materials published in Russia are now wrong ideologically. The market is not so empty as before, but the ELT materials in shops and libraries are often inappropriate. It is expensive to import books, audio and video cassettes. The common practice of photocopying ('pirating') language courses, though hampered by the lack of photocopiers and other equipment, is thriving. The question now is whether to purchase or publish materials. For economic and financial reasons publishing FLT materials under licence by Russian publishers seems to be more realistic and promising. However, to make this option possible, the following recommendations for the FLT materials needed by Russian teachers at present should be implemented:

(a) The FLT materials must be nationally oriented. Unfortunately, all too often the same definitions and grammar rules are repeated from textbook to textbook regardless of the national knowledge, experience and needs of the student. The difficulties with grammar books are increased by the terminological mess; Russian grammar books and textbooks use far more terminology – and of more obscure and elaborate character – than their European counterparts.

(b) As for teaching vocabulary, the success of FLT in this respect largely depends on the thematic and educational value of the layer of language to be learnt. Many topics, naturally, are at the very end of the list of priorities of Russian students for obvious social, cultural and historical reasons (such as, for instance, hotel registration, hiring a car, bank, hairdresser's, travel agency, etc.).

These recommendations pre-suppose a larger scale of co-operation between Western and Russian authors, and between textbook writers and teachers of English as a foreign language. It is my firm belief that this is the most efficient way to achieve good results and to settle the urgent problem of ELT materials in Russia.

Ideally, we would like to have Russian-oriented materials by native-speaking authors with commentaries written for Russians by Russian teachers of foreign languages (e.g. *The Bensons*, Rawson Jones, 1991). Such materials are ideal for many reasons: practical (obvious), theoretical (hidden collocational stumbling-blocks) and psychological (not to frighten away a potential student).

(5) *Lack of equipment.* There is an extremely acute lack of equipment for FLT. Put simply, there is next to nothing. No computers, very few videos, no photocopying machines, no cassettes, and no paper. Even our blackboard theories are hampered now by the absence of chalk. I am far from exaggerating the role of technical aids in ELT, as we are only too used to having none, but now the situation is both absurd and ludicrous.

(6) *Competition.* A new, hitherto unknown danger in this country is the competition in the private, i.e. commercial sector. The problem for FLT at the university level is now simply one of survival.

(7) *FLT methods.* The obsession with the communicative approach, the famous dialogues on practical, every day, often artificial and unnecessary subjects for a Russian student oust the traditional texts and ignore the function of language as the treasury of culture. This results in a decrease in the level of literacy and an increase in the number of mistakes in grammar and syntax.

However, I do not wish to end my survey of FLT in Russia on a sad note. There are grounds for optimism when we consider that we have something which is more important than all the above-mentioned problems: we have enthusiasm, eagerness, interest and a firm belief that the most important things required for ELT is a good teacher and hard work on both sides – the student and the teacher.

References

Green, S. (1990) Modern languages and attainment targets. *Language Learning Journal* 2, September.

Powell, S. (1992) Becoming language wise: Learning from one another. *Language Learning Journal* 6, September.

Rawson Jones, K. (1991) *The Bensons*. Modern Language and Learning Systems.

10 Anglo-Nigerian Pidgin in Nigerian Education: A Survey of Policy, Practice and Attitudes

CHARLES C. MANN

> *Africans and Asians alike viewed an English academic*
> *education as the means to social and economic advantage*
> *and, for some, eventual political power. Anything less*
> *was regarded as second rate. (Whitehead, 1982: 58)*

Introduction

Traditionally, the literature on definitions and descriptions of pidgins and creoles[1] is replete with derogatory epithets, e.g. 'corrupt', 'bastardised', 'marginal' (forms of their so-called superstrate languages). However, and as also suggested in Mann (1988: 93), Hall (1955: 30) points out that 'there is no such thing as "corruption" in linguistic history, only change'. He reports (1955: 13) that an Australian critic called Neo-Melanesian – the pidgin of Papua New Guinea – 'every-man, no-man language', and that in July, 1953, the Trusteeship Council of the United Nations in that region 'condemned the use of Pidgin in the Territory of New Guinea, and demanded that Pidgin be immediately "abolished"'. Today, it is the language of Parliament in Papua New Guinea.

In spite of increased awareness, since Hall's work, of the origins, processes of formation, nature and relevance of these languages to linguistic theory, pidgins and creoles continue to be socially perceived as lesser languages, and the 'poorer cousins', even if Decamp (1971: 16) rightly remarks that 'In fact, we can never know how many of the "normal" languages of the world originated via this pidgin-creole process'. The low social prestige they suffer, consequently, is so regular as to suggest that it is a salient feature of their definition.

Anglo-Nigerian Pidgin (ANP) is an endogenous, Atlantic pidgin, believed to have evolved from language contacts between the natives of the coastal areas of present-day Nigeria and, firstly, Portuguese sailors (fifteenth century) – giving rise to 'Negro-Portuguese' (Brosnahan, 1963: 23); then, British traders, missionaries and colonisers (eighteenth century), undergoing, thereby, a process of re- and adlexification (towards English). Variously called 'Nigerian Pidgin English', 'Nigerian Pidgin', 'Broken English', or simply 'Broken', ANP is, today, a regular feature of urban language communication in Nigeria, even if it is regarded, generally, as having its stronghold in the multilingual Delta region (Warri, Sapele and Effurum). While it is, by all indications, going through a process of creolization, i.e. structural complication, elaboration and extension in use, it is regarded by some (Elugbe & Omamor, 1991) as having 'nativised' in the Delta.

Today, ANP's sociocommunicational utility, as an interethnic *lingua franca*, is in expansion. In fact, as suggested by Mann (1993), it has undergone a process of language (function) naturalisation (or 'readjustment') with the university youth, in that it is now used between students sharing a common mother tongue, as a language in its own right, and it is no longer necessarily viewed as an 'auxiliary'. According to Marchese and Schnukal (1980: 1), 'Though often ignored and only partially documented, Nigerian Pidgin English (NPE) may be spoken by more people than any other language in Nigeria'. A similar view – though qualified with specific reference to urban centres and interethnic communication – can be found in Mann (1993). ANP is, at present, liberally used in the media for newscasting, drama sketches, discussion and record request programmes, and, more popularly, advertising. Furthermore, radio and TV drama presentations and advertisements in ANP are, more often than not, the most popular, in terms of public appeal. While there have been attempts to graphise it (Saro-Wiwa, 1985; Fatunde, 1986) for literary purposes, there is, as yet, no standard orthography.

The formal language situation in Nigeria, today, is that English is the official language (of instruction, government and banking); while Hausa, Yoruba and Igbo – languages of the three (demographically) dominant tribes – enjoy official recognition for legislative matters, and in education, as subjects of instruction at secondary and tertiary levels. By the same policy, languages of minority tribes (e.g. Efik, Ijaw, Urhobo) can be used as media and subjects of instruction at the primary level, in their role as mother tongue(s) (MT), or languages of the immediate community (LIC). Nowhere, today, however, is ANP officially recognised as liable to play a role in the Nigerian educational establishment.

This paper surveys the main states and trends of educational policy and practice in Nigeria – both pre- and post-independence – with specific reference to language education, and in relation to ANP. It also presents and evaluates questionnaire-based data, from six urban centres in southern Nigeria, on attitudes of the principal actors in the educational establishment towards ANP, in an attempt to better appreciate where this language stands currently in this crucial domain of Nigeria's national life, and in the context of new, world developments. An attempt is made to interpret the attitudes expressed in the survey from a sociopsychological perspective.

Language Policy and Practice in Nigerian Education

The pre-Independence era

Although the 1st Educational Ordinance for West Africa (1882) decreed the sole use of English in teaching, subsequent official pronouncements and actions on language education in the colonies[2] prescribed the use of the natives' mother tongue(s) in the early stages of primary education. The missionaries were the first to take an interest in indigenous languages 'to teach basic literacy so that pupils could read the Bible and memorise the catechism. This often resulted in pioneering instruction in vernacular languages and translating the Word of God into these same languages' (Watson, 1982: 13). Likewise, the other two funding agencies of colonial education had their vested interests in language education: trading companies and government required numerate and literate natives to function as administrative and court clerks, etc. The attraction of the colonial school is summarised by Watson (1982: 26) thus: 'many of the students who attended saw the European language and the examination qualifications as a route to employment in government service or in business and commerce'.

In practice, there were inadequacies in teaching staff, teacher-training and the provision of relevant textbooks; educationists decided locally on texts used, curricula and syllabi, with state control being exerted only through grants-in-aid, payment-by-results and inspection. Awoniyi (1976: 37) describes the colonial government's attitude towards mother tongue education, in spite of its seemingly commendable official stance, as '"benevolent tolerance" without any systematic planning'. If it is any consolation, we are informed (Watson, 1976: 9–10) that primary education was introduced in England only in the 1870s; universal secondary education came well after World War II;

and 'if a policy of *laissez-faire* was pursued in most British colonies in the nineteenth century this reflected the prevailing pattern in England'.

The post-Independence era

The colonial legacy in language education was carried over, initially, with little or no tinkering after Independence. Excepting the Northern Region, the mother tongue (or language of immediate community) was used for instruction for the first three years of primary education, while English was studied as a subject – these roles being reversed for the three remaining years. English is the language of instruction at secondary level, with the possibility of studying the "major" languages as electives (French, and possibly Arabic, were compulsory for the first three years, after which they became electives). English, while being the language of instruction in the newly-established universities, is also compulsory in the first year as a remedial subject, given the unsatisfactory standards attained by some students on admission.

In 1967, the division of the Federation into 12 states led to some local liberties being taken with policy through language education experimentation: the Western state's six-year (mother tongue) primary school project (Afolayan, 1976); and the Rivers Readers' Project on the formalisation of mother tongues in Rivers state, and provision of primers, thereof (Williamson, 1976).

In 1977, the National Education Policy made it mandatory, for the first three years of secondary education, that pupils study one major Nigerian language, in addition to their own (after which these became electives). This meant that language studies constituted as much as a third of the curriculum, which comprised 12 subjects. At tertiary level, the inclusion of Nigerian languages as subjects of degree study in departments of linguistics is a reflection of a growing interest in indigenous languages. These languages are, generally, also used for newscasting, drama sketches, discussion programmes and advertising in radio and TV.

One should add that the 1979 Constitution[3] gave legal stamp to the role of English as the official language of the Federation, and to Hausa, Yoruba and Igbo ('when adequate arrangements have been made therefor') as languages of the National Assembly; as well as to local language(s) selected by State Assemblies for their business ('as the House may by resolution approve').

In practice, the same *lacunae* in implementation that dogged policy in colonial times, were to be found: inadequate planning for teacher-training needs for mother-tongue education (Bamgbose (1992: 572) reports that of the 48,854 teachers required, only 6,383 were available); lack of textbooks and other study materials; and no feedback, or review systems. In effect, the urban vs. rural, and élite vs. ordinary school duality of the colonial heritage has been maintained.[4]

Attitudinal Survey

This questionnaire-based survey sampled the attitudes and perceptions of pupils/teachers and students/lecturers in six urban centres in southern Nigeria (Calabar, Port-Harcourt, Warri, Benin, Lagos, and Ibadan) towards ANP. Twenty subjects were sampled (per group) in each centre, divided equally among the subgroups and sexes, i.e. five of each, to give a total of 240 subjects. The sampling rationale was based on prevailing ethnic representativity at state and centre levels. Ibadan, given its relative linguistic homogeneity, with Yoruba being the *lingua franca*, served as an inclusive control centre. Thus, while Ibadan has a different linguistic aspect from the other five, which could be said to belong to the 'Pidgin zone', Ibadan is, nonetheless, a southern Nigerian urban centre and its scores, though examined apart, were taken into consideration for overall evaluation. The four-part questionnaire gathered information on the subjects':

- personal details (age, sex, religion, tribe, etc.);
- verbal repertoire;
- contact details (with ANP); and
- attitudinal dispositions towards ANP's nature, promotion in certain domains, and possible adoption as a future official language (with reasons advanced).

The survey scores indicated in Tables 10.1 and 10.2 (and other main scores) are presented, analysed and discussed below. Figure 10.1 presents the inter-centre analysis of approval for ANP as an official language.

Results and Analyses: Secondary Level

Sample profile

(Numbers presented in the summaries of results are rounded percentages.) The four main tribes represented by the pupils were: Yoruba (30%), Edo (13%), Efik (8%), and Ibibio (8%). Most were 15–19 years old (82%); and trilingual (40%) – ANP ranked as their first third language, and 67% believe they speak it well. The greater number (45%) claimed they first came across ANP when they were 5–9 years old, at school (21%), and through peers (63%).

Table 10.1 ANP (Attitude) scores at secondary and tertiary levels

	Secondary (%)				Tertiary (%)				Overall
	Pupils n=60	Teachers n=60	Mean-Ib* n=100	Mean n=120	Students n=60	Lecturers n=60	Mean-Ib* n=100	Mean n=120	Mean n=240
ANP as language									
1 In your opinion, is ANP a language?	70	83.3	82	76.6	88.3	80	88	84.1	80.3
2 In your opinion, is ANP a 'normal' language?	35	53.3	50	44.2	56.7	46.7	52	51.7	47.9
3 In your opinion, is ANP a variety of English?	53.3	70	65	61.7	81.7	63.3	72	72.5	67.1
ANP as school language									
4 Should ANP be taught in schools?	25	21.7	27	23.3	25	25	26	25	24.1
5 Should ANP be used to teach in schools?	33.3	33.3	37	33.3	33.3	33.3	36	33.3	33.3
ANP as official language									
6 Should ANP be adopted as the official language?	30	40	38	35	35	33.3	35	34.1	34.5
Favourable reasons:									
a ANP is efficient, easy to learn, spoken by most	25	35	33	30	28.4	20	24	24.2	27.1
b ANP aids interethnic communication	3.3	1.7	2	2.5	3.3	3.3	3	3.3	2.9
c ANP is ethnically neutral	1.7	3.3	3	2.5	3.3	10	8	6.6	4.5
Unfavourable reasons:									
d ANP retards learning of English (in children); leads to exam failures	41.7	43.3	38	42.5	18.3	23.3	18	20.8	31.7
e ANP is not standardised	8.3	8.3	8	8.3	16.6	16.7	19	16.7	12.5
f ANP is not understood by everyone	1.7	1.7	1	1.7	11.7	1.7	7	6.7	4.2
g ANP is not a world language	11.6	3.4	9	7.5	11.7	11.7	12	11.7	9.6
h ANP is not indigenous	5	—	3	2.5	3.3	5	4	4.2	3.3
i ANP does not sound 'sweet'	1.7	3.3	3	2.5	3.3	5	4	4.1	3.3
j ANP is a 'no man's language'	—	—	—	—	1.7	1.6	2	1.7	0.9

*Mean-Ib = Mean excluding Ibadan, i.e. mean of Pidgin zone, or the average for the five centres: Calabar, Port-Harcourt, Warri, Benin and Lagos only

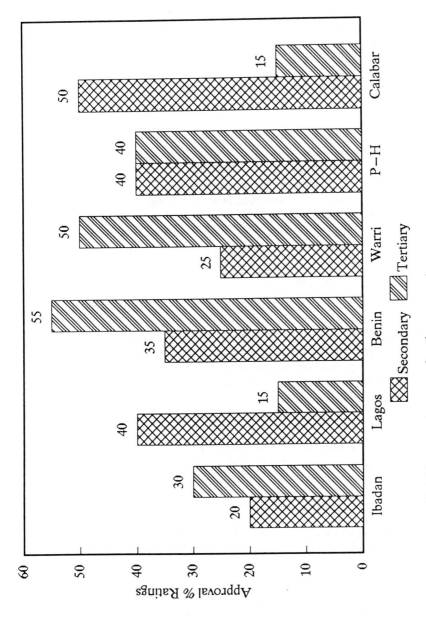

Figure 10.1 ANP (as official language) approval rating per centre

The (main) ethnic composition of the teachers was: Yoruba (25%), Ibo (20%), Edo (15%), and Efik (8%). 48% were in the age range 30–39 years, while 40% were between 20–29 years. The greater number (47%) were trilingual, with ANP, again, being ranked as the most popular third language and 70% claimed they speak it well. 30% indicated they came across ANP, for the first time, between the ages of 1–4 years; and 27%, between 10–14 years. The school is, again, indicated as the most popular place of contact (30%), and peers (65%) as the primary agents.

Attitudinal Dispositions

(1) ANP appears to have enjoyed more favour, regularly, from teachers than pupils, in relation to perceptions of its (language) nature and status (Questions 1–3). The scores of both subgroups converge a lot more on issues of its possible (formal) applications and promotion (Questions 4–6): 25% of pupils would like to see it taught as a subject, and 22% of teachers. 33% of all subjects combined would not be against it being used to teach; curiously, 40% of teachers would like it adopted as official language, compared to 30% of pupils.

(2) ANP's accessibility, as a language, is the strongest point in its favour, as far as the pupils are concerned, followed by its use as a mediating language between the different ethnic tongues. The three most remarkable (negative) scores for ANP with the pupils are, respectively: their view that it impedes educational progress in English (this is also the most important factor at 42%), that it is not a world language, and that it is not standardised. A lot more teachers appreciate its ease of acquisition (35%), and find the consideration of its apparent politico-ethnic neutrality more important (3%), as a factor in its favour, than its function in interethnic communication. The number of teachers who believe it would hinder education in English is close to that of the pupils (43%), but, again, the teachers found its lack of standardisation a more worrying problem than the fact that it is not an internationally recognised language.

(3) In the Pidgin zone (i.e. Calabar, Port-Harcourt, Warri, Benin, and Lagos), a very high percentage of the subjects (82%) regard ANP as a language, half of them believe it is a 'normal' language, and most feel it is a variety of English (65%). 27% would like it taught as a subject; while 37% think it should be used as a medium of instruction. Almost 40% favour its adoption as an official language. The main rankings of reasons advanced follow the pattern of the teachers' scores.

(4) Predictably, all the final means for the group are reduced under the influence of the low scores from the control centre Ibadan (Ibadan-only figures are not presented in Table 10.1), where only 5% favour it being taught; 15%, the possibility of using it to teach; and a mere 20%, its adoption as official language. Only three (unfavourable) reasons are offered here in the control centre: [d] (65%); [e] (10%); and [f] (5%). Overall, the scores from all centres at the secondary level show that 23% of those sampled support teaching ANP in schools; 33% would not mind it being used to teach; and slightly over this same number would like to see it adopted as official language.

Tertiary Level

Sample profile

The three main constituent ethnic groups in the students sample are: Yoruba (33%), Edo (17%), and Urhobo (8%). Most of them (87%) were in the age range 20–29 years, are trilingual (43%), use ANP as their dominant third language, and 73% claim to speak it well. The greater number (45%) indicate having come across ANP for the first time in the age range 5–9 years, and 33% in the age range 1–4 years. Most claim to have had contact with ANP for the first time in the domains 'at home' (43%), (the school coming second best here with 18%), and the agents of contact were family (43%) and peers (43%).

The main (ethnic) composition of the lecturers sampled is as follows: Yoruba (23%), Ibo (17%), Edo (13%), and Urhobo (12%). Most were 30–39 years old (58%), and quadrilingual (43%). ANP ranked as their dominant third language, with 67% claiming to speak it well. 27% had their first contact with ANP between the ages of 10–14 years, and 25% between the ages of 1–4 years. This initial contact took place, for the greater number (33%) at school, and through peers (65%).

Attitudinal Dispositions

(1) The trend of scores for Questions 1–3 seems to be reversed for the third-level group, i.e. students appear to have responded consistently more positively than lecturers; all their scores, except for teachers on Question 6, are more than (or equal to) those of the other subgroups. The fact that ANP is easy to learn, and accessible to the majority of Nigerians is, in their view, its most positive feature. The students also have the most evenly spread scores for factors mitigating against its adoption as an official

language. Interestingly, the fact it is not (nationally) understood by all, is as important an inhibiting factor as its lack of an international communicational status. Incidentally, their score for the likelihood that ANP would hinder educational progress in English is the lowest (18%).

(2) In spite of the significant differences in scores for the first three questions, the lecturers' ratings on Questions 4–6 converge with those of the students, and are very similar to those of the subgroups in the secondary. Noticeably, they record the lowest score (20%) for the statement that ANP is efficient and easy to learn (6a), but the highest, in appreciating its politico-ethnic importance (10% on 6c). The lecturers' scores regarding reasons against the adoption of ANP as an official language (6d–j) are also more evenly spread: their appreciation of the need to standardise ANP is the highest (17%) – almost equalled by the students – and is double that expressed by pupils and teachers, as individual subgroups. They also emphasise most the drawback that ANP is not indigenous (7%).

(3) In the Pidgin zone (i.e. excluding the Ibadan scores) the third-level students recorded higher scores than the second-level pupils regarding ANP's language status (Questions 1–3), but converge with the latter regarding its position in schools and official status (Questions 4–6). ANP's lack of standardisation is its most significant drawback (19%) for third-level students in the Pidgin zone, whereas its claimed contribution to exam failure is the most important factor for second-level pupils.

(4) In contrast to the second-level scores, the margin between the third-level scores from Ibadan and the Pidgin zone (comparing the means excluding and including Ibadan) is much closer regarding ANP's status as a language (Questions 1–3), both groups appearing to converge on questions regarding its position in schools and its official status (Questions 4–6). Politico-ethnic considerations rate second for lecturers and students, in terms of favourable reasons for choosing ANP as official language. With regard to reasons against the adoption of ANP as an official language 6[d–j], their mean for [d] is half that of pupils/teachers; but for [e], double the score for the second-level respondents. As was the case with the latter, 25% would be happy that ANP is taught as a subject, 33% would approve its use as a medium of instruction, and an almost similar proportion would favour its adoption as an official language.

Synthesis and Discussion

Overall scores indicate that a healthy 80% regard ANP as a language, about half think it is a 'normal' language and most (67%) perceive it to be a variety of English. Regarding more formal concerns, 24% approve of it being taught as a subject; 33% would not mind it being used as a medium of instruction; and over 34% would like it adopted as official language. Interestingly, more respondents were apprehensive of the idea of teaching ANP as a subject than of using it as a medium of instruction, or an official language (mean deviations: Questions 4–5 = 9.1; Questions 5–6 = 1.3). The best approval ratings, overall, come from Benin, followed closely by Port-Harcourt (see Figure 10.1).

Evidently, ANP is the most popular third language among the respondents. The school is, overall, the *primary locus* of contact with ANP, and peers are its *primary agents*. ANP is, therefore, an active language of the school playground. Considerations of the influence of independent variables reveal correlations between approval ratings, gender, and ethnic origin. Approval ratings of male respondents are double, overall, those of female respondents; Yoruba respondents tend to have a lowering effect on ANP's approval ratings, and only 10% of Yorubas sampled approve its use as a subject of instruction.

A recategorisation of reasons advanced for ratings in Questions 1–6, under broader headings (see Table 10.2), shows more clearly that while broadly speaking, educational reasons are the most important for respondents from the second-level, communicational ones are the priority for third-level respondents.

Table 10.2 Reasons for ANP approval ratings: categorisation into macro-domains

	Secondary	Tertiary
1. *Communicational*		
(a) Sociocommunicational/functional-integrative (6a)	30.0	24.2
(b) Interethnic communication:		
'ANP aids interethnic communication' (6b)	2.5	3.3
'ANP is not understood by everyone' (6f)	1.7	6.7
(c) World communication: 'ANP is not a world language' (6g)	7.5	11.7
Total:	41.7	45.9
2. *Educational/socioeconomic*		
(a) Instructional: 'retards learning, leads to exam failure' (6d)	42.5	20.8
(b) Standardisation: 'ANP is not standardised' (6e)	8.3	16.7
Total:	50.8	37.5
3. *Ethnic identity/authenticity*		
(a) Authenticity: 'ANP is not indigenous' (6h)	2.5	4.2
(b) 'ANP is a "no man's language"' (6j)	0.0	1.7
Total:	2.5	5.9
4. *Politico-ethnic:* 'ANP is ethnically neutral' (6c)	2.5	6.6
5. *Sociomoral:* 'ANP does not sound sweet' (6i)	2.5	4.1

One could posit that this is related to the more prescriptive perspective taken in secondary education, as compared with the greater liberalism promoted in tertiary education. The most telling factor in the subjects' attitudes is the apprehension that ANP would hamper education in English, and lead, eventually, to lower educational standards. In sociopsychological terms, it could be suggested that this is a pragmatic viewpoint, based on the social exchange theory, i.e. decisions we take in society are grounded on our evaluation of the rewards they could generate. There is also a hint of Tajfel's (1974) theory of intergroup distinctiveness, whereby 'people experience satisfaction in the knowledge that they belong to groups which enjoy some superiority over others' (Giles & Smith, 1979: 52).

Conclusion

It is very unlikely that there will be a significant challenge to the role of English as Nigeria's official language in the foreseeable future. The recent enhancement of the capitalist ideology – whose principal agents and actors are Anglophone or 'anglophonising' – following the collapse of socialist systems in the Soviet Union and other east European countries, can only reinforce its status on the world stage. It would equally enjoy some fillip from contemporary tendencies to establish supranations (e.g. the European megastate), which would, necessarily, require a convergent medium of communication. Given that English remains the language of education, and, therefore, the passport to educational qualifications and (upward) socio-economic mobility, these two pulls or forces, the national and the international, will continue to constitute its attraction to Nigerians. Moreover, it is unlikely that those who used it to attain an élite status, will be sympathetic to a change that puts their position in jeopardy.

However, it is my contention, though hypothetical, that English is too typologically distant – linguistically, psycholinguistically and socioculturally – to serve the higher goal of liberation and emancipation from underdevelopment. The aspiration must be to have an official language which is more relevant and accessible to the sociocultural existence, or 'world view', of the people. Misconceptions of their competence in English are widespread among Nigerians. In fact, few Nigerians possess a standard mastery of English, even fewer use it grammatically correctly and only about 10% are literate in it (Bamgbose, 1992). This state of affairs cannot be explained away, in my view, by reference to the ineffectual literacy campaign. The greater majority of Nigerians are denied, through English, an opportunity to take part fully in the national debate, with implications for the growth of indigenous languages and their use in ideation, full self-expression, and sense of self. In fact, it might very well not be an overstatement to say that English is, today, a language of captivity and deprivation in Nigeria. Curiously, this author is not aware of any nation that attained greatness through an imposed foreign tongue that did not 'nativise'.

The results recorded from the survey on ANP can only be described as promising for a language that is not standardised, suffers from low social prestige, but, most importantly, enjoys no official recognition. Given its omnipresence in urban sociocommunication, it is high time ANP enjoyed more respect and appreciation from all those concerned with language planning and policy in Nigeria. There are, clearly, implications for cost, planning, interethnic tensions, and sociopsychological reorientation, in any discussion of language policy change or modification. However, these must not be dissuasive excuses. Government and academics must reinforce their interest in the study and formalisation of Nigerian languages, and follow, attentively, their evolution in society, so as to better determine what roles they could be made to play. They must be given a chance to fulfil the three types of language 'adequacy' defined by Whinnom (1971: 108): contextual, referential and literary. After all, a language is only as developed as the communicational challenge it gets. The present vitality of ANP in socio-communication is established, and growing still. This, in some respects, already vindicates Hymes' (1971: 3) hope that pidgins and creoles, which have traditionally been called the stepchild of linguistic theory and research concerns, would, one day, prove a Cinderella. Our next obligation is to give Cinderella her shoe!

Notes

1. See Hymes, 1971; Valdman, 1977; Mann, 1988, for discussion.
2. The Phelps-Stokes Commission (1922), the 1st Report (HMSO, 1925) of the Advisory Committee on Education in the Colonies, the inauguration of the International Institute of African languages and cultures (1926), and the 1927 Memo of the Conference of Colonial Officers.
3. Chapter 5, Part I, B.51 and Part II, A.91, respectively.
4. See Oladejo (1992) for discussion of vagueness and loop-holes of the 1977 National Policy in Education.

References

Afolayan, A. (1976) The six year primary project in Nigeria. In A. Bamgbose (ed.) *Mother Tongue Education* (pp. 113–34). London: Hodder & Stoughton.

Awoniyi, T. (1976) Mother tongue education in West Africa: A historical background. In A. Bamgbose (ed.) *Mother Tongue Education* (pp. 27–42). London: Hodder & Stoughton.

Bamgbose, A. (1992) Language policy and practice in education: The Nigerian experience. *Bilingualism & National Development* 2, 564–75.

— (ed.) (1976) *Mother Tongue Education*. London: Hodder & Stoughton.

Brosnahan, L.F. (1963) Some historical cases of language imposition. In J. Spencer (ed.) *Language in Africa: Papers of the Leverhulme Conference on Universities and the Language Problems of Tropical Africa* (pp. 7–24). Cambridge: Cambridge University Press.

Decamp, D. (1971) The study of pidgin and creole languages. In D. Hymes (ed.) *Pidginization and Creolization of Languages* (pp. 349–70). Cambridge: Cambridge University Press.

Elugbe, B. and Omamor, A. (1991) *Nigerian Pidgin*. Ibadan: Heinemann.

Fatunde, T. (1986) *Oga na tief man*. Benin: Adena.

Federal Ministry of Information. (1977) *National Policy in Education*. Lagos.

Giles, H. and Smith, P. (1979) Accommodation theory: Optimal levels of convergence. In H. Giles and P. St. Clair (eds) *Language and Social Psychology* (pp. 45–63). Oxford: Blackwell.

Hall, R. jnr (1955) *Hands Off Pidgin English!* Sydney: Pacific Publications.

Hymes, D. (ed.) (1971) *Pidginization and Creolization of Languages*. Cambridge: Cambridge University Press.

Mann, C. (1988) Traditional notions on Pidgins and Creoles: A review and a contemporary view. *Ilorin Journal of Language and Literature* 1, 89–97.

— (1990) Choosing an indigenous official language for Nigeria: Perspectives & procedures. *Language and Nation*. BAAL, 6, 91–103.

— (1993) The sociolinguistic status of Anglo-Nigerian Pidgin: An overview. *International Journal of the Sociology of Language* 100/101, 167–78.

Marchese, L. and Schnukal, A. (1980) Nigerian Pidgin English: A progress report. Paper presented at the Inaugural Meeting of the Linguistic Association of Nigeria, Ibadan.

The Constitution of the Federal Republic of Nigeria. (1979) Lagos: *Daily Times*.

Oladejo, J.A. (1992) How not to embark on a bilingual education policy in a developing country: The case of Nigeria. *Bilingualism and National Development* 1, 413–29.

Saro-Wiwa, K. (1985) *Sozaboy*. Port-Harcourt: Ewell Saros.

Tajfel, H. (1974) Social identity and intergroup behaviour. *Social Science Information* 13, 65–93.

Valdman, A. (1977) *Pidgin and Creole Linguistics*. Bloomington: Indiana University Press.

Watson, K. (ed.) (1982) *Education in the Third World*. Kent: Croom Helm.

Whinnom, K. (1971) Linguistic hybridisation and the 'special case' of pidgins and creoles. In D. Hymes (ed.) *Pidginization and Creolization of Languages* (pp. 91–115). Cambridge: Cambridge University Press.

Whitehead, C. (1982) Education in British Colonial dependencies 1991–1939: A re-appraisal. In K. Watson (ed.) *Education in the Third World* (pp. 47–60). Kent: Croom Helm.

Williamson, K. (1976) The Rivers Readers Project in Nigeria. In A. Bamgbose (ed.) *Mother Tongue Education* (pp. 135–53). London: Hodder & Stoughton.

11 Issues of Ethnic Participation in Language Planning in an Age of Ethnic Empowerment: Observations from Guatemala

KATHERINE LANGAN

Introduction

In Guatemala 15 years ago it was unimaginable that there would be govern-ment sponsored and supported bilingual education programmes in Spanish and Mayan languages. Despite decades of serious study by linguists and anthropologists, the majority of Guatemalans (including Mayas) did not appreciate the linguistic complexity and beauty of the 22 different Mayan languages spoken within the borders of the country. These languages were disparagingly referred to as 'lenguas' or 'dialectos' and dismissed as not being 'real' languages. School teachers would tell the Mayan children to stop using their mother-tongue, because it was not a real language and took up space in the brain which could be more profitably used to study Spanish and learn school information.

Now there is a well-established bilingual programme. It runs for five years, from a pre-school preparatory year through grade four and there has been discussion about extending the programme through all six primary grades. All aspects of the programme: curriculum and text development, additional reading resources preparation, teaching, evaluation, supervision and plan-ning are done by Mayas, or at least with Mayas. This is a new sociological group, the Mayan professional, who is not just moving into the dominant

Latin culture, but trying to stay faithful to being a Maya. This group is the focus of this paper.

Firstly, I will briefly describe the members of the group who form the basis for this study, then I will discuss three aspects: objectivity, professionalisation, and cultural conflicts as they pertain to this group as both affected by and effecting societal changes. Finally, I will raise some questions directed toward tertiary educational and adult training institutions which may help in the design of programmes designed to professionally upgrade marginalised ethnic groups.

The Population

This study falls within the realm of Ethnography because the data come from field observations over time by a participant observer. It is different from most ethnographies because the subjects came to me in the university classroom, instead of me going to them. The principal subjects are a group of 64 students (58 Mayas and six Latins), most of whom I taught for two semesters or more, some of whom I worked closely with as director of final seminar or thesis mentor. This group constitutes about half of all linguistics students in Guatemala during the years 1991–1993. The Latin students will be mentioned from now on only for contrast with the Mayan students.

The students were enrolled in the undergraduate (Profesorado) or graduate (Licenciatura) programmes at either Rafael Landivar University (URL) or Mariano Galvez University (UMG). Some students took classes at both institutions.

The Mayan students all had full-time jobs, almost all were married, most had children, and less than 10% lived in Guatemala City (where the universities are located). The majority of students were teachers (not always in bilingual schools) or worked in other aspects of the bilingual education programme. The majority came from Kaqchikel-speaking towns, but there were also Mam, K'iche', Q'eqchi', Poqomchi, Akatek, Popti', and Qanjob'al speakers in my classes.

Among the students who commuted to classes, the one-way travel time ranged from one to 17 hours. To accommodate a non-resident student population, classes were held at weekends. URL conducted all classes on Saturday (8.00 am – 5.00 pm). UMG held two classes on Friday (4.30 – 9.00 pm) and three on Saturday (7.30 am – 2.00 pm). After classes were finished on Saturday, students would rush for buses to begin the journey home for another week of family, work and study. Several students had to walk about an hour to get to a telephone.

While not every student was academically brilliant, they were almost all highly motivated with a zeal associated with visionaries and missionaries. Overall, the students were dedicated, conscientious, co-operative, academically under-prepared for university level work, overworked, and determined to succeed not just for job reasons, but for cultural survival.

Much more could be said about the circumstances and character of these students, but this is a general picture. More information will be given in the following sections.

Students as Agents of Change and Maintenance

As mentioned above, I want to focus on how this tertiary educational experience provides insight into the conduct of these students as agents of change and maintenance. I will begin by discussing objectivity.

Objectivity

Among scientists (social or natural) objectivity is considered fundamental to good research. Even while acknowledging the advantages of insider insight, that insight is useless unless one can identify, describe and explain any given phenomenon. Saville-Troike's (1982: 4) point about insider ethnographies can be applied to any methodology. She says:

> . . . discovering patterned behaviour which operates largely unconsciously for the native investigator presents quite different problems for 'objectivity'.

Here, then, is the first point where there is conflict between the culture of the university and the culture of the Mayan nationalists. The university looks to objective research as the fundamental starting point, while the students count on rhetoric and a sense of moral motivation.

This conflict rests in the difference between quasi-logical and analogical patterns of proof as expounded by Koch (1983). In quasi-logical argumentation 'ideas are persuasive' and 'institutions make decisions', while in analogical argumentation 'culture is persuasive' and 'history/tradition make decisions'.[1] One of the most common authorities within Mayan culture is some form of 'Our ancestors say'. What the ancestors say preserves and perpetuates the culture. Traditionally, the elders of a community or those who have achieved status as elders by their position in institutions will pass along the ways of the ancestors. What is particularly interesting about the university students is their perception that their destiny, purpose and mission is to assure the continuance of Mayan languages and culture while gaining parity in the larger socio-political entity of Guatemala.

This is problematic. While teaching a class on dialectology the students were instructed to do a limited geographical survey to look for variants, describe the variants and then discuss the implications of regional variation for language standardisation. None of the approximately 30 students in this course referred to their linguistic data as a departure for standardisation. Instead, the responses were the most overt statements of the perception the students had of their own responsibility to bring their languages and culture into the next stage of Guatemalan society. They referred to the ancestors' counsel for unity and the history/tradition of unity and harmony before the Conquest. Often the students concluded that unification is imperative for the continuation of the culture.

It was obvious that the students have a clear sense of what ought to be, but a more vague sense of what 'is'. Empirical data are not the first recourse for proof, but the rhetoric of Mayan nationalism. Of course, the rhetoric is important, because data will not effect change. Data only tell you how far you have to go to achieve change. But rhetoric can be oppressive if differing views are not treated with respect and rhetoric alone can lead to fallacious conclusions.

Another issue is the ability of students to objectivise and articulate salient information from their own experience. Both in class and in thesis sessions obvious information was not seen until it was pointed it out to them.

The students' objectivity is limited by two things. First, a lack of in-depth training in research and sociological methodology. Secondly, the intensity of their feeling for the maintenance of their own languages and cultures. Neither of these limitations is terminal, but both have to be recognised by the students themselves.

In the future, these students will be called upon to shape policy and pro-grammes. If they cannot see from where they are starting, it will be difficult for them to design and then evaluate effective programmes without a certain level of objectivity. If programmes are run only on rhetoric, I suspect a low rate of accomplishment will be the result, given the lack of concurrence within the Mayan community on educational issues, including the shape of the alpha-bet and the acceptability of standardised varieties.

The students in the programme need to be agents of change by redefining group membership beyond town boundaries, which is the definition for the majority of Mayas. Yet these same students do not consciously take this level of identity into account because of the nationalist unity rhetoric. Of course, the idea of unity is not just nationalistic rhetoric. It resonates with the existing 'us–them' social division between Mayas and Latins. However, there is also a great deal of social division between different towns whose dialects are mutually intelligible.[2] I will return to different aspects of this issue below.

To convince the Maya of the need for unification rhetoric will be extremely important. To convince funding agencies, sceptical bureaucrats and outside consultants of the validity and success of programmes these students will have to use the arguments of data and syllogism. In addition they will need to pass along that perspective among their own, both on the work and cultural level.

So, these students have to change their own mode of argumentation and proof and pass along that perspective to their home communities. As they undergo the change process they also transmit the different patterns within the Mayan society.

Internal conflict in Mayan society

The issue of objectivity is closely connected to the issue of the internal conflict within the Mayan segment of Guatemala. Inter-ethnic conflict is a worldwide phenomenon. The conflict between exploiting ethnicities and exploited ethnicities has received a great deal of attention in the press and in professional literature in many areas, e.g. geolinguistics and educational parity. In Guatemala, the majority of attention has focused on this aspect of conflict – the powerful Latins versus the powerless Indigenous. This could give the false impression of widespread unity among all the Mayas regarding the types of changes and programmes implied by the implementation of bilingual education. For these visionary students there is a real possibility that they will find themselves, as Edwards (1985: 39) said, '. . . substituting one set of shackles for another'.

As already indicated, there is considerable diversity of opinion among Mayas *vis-á-vis* bilingual education issues: from macro level questions about the need for bilingual schools to micro level issues pertaining to alphabets, standard forms of the languages, etc. The university students are very much in favour of bilingual education, legal linguistic parity, language standardisation and other issues related to nationalist movements. This group, however, is a numerically small sub-section of the larger population.

Among the larger population, there is still diversity of opinion. Some people are for bilingual education – others are not (Menchú & Xulú, 1993). Some parents send their children to other towns to avoid bilingual schools – others try to promote bilingual education in the classroom even if the school is not designated as part of the bilingual programme. If the school officials are not open to bilingual classrooms, private programmes may be started

(Barrientos *et al.*, 1992). Some people verbally promote the idea of bilingual education, but their actions work against it (Hurtado, 1993). While some success can be reported, there is no widespread acceptance for written forms of Mayan languages. The best documentation is found for the K'iche' area (Henne, 1985).

There is even a difference of opinion on whether the speaking of a Mayan language is crucial to being Mayan (Langan, 1993). Historically, the Maya have associated in-group membership with speaking the in-group language.[3] The main division of Mayan society has been 'us' and 'them'. 'Us' does extend to include all Maya in opposition to Latins. However, when asked if the people from a town only a few kilometres distant, speaking a mutually intelligible variety speak the same language, the answer is usually negative.[4] For most of the normal population basic linguistic identity is limited. 'Our language' refers to the regional dialect spoken in 'our town'.

For the students and nationalists, linguistic identity is the whole dialect chain; some are hoping for unification of the dialect chains within a language family. The ideological conflict concretises in the standardisation process: alphabetic graphics, lexical items, grammatical and syntactic strategies.

The classic example of this conflict is the alphabet reform of 1986. The leadership of the nationalist movement advocated change from the previously authorised alphabets, in part because the reformed version moved away from certain Spanish spelling conventions and so made the written form of the languages look very different from written Spanish. Another hope for the reform was the unification of spelling as a step toward written standards. Many of those who had learned to read using the old alphabets (which were based on town or regional dialectic features) responded quite negatively, wondering if they would still be able to read and write in their languages. These readers felt threatened by the change, yet the proponents did very little to alleviate the fears of disenfranchisement, preferring legislative fiat in the form of a presidential decree to the slow process of re-educating the reticent population.

The bilingual education programme is functioning on the implicit premise of unification. This unification is based on the perception of past historical unity and the desire for the past and future benefits of larger group solidarity. Edwards (1985: 43), commenting on Smith, describes this aspect of nationalism:

> Nationalism may be described as 'the myth of the historical renovation' in the process of which 'a pristine state of true collective individuality' is rediscovered, nurtured and used to forge an identity needed for the present and the future.

It is not my purpose to discuss the merits of nationalistic unity. However beneficial such unity may be, there has been little or no effort at achieving consensus among speakers about this decision, or even what "unity" means. The students, who want to maintain and preserve their cultures, are now using language to change not only linguistic diversity, but also the basic identity factors and the very process of decision-making.

The university courses which I was assigned to teach frequently touched on this issue. Overtly bringing up the topic of intra-group imperialism always generated considerable discussion in the classroom, usually ending with a frustrated demand for more training so that such an undesirable situation could be avoided. It always appeared easier for the students to accept that they were agents of change of Latin ideas, methods, and practices, rather than of Mayan customs, ideas, and practices.

In summary, these students were being trained to be change agents without actually bringing that aspect of bilingual education into focus. This creates a paradoxical situation for the students who are committed to both change and preservation. This paradox is not insurmountable, but requires that the students both see the paradox and have time to deal with it.

Questions and Suggestions

There is no such thing as a perfect programme. Anything can be improved and it is easier to criticise than to create. However, my experience with these students raised serious questions about the whole structure of tertiary education for situations like Guatemala.

The most fundamental question is: is it realistic to expect students to assimilate not only information, but a different perspective of valid argumentation using intensive programmes over limited time? If the goal of such programmes is to really prepare individuals who are independently capable of performing at a professional level, then the answer is 'no'. The curriculum and academic structures must be modified to give the students the opportunity to recognise and grapple with the course content and the social issues which can create dilemmas. The students in Guatemala had no desire to prolong their course of study, but they also wanted to feel qualified at the end of the programme. Interviews with students who had finished or were about to finish indicated that they were acutely aware of the inadequacies of the programmes. At the end of their study and thesis the feeling was that they were just beginning to understand the theories and to have ideas about application for their own specific areas of work and their study time was now over. The best students as well as the slower ones felt this way. None of them were prepared enough to begin teaching others except at the most basic levels.

It must be clearly stated that this is not because the students lack intellectual ability, but they did not have the time to deal with the amount of information they were expected to acquire. There was almost no opportunity to talk with faculty outside of class. The time pressure was worse at the university which received funding from USAID for four years to prepare qualified professionals. Under this regime, students had one semester to write their thesis and there was no way to take fewer than five courses per semester.

This raises the question: can training programmes be designed which will take into account the students' real situation and needs? If national or international entities really desire the participation of previously marginalised populations, then other models will have to be found. The distance education model seems appropriate. Establishing regional centres with taped lectures and readings could help the students have more time to study and they would have to spend less time on overcrowded buses.

Contact time with faculty could be increased by including tutorial sessions in the curriculum and/or assigning mentors for the whole time, not just for the thesis or seminar courses.

Finding faculty has been an issue. Many linguists and anthropologists have field time in Guatemala, very few plan their trips to allow for participation in the university programmes. The academic year does not coincide with most European or North American systems. However, it might be possible to include university students in field research, following an apprenticeship model. This option and the option for teaching would be feasible for graduate students who are in the country doing their own thesis data gathering. Since so many institutions and scholars from developed countries are interested in the peoples and events of countries like Guatemala, surely professional organisations and associations could organise apprentice match-up programmes for the enrichment of all concerned.[5]

This match-up idea may also provide a handle for another question: how helpful are training programmes which do not allow for the recruitment and training of future trainers from the target population? One of the greatest problems which I see is that the current tertiary educational opportunities in Guatemala do not provide sufficient depth for the graduates to take over the teaching functions. There are no masters programmes in linguistics, certainly no doctorate programmes. While many of the students have the potential to become outstanding professionals at the international level, they need more time to become proficient in the field. Again, institutions which enjoy working in such countries could establish dedicated scholarships/fellowships for promising students. Perhaps some sort of partnership could be established between Guatemalan and outside universities to provide at least a masters level programme.

The design of such a programme may need to be quite creative: for example some intensive classroom time, followed by a correspondence mentoring, with participation in field research and a year or two for directed thesis work.

There are many other suggestions which could be made. But I would like to conclude with a reminder that, while I have described the experience of Guatemala, I do not believe that experience to be unique. It is my hope that the issues raised here may help in designing programmes which do not stop half-way in preparing previously marginalised people to confidently take control of their destiny and to contribute significantly to the well-being of their ethnic groups and countries.

Notes

1. There are several other characteristics in Koch's description which cannot be included here.
2. Julia Richards (1987) gives an excellent example of this in her study of the Lake Atitlán towns.
3. This is not the only criterion, of course. There are non-Mayas who speak Mayan languages. These people can form a distinct group in the town where they live. For a good description of this see Reina, 1966.
4. The exception is the Q'eqchi' area in state of Alta Verapáz.
5. There are a few examples of this sort of mentoring process. The majority of the students who enter the university programmes had their initial exposure to the linguistic study of their own language through such contacts.

References

Barrientos, V. de, Rolando Chacach Catú, y Manfredo López Buatista (1992) Escuelas privadas mayas en Guatemala. *Boletín de Lingüística* 35, 1–4.
Edwards, J. (1985) *Language, Society and Identity.* Oxford: Basil Blackwell.
Henne, M.G. (1985) Why mother tongue literature has failed to take root among the Maya Quiche: A study in the sociology of language in a field programme of the Summer Institute of Linguistics, 1955–1982 Guatemala, Central America. Unpublished MA thesis. University of Texas, Arlington.
Hurtado, A.D.H. (1993) Actitudes sociolingüísticas hacia los idiomas Popti' y español por parte de los maestros de las escuelas oficiales del perimetro urbano de Jacaltenango. Unpublished Licenciatura thesis. Universidad Rafael Landivar.
Koch, B.J. (1983) Presentation as proof: The language of Arabic rhetoric. *Anthropological Linguistics* Spring, 47–60.
Langan, K. (1991) Language proficiency, use and attitudes in Santo Tomás Chichicastenango: A study of language competition. Unpublished PhD dissertation. Georgetown University.

Menchú Chuc, R.V. and Xulu, M.A.T. de. (1993) Actitudes de los padres de familia, mayahabantes e hispanohablantes, hacia la educación bilingüe para todos en Totonicapán y Patzún. Seminario: Lingüística, Educación y Sociedad. Guatemala: Universidad Mariano Galvéz.

Reina, R.E. (1966) *The Law of the Saints: A Pokomam Pueblo and its Community Culture*. Indianapolis, IN: The Bobbs-Merrill Company, Inc.

Richards, J.B. (1987) Language, education and cultural identity in a Maya community of Guatemala. Unpublished PhD dissertation. University of Wisconsin, Madison.

Saville-Troike, M. (1982) *The Ethnography of Communication* (Language in Society 3). Oxford: Basil Blackwell.

12 A Psycholinguistic Study of Pronunciation of Bilinguals: The Case of Belgium

M. SPOELDERS, A.Z. GUIORA, K. VAN LEEUWEN,
C. MEULEMAN, F. VAN BESIEN, A. VYT and G. DE SOETE

Introduction

It is a well-known fact that adults find it difficult to acquire native pronunciation in a second language (L2), although they are able to acquire native proficiency at the level of syntax or lexicon, for example (Scovel, 1969). Several explanations have been suggested. They can be grouped in three major categories (cf. Vyt & Van Besien, in preparation). A first series of explanations centres around the inability of speakers to acquire native-like L2 pronunciation after a certain age due to maturational restrictions. A second kind of explanation revolves around a set of psychological factors rooted in motivational components, learning strategies, or habits which do not encourage an individual to try to accomplish native-like L2 pronunciation but rather prevent him from doing so. For example, a facility argument involves the assumption that use of two languages with one and the same pronunciation system may be easier and more economical. The third category also has its roots in the psychological realm but is related to socio-emotional mechanisms linked to identity development. This kind of explanation has been suggested by Guiora. According to Guiora (1992: 28), 'pronunciation is a marker, separating natives from non-natives, a marker of group language identity, and the core of an individual's "language ego".'

The construct of 'language ego' refers to the 'totality of identity formants and determinants, cultural and individual, shaped and carried by language' (Guiora, 1992: 50). Pronunciation of the language, being a well-defined, observable behaviour, is seen as the core of this language ego. The way people sound represents them as individuals and as members of a group. Hence, when acquiring L2 pronunciation, inhibitions come to the fore. Indeed, full acquisition of native pronunciation in L2 would imply sustaining a double language ego. Only under special conditions are adults able to suppress those inhibitory forces. Under the influence of alcohol (Guiora *et al.*, 1972), hypnosis (Schuman *et al.*, 1978) and Valium (Guiora *et al.*, 1980), adults have been shown to approximate native-like pronunciation in a second language. These different agents act as disinhibitors, producing a temporary change in language ego boundaries in the form of greater permeability.

Should people who consider themselves as natural bilinguals be viewed as having two language egos? If so, this would mean that they would show native pronunciation in both languages. Following Guiora's hypothesis bilinguals can only have native pronunciation in one language. Guiora & Schonberger (1990) tried to empirically validate this corollary in the Haifa setting.

They tested the following hypotheses:

(a) most natural Hebrew-English bilinguals (in perfect command of both Hebrew and English) will speak Hebrew (the school language) without a trace of a foreign accent, but will have a slight foreign accent in English (the home language);

(b) while it may be possible for some bilinguals to speak English without an accent, no one will speak Hebrew with a foreign accent. It was hypothesised that native pronunciation would be found in Hebrew because it is the dominant language for these bilinguals: although English was and continues to be the main home language, true nativeness is reserved for the dominant language (Hebrew) and the other language (English) will be marked.

27 out of 29 subjects tested by Guiora and Schonberger displayed native pronunciation only in one language. One subject spoke both languages with a foreign accent and the judges could not agree about the performance of the last subject. With the exception of this one subject there was perfect agreement between the judges regarding the performance of all the other subjects. Of the 27 subjects who showed native pronunciation in one language only, 25 spoke Hebrew like a native and only two spoke English like a native. The results confirmed the hypotheses posited. Most natural bilinguals were found

(a) to produce native pronunciation only in the dominant language;

(b) not to speak the dominant language with a foreign accent; and

(c) to speak the non-dominant language with a slight foreign accent.

Belgium as a trilingual country offers an opportunity to replicate the Haifa study. The respective dominance positions of the three national languages (Dutch, French and German) in their corresponding territories, create favourable, albeit complex, conditions for studying bilingual behaviour. The hypothesis is that Dutch-French bilinguals living in the Dutch-speaking part of Belgium will have native pronunciation in only one language, i.e. in Dutch.

Experiment I

Subjects

The subjects of this study were 29 Dutch-French bilinguals with French as a 'home language' and Dutch as their dominant or 'school language'.

The subjects present the following profile:

- they were born and raised in Belgium;
- they are high school students between 14 and 18 years old;
- both their parents speak the same language at home, i.e. French;
- they are self-proclaimed bilinguals;
- they have acquired both languages simultaneously, i.e. they have acquired one language at home (their parents' language, i.e. French) but were sent, before the age of four, to a school where the language of instruction was the other language, i.e. Dutch;
- they still use their parents' language at home, and the other language at school. Outside the school situation they use both languages, depending on circumstances.

Subjects in this study were carefully selected. School principals of four secondary schools in Ghent – a town in the Dutch-speaking part of Belgium – provided lists with names of students they believed to be speaking French at home.

An introductory letter, not revealing the real purpose of our study, was sent to equal groups of boys and girls belonging to the same age category. In the letter the subjects were asked to participate in a study that proposed to explore the possibility of presenting TV and radio programmes in more than one language.

In a telephone follow-up the subjects were asked to confirm their co-operation. It was established that the subject did indeed speak French at home.

Procedure

In order to compare the pronunciation of bilinguals in their two languages, spontaneous spoken language samples were needed (Thompson, 1991). Therefore a structured interview was used. A topic was chosen which was supposed to be of some interest to people between 14 and 18 years of age: '(free) radios and television', with questions like: 'What are your favourite radio programmes? What kind of programmes would you like to make? Do you think publicity is a good thing? What is the best time to broadcast programmes? What do you think about the use of jingles?, etc.'.

Three Dutch and two French native speakers were trained as interviewers and the interview procedure was rehearsed several times. They made appointments with the subjects to be interviewed. The interviews were conducted at the homes of the subjects in order to let them feel comfortable and to reduce the level of anxiety they could possibly experience when being interviewed. The conversations were recorded with a small, unobtrusive tape-recorder. The use of such a recorder may have caused the loss of certain samples on account of insufficient quality. 58 recordings were made in all. Subjects were rewarded for their co-operation.

Extracts of about two and a half minutes were taken from each interview and put together on a tape.

Two dummies in each language (i.e. two Dutch monolinguals and similarly two French monolinguals) were added to the list of interviews before they were presented to two rating judges per language.

The judges/raters were asked to answer the following question after each language sample: 'Does the speech segment sound native according to you, yes or no?' The judges had their attention drawn to the fact that dialectic variants also belong to the native language. In order to avoid too analytical an approach to the pronunciation evaluation, the judges listened only once to each extract.

The judges – as was the case in the Haifa study – were two native Dutch-speaking linguists from Ghent University for the evaluation of the Dutch interviews and two native French-speaking linguists from Liege University for the evaluation of the French interviews. In order to check rating consistency, the judges were asked to re-evaluate the same interviews two months later and in a different order.

Results

Table 12.1 summarises the results. 16 out of the 29 subjects were judged to have a *native Dutch pronunciation* by Judge I and 13 out of 29 by Judge II.

Table 12.1   Ratings of Dutch and French language samples (Experiment I)

	Ratings by Dutch speaking judges (N = 2)				Ratings by French-speaking judges (N = 2)			
	Judge I		Judge II		Judge I		Judge II	
	n-ns	ns	n-ns	ns	n-ns	ns	n-ns	ns
Test	13	16	16	13	12	17	13	16
Re-test	13	16	18	11	12	16	14	12

n   = native speaker
n-ns = non-native speaker

Both the judges agreed on 12 subjects having native Dutch pronunciation but they also agreed on 12 subjects whom they found not to have native Dutch pronunciation. Quite surprisingly the judges disagreed on five out of the 29 cases.

As regards the results of the re-test, 16 subjects were judged to have native Dutch pronunciation by Judge I and 11 subjects were found to have native pronunciation by Judge II. Both judges found nine subjects to have native Dutch pronunciation and 11 subjects to have non-native pronunciation. The judges disagreed on nine out of the 29 cases. As far as the dummies are concerned, the judges agreed but the same dummy was found to be 'non-native'.

As far as the *intra-judge reliability* is concerned, Judge I took a different decision at the re-test in seven out of 29 cases. Judge II did so in eight cases. Moreover, both the Dutch judges agreed on the dummies but they did find one of them to be 'non-native' in the test as well as the re-test. This, of course, shows the vulnerability of a rating procedure using only two judges.

17 out of the 29 subjects were judged to have a *native French pronunciation* by Judge I and 16 out of 29 by Judge II. Both the judges found 15 subjects to have native French pronunciation but they also agreed on 11 subjects whom they found not to have native French pronunciation. The judges disagreed on three out of the 29 cases. Both the French judges agreed on the dummies: both were judged to be native French speakers.

As regards the results of the re-test, 16 subjects out of the 28 subjects were judged to have native French pronunciation by Judge I and 12 subjects out of 26 were found to have native pronunciation by Judge II. Both judges found 11 subjects out of 26 to have native French pronunciation and 11 subjects to have non-native pronunciation. The judges disagreed on four out of the 26 cases. As far as the dummies are concerned, one of the judges surprisingly found one of the dummies not to have a native French pronunciation.

In five out of the 28 cases Judge I changed his judgement in the re-test whereas Judge II did so in eight out of his 26 cases.

Discussion of the Results

The above results did not appear to uphold the straightforward Haifa findings. On account of the low intra-judge reliability it was decided to add to the number of judges and submit the extracts to two new enlarged rating groups. An increase in the number of judges, moreover, would make it possible to use a statistical tool in order to fine-tune data analysis. It might be interesting to point out that the judges themselves, having been debriefed, admitted they encountered problems in judging the nativeness of certain pronunciations. In light of this the problem of defining native pronunciation in Belgium had to be confronted for the first time. One of the main problems in the Ghent area was, for one, the pronunciation of the [R].

Considering the above results, the Haifa-hypothesis does not appear to be upheld. However, in view of the low inter and intra-judge reliability it was decided to design a second experiment in order to be able to use an appropriate statistical tool.

Experiment II

Subjects

Subjects were the same as under Experiment I: a group of 29 French–Dutch bilinguals from the Ghent area.

Procedure

The Dutch interview extracts were presented to a group of 34 Dutch native speakers, final year students of two Flemish Colleges for Interpreters and Translators. The French interview extracts were presented to a group of 50 French native speakers, students of the Department of Economics of the Catholic University of Mons. The divergent student numbers are merely a matter of student availability. The student-raters were made to listen to the language extracts in a language laboratory, once and only once for reasons stipulated above under Experiment I.

Results

Table 12.2   Ratings of Dutch and French language samples (Experiment II)

Subjects	Ratings by Dutch-speaking judges (N = 33)		Ratings by French-speaking judges (N = 50)	
	n-ns	ns	n-ns	ns
F.M.	13	16	25	25
M.A.	27	6	19	31
N.J.	1	32	8	42
V.T.M.	12	21	50	0
C.S.	12	21	30	20
H.K.	9	24	17	33
BE.S.	9	24	27	23
BR.S.	2	31	21	29
V.A.F.	10	22	23	27
M.M.	1	32	40	10
Z.K.	31	2	10	40
D.P.V.	3	30	0	50
C.E.	1	32	3	47
D.I.	27	6	3	47
R.B.	10	23	48	2
V.B.	1	32	45	5
D.J.-F.	1	32	6	44
V.V.	7	26	44	6
R.G.	21	12	33	17
V.D.G.	6	27	35	15
D.T.	0	33	49	1
V.O.E.	7	26	19	31
D.F.	0	33	49	1
G.S.	4	29	8	42
M.L.-G.	6	27	21	29
H.C.	0	32	32	18
L.F.T.H.C.	5	27	32	18
d.S.M.	8	25	40	10

n   = native speaker
n-ns = non-native speaker

Table 12.2 gives an overview of the results. Due to poor recording quality, not all the Dutch judges expressed their opinion and the number of subjects was reduced to 28.

In the Haifa study, using only two judges, 27 out of 29 subjects displayed native pronunciation in only one language. In the present study there are only three subjects (V.B, D.T. and D.F.) who were found to display native pronunciation in Dutch by an overwhelming majority of the judges. Completely unexpectedly, two subjects (Z.K. and D.I.) were almost unanimously judged to have native pronunciation in French only. Five subjects (N.J., D.P.V., C.E., D.J-F. and G.S.) were judged to display native pronunciation in both languages. In the remaining cases the judges wholeheartedly disagreed, not only between the two rater groups, but also within each group.

A special likelihood ratio statistic was devised for testing the hypothesis (full details on the rationale and results are available from the authors). As a result, the hypothesis asserting that each subject displays native pronunciation in only one language, must be rejected. Moreover, it clearly appears that the divergent results are not due to a few aberrant subjects or interviewees but that the hypothesis fails to be supported by a majority of the subjects.

General Discussion

Any meaningful interpretation of the findings will have to account for the unequivocal and contrary findings of the Ghent and Haifa studies.

In the first instance it would appear to be necessary to re-examine the research methodology. What about the intrinsic value of yes/no statements and could a supplement of (more valid) information have been culled from a multiple point scale? How far could the rater origin have influenced the ratings? How far could a French sounding uvular [R] sound familiar to a rater of the Ghent region where the sound is not uncommon at all, but sound definitely foreign to a rater of other Flemish regions? Do we have a rater expectancy problem: how many raters will have expected to answer 'yes' 30 times!? Finally, how far could the quality of the recordings (which had to be as inobtrusive as possible) have influenced the ratings?

Next the question ought to be asked whether the idiosyncrasy of the Belgian situation allows a valid replication of the original study at all. To what extent can children of English-speaking immigrants in Israel be compared to French-speaking children in Flanders? Does Hebrew as a dominant language in Israel have the same status as Dutch as a dominant language in Flanders? The Belgian situation is very complex, indeed (Spoelders & Van de Craen, 1992; Laine,

Van Leeuwen & Spoelders, 1994). In the course of history the status of French in Flanders has undergone drastic changes, evolving from a self-evident dominant language used by the higher social classes to what has gradually been thought of as only a second national language (or has it?). It might very well be that traditional French-speaking Flemish have not yet recovered from this 'trauma': to all intents and purposes their true nativeness may still rest with the French language.

Finally there is the concept of dominance and, for that matter, that of the language ego, both concepts being at the very core of the hypothesis underlying the present study. Indeed, up until now the concept of 'dominant language' had been used in an exclusively sociolinguistic sense. However, in the Belgian situation as described above, the dominance of French versus Dutch might be a matter of an individual's choice. Should we opt to define dominance in a psycholinguistic manner, this may allow us to offer an explanation for the differences in pronunciation. Moreover, language ego being a maturational concept, and indulging in a developmental psychological approach, one might wonder about the various stages of completion of the subjects' language egos. It follows that pronunciation might not be the ultimate marker or 'litmus test' of the language ego it was suggested to be – without contesting the veracity of the language ego concept itself and most certainly not its heuristic value. Future research may have to focus on alternative markers (of a syntactic or lexical nature?) in an attempt to come to firmer grips with the evasive but ever alluring language ego concept.

Acknowledgements

The authors gratefully acknowledge the comments of the other members of the RUG Bilingualism Research Group: J. Boulima, A.-M. Cotton, W. Hanssens, M. Hinderdael and L. Van Damme.

The research was performed with grants (to M. Spoelders) Nr. 8.0030.92 of the Belgian National Fund for Scientific Research, and Nr. 01112092 of the RUG's own Research Fund. The RUG Bilingual Research Group would like to thank: J. Taeldeman and his collaborators (Department for Dutch Linguistics, RUG), Chr. and J. Delcourt (Department for Romance Languages, Université de Liège), the Directors of the Institutes for Interpreters and Translators (VLEKHO, Brussels and PHVT, Ghent) and M. Geerinck and his collaborators (Language Department, Facultés Universitaires Catholiques de Mons) for their assistance in judging the interviews.

References

Guiora, A.Z. (1992) Notes on the psychology of language. *Scientia Paedagogica Experimentalis* 29 (supplement).

Guiora, A.Z., Acton, W.R., Erard, R. and Strickland, F.W. (1980) The effects of benzodiazepine (Valium) on permeability of language ego boundaries. *Language Learning* 30, 2, 351–63.

Guiora, A.Z., Beit-Hallahmi, B., Brannon, R.C.L., Dull, C.Y. and Scovel, T.S. (1972) The effects of experimentally induced changes in ego states on pronunciation ability in a second language: an exploratory study. *Comprehensive Psychiatry* 13, 5, 421–8.

Guiora, A.Z. and Schonberger, R. (1990) Native pronunciation of bilinguals. In J. Leather and A. James (eds) *New Sounds 90*. Amsterdam: University of Amsterdam.

Laine, E.J., Van Leeuwen, K. and Spoelders, M. (1994) On secondary school students' language attitudes in Belgium: A research note. *Interface. Journal of Applied Linguistics* 8, 2, 79–86.

Schuman, J.H., Holroyd, N., Campbell, N. and Ward, F.A. (1978) Improvement of foreign language pronunciation under hypnosis: A preliminary study. *Language Learning* 28, 1.

Scovel, T. (1969) Foreign accents, language acquisition, and cerebral dominance. *Language Learning* 19, 245–54.

Spoelders, M. and Van de Craen, P. (1992) Aspetti sociolinguistici, educativi e politici relativi al bilinguismo in Belgio. *Il Quadrante Scholastico* 53, 60–74.

Thompson, I. (1991) Foreign accents revisited: The English pronunciation of Russian immigrants. *Language Learning* 41, 177–204.

Vyt, A. and Van Besien, F. (in preparation) Age-related differences in acquiring second language pronunciation proficiency: A framework for explanations.

13 Mixed Discourse as a Reflection of Bilingual Proficiency

AD BACKUS

Introduction

This paper suggests arguments for an idiolect-based model of linguistic description, which, it is claimed, is especially valid when studying language contact. This will be illustrated with data from one bilingual community in particular: the Turkish community in Holland. First, a necessarily sketchy outline of the model will be provided, followed by a description of the Dutch–Turkish language mixing data on which I am basing the discussion. The main claim will be that the data reflect successive stages in the development of immigrant Turkish and that these stages can be described as different versions of the bilingual vernacular: one of the registers every speaker in a bilingual community needs for daily communication. In each case, this vernacular can be characterised as a mixed lect, since it consists of elements from both languages.

Linguistic Description

It is my contention that linguistic description should be bottom-up, meaning that our goal should be to describe speakers' idiolects. However, since a range greater than that is required, we must also abstract away from the individual as much as possible, to arrive at descriptions of 'languages' or 'lects'.

Variation and change in idiolects

While advocating an idiolect-based approach, it must be acknowledged that it is extremely difficult to describe idolects adequately, for at least three reasons.

One is that passive knowledge is part of the idiolect. How can we make an inventory of what a speaker knows if the only data to which we have access is what s/he produces?

Another reason is that idiolects are dynamic and subject to constant (minor) change. Describing every sound, word, and pattern the speaker has ever uttered, and keeping track of these 24 hours a day, while at the same time continuously computing relative frequencies of words and patterns, plus allocating every word and sentence pattern to a certain register, is a more than daunting task. To add insult to injury, it is not even enough: we still have no way of knowing whether the speaker knows a certain word or construction even though s/he has never used it. However, these two problems have to be dealt with by every theory of language, and offer no principled grounds for rejecting an idiolect-based approach. It seems reasonable to say we can settle for a description of what a certain group of idiolects have in common.

The third problem lies in the fact that variation can be located in one and the same idiolect. Our grammar must comprise all the different registers an individual knows or uses. In most societies a speaker needs to modify his/her language use depending on the situation. How sharply these registers are delineated again depends on social circumstances (cf. Gumperz, 1968: 465). Linguistically speaking, the differences between them are gradient in nature. Whether something is a better or a worse example of a certain register depends on judgement: it varies from speaker to speaker. It is of course possible to assign the word *conventionalisation* to a formal register and the phrase *what becomes normal to say* to an informal variety, but the difference is still one of degree. What makes the assignment possible is that the two expressions are so far apart on the register continuum that they qualify as fairly typical examples of their respective categories.

Variation on both the community and the individual levels can be described if we make use of the notion of prototype. Prototypes are useful as a descriptive device in many areas, including typology, dialectology, historical linguistics, sociolinguistics, and conversational analysis. Thus they allow us to classify speech data as Dutch rather than German (and by extension, as English rather than, say, Arapaho), as Norwich English rather than Scots English, as Modern rather than Elizabethan English (Fife, 1992), as formal rather than vernacular English, or even as representing the same speaker speaking to his/her mother rather than to his/her partner (cf. Weinreich, 1968: 307). In short, it allows us to lump together any group of idiolects which show similarities in a certain way.

Bilingual Idiolects

In bilingual cases, idiolects usually consist of varieties which are more sharply distinguished than is the case in stylistic variation in monolinguals. Nevertheless, the same model of description applies. In the bilingual community the list of registers includes 'talking to another bilingual' and 'talking to a monolingual of Language X or Y'. This paper focuses on the register associated with conversations between bilinguals, which I will call the 'mixed lect', consisting of material from both of the bilingual's languages. For most bilingual communities, as long as they are not too diglossic, the mixed lect is the basic vernacular, i.e. the most common, unmarked way of speaking within the community.

Though every bilingual idiolect in these communities contains this mixed lect, it does not have the same make-up in every idiolect in a given community. Even idiolects in close contact, like those of two relatives, do not necessarily have the same mixed lect. This paper explores specifically differences between the mixed lects of different generations of Turkish immigrants in Holland.

To circumvent the change problem mentioned above, I define a lect as the set of conventionalised units, which include words, combinations of words as well as patterns. The set of units is the grammar of a lect (or a language); the subset of patterns, its syntax (Langacker, 1987). An instance of change is the occurrence of a new element in someone's idiolect. Conventionalisation is a process by which a new element becomes entrenched in a speaker's grammar as a unit of the language. At least theoretically, it is also possible that a change is constituted by the loss of unit status for a certain element. This process, which we can label attrition, is hard to pin down, partly because we do not know too much about passive linguistic knowledge, and also because levels of entrenchment can vary. It is a much slower process than conventionalisation and hence it usually takes place between sets of idiolects distant in time (e.g. generations) rather than within an idiolect. For conventionalisation this is true to a somewhat lesser extent. Readily available examples of attrition and conventionalisation in immigrant languages are the decreased use of vocabulary specifically connected with the society left behind and the acquisition of cultural loans from the new language, respectively.

Immigration provides us with a fruitful context for studying processes of change. Immediately upon arrival, the immigrant vernacular turns into a mixed lect. What makes the immigration case more fruitful than, for example, the case of somebody getting a new job, is that the mixed lect of the immigrant contains much clearer and more dramatic differences between the contributing languages/lects. That is, though the processes of change are the same, they are more easily studied in a bilingual context than in a bidialectal, or bisocial

one. But in principle there is no difference between somebody who suddenly
has to start using academic jargon because of a new job and somebody who
has to start using words from a new language because s/he has emigrated. In
both contexts there were lexical gaps in the lect they used to speak and these
are filled.

In bilingual cases it is simply easier to state where a certain element came
from. However, through codeswitching and convergence (cf. Johanson,
(1993), who classifies both phenomena under the single process *code-copying*)
this picture will soon be complicated. Soon we will not be able to state
unequivocally that an L2 element is really L2; it may just as well be a conventionalised element in the mixed lect.

Another reason why immigration is an interesting context for this kind of
research is that there is a great deal of variation, due to great differences in
linguistic competence. Following the development of the mixed lect through
time is the main goal of this paper. In order to do that, we will look at three
different groups in the immigrant community, distinguished according to
proficiency in L2.

To sum up, three problems of an idiolect-based approach were identified
above: passive knowledge, change (the dynamic aspect of idiolects), and
variation (idiolects break down into several registers). The first one is a serious
problem which cannot be solved for the moment; the other two can be solved
if we adopt the notion of prototype as a descriptive device. It can help us to
distinguish registers from each other, and the change problem can be tackled
by focusing on successive stages of an idiolect, or, more easily, by looking at
different groups along the change continuum. This paper will document how
the mixed lect common to all Turkish-Dutch idiolects in Holland, has changed
over time.

The Dutch Turkish Mixed Lect

The Turkish community in Holland is fairly young. The first immigrants
arrived in the 1970s when most of them were between 20 and 40 years old.
A second generation consists of their children, some of whom were born in
Turkey and came to Holland in their early teens (called 'intermediate' generation from now on) and some of whom were born and raised in Holland. Finally
there are fairly recent young immigrants who have mainly come to Holland
as spouses of second generation members. As far as Dutch proficiency goes,
there are three fairly recognisable sub-groups: virtual monolinguals, who
never went to school in Holland (first generation, including recent arrivals),
Turkish-dominant bilinguals, who came to Holland when they were of school

age (intermediate generation), and balanced bilinguals, who have had all of
their schooling in Holland (second generation). All data reported on are
taken from self-recorded spontaneous conversations between peers.

The first generation

The following examples are typical for recent arrivals:

(1) ben yedi, sekiz ay sonra gine bir kursa başladın, oda **Tilburg-Noord**'daydı
    I seven eight month later again a class started-1sg it-CONS T-N-LOC-
    PRET
    'Seven or eight months later I started another class, which was in
    Tilburg-Noord'.
(2) Zaten bu ayın yirmisinde şey var **Hemelvaart** . . .
    anyway this month-GEN twenty-AGR-LOC thing is Ascension Day
    'Anyway, on the twentieth of this month there's this thing, Ascension Day'
(3) geldiğimde iki ay **nieuwkomers**'a gittim . . .
    coming-1sg-LOC two month *newcomers*-DAT came-1sg
    'When I came, I went to the *nieuwkomers* class for two months'
(4) **Oke** dedi yapmana gerek yok, **herhaling**'da.
    OK said-3sg doing-2sg-DAT necessary not, repetition-LOC
    'You don't have to get an "*OK*" in the repetition task'
(5) bak ne güzel konuşuyor: **ja** diyor Hollandaca, gördünüzmü?
    look how nice talk-3sg: yes say-3sg Dutch, saw-2sg-Q
    'Look, how nicely she says that: she says *ja* in Dutch, did you guys see
    that?'
(6) evet **terras**'da oturuyorlar. Orada bir **friet**'çi var böyle gumar oynanan
    yerler var.
    yes terrace-LOC sit-3pl. there a chips-AG is such gamble playing place is
    'Yes, they're sitting on the terrace. There's this chips place there, where
    there's one of those gambling places'

Dutch elements mostly fill lexical gaps. Most obvious in this respect are
proper nouns, like *Tilburg-Noord* in (1). Lexical gaps are treated as a gradient
category. As a limiting case, there are Dutch words which have no competition
at all from Turkish elements, like proper nouns. Presumably, *Hemelvaart* in
(2) is also situated quite near this extreme. A little further down the line are
words which belong to the jargon of semantic fields which the immigrants
associate with Dutch, notably the language class (*nieuwkomers* is the name
of the class, cf. also *herhaling* in (4)) and 'going out' (cf. *terras* and *friet* in (6)).
In addition, Dutch elements appear in quotations, as in (4) and (5). A final
characteristic of this early mixed lect is the use of the Turkish word-formation
suffix -*ci* on the Dutch noun *friet* to form the agentive noun *frietçi*: someone
who sells *friet*.

The intermediate generation

The mixed lect found in speakers of the intermediate generation is characterised by a large number of Dutch content words used in grammatically Turkish sentences, along with a considerable amount of intersentential codeswitching (cf. Backus, 1992). Typical examples include:

(7) O *blonde*'dan alıyordum, ***Burgemeester van Damstraat***'daydı.
   that blonde-ABL took-PROG-1sg, BvD-street-LOC-PRET
   'I was taking [lessons] from that blonde girl, in the Burgemeester van Damstraat it was'.

(8) Şimdi o *afstuderen* yaptı.
   now she graduate did-3sg
   'Now she's graduated'

(9) ***Cassetterecorder***'nan *friettent*'e gidelim lan!
   tape-recorder-WITH chip-shop-DAT let's go hey
   'Hey, let's go to the chip shop with the tape recorder'.

(10) bir sürü *taal*'ları *beheersen* yapıyorken
    a lot language-PL-ACC know do-WHILE
    'while he knows a lot of languages'

(11) *op kamers wonen* yapacağım
    in rooms live do-FUT-1sg
    'I'll be living on my own'

(12) guzel yemek pişiriyorsa *dan zou ik wel komen*
    'if he'd cook a nice meal then I would come'

(13) Köln'e gittik, trenle. Ama *kost veel man, 77 gulden, heen en weer*
    'we went to Cologne, by train. But it's expensive, man, 77 guilders, round trip'

In this version of the mixed lect, the notion of lexical gap is stretched beyond its usual limits. Dutch freely contributes content words, both nominal and verbal, and mostly in semantic areas associated with Dutch-speaking situations. These words fail to enter the vernacular, not because there is no Turkish equivalent present in the bilingual lexicon, but rather because the concepts they represent have stronger links with the Dutch lemmas than with the Turkish lemmas. Elements from the fields of education (*afstuderen*, *taal beheersen*) and social life (*cassetterecorder*, *friettent*, *op kamers wonen*) stand a good chance of originating in the Dutch part of the lexicon, in addition, of course, to true lexical gaps (*Burgemeester van Damstraat*). Note that there is a larger range of Dutch elements than was the case in the first generation. Not only are there verbs and adjectives as well as nouns, there are also larger collocations (*taal beheersen*, *op kamers wonen*), and even clauses and sentences.

The second generation

Yet a different picture is offered by data from the second generation:

(14) Ha, *Utrecht*'te miydi o?
     O, Utrecht-LOC O-PRET that
     'Oh, was that in Utrecht?'
(15) *misbruikt* diyorlar ya
     abused say-3pl INT
     '"Abused", they say, right?'
(16) iki gün önce *bioscoop*'a *vragen* yaptıydım
     two day before cinema-DAT ask did-PRET-1sg
     'Two days before I had asked her out to the cinema'
(17) Hollandalılar *echt spontaan* eline alıyorlar
     Dutch-pl real spontaneously hand-3-DAT take-3pl
     'The Dutch take things into their hands real spontaneously'.
(18) Türkiye'ye gidinci *bent geen Turk, hier ben je ook geen Nederlander*
     yani, *je bent gewoon* karışık.
     'When you go to Turkey you're not a Turk and here you're not Dutch,
     you see, you're just mixed'.
(19) çok yapınca *dan is het niet meer erg* ama birincisini yapan *die is gewoon*
     de kötüsü.
     'when many do it, then it's all right, but the first one who does it
     she's just the worst'
(20) ondan sonra ne oldu ben ikinci bölümünü kaçırdım; *dat had ik gemist*
     toen hani şey vardı ya
     'then what happened, I missed the second part; I had missed it then,
     there was something'
(21) *hij was* garıptı, *ja, echt* garıp
     he was weird-PRET, yes, really weird
     'he was weird, yeah, real weird'.

The quintessential type of language mixing in this third version of the mixed lect is regular alternation of the two codes, as in (18)–(20). Intrasentential CS for lexical gaps (*Utrecht*), quotations (*misbruikt*) and the occasional Dutch content word (*bioscoop, vragen, echt spontaan*) still occurs, but is far less frequent than switching at clause and sentence boundaries. Since intrasentential CS occurs in both directions (cf. *garıptı* in (21)), it is impossible to assign one language as the matrix language for the entire conversation.

Discussion

Above we briefly examined some characteristics of the Turkish–Dutch mixed lect at various stages in its development. In the idiolects of first generation speakers, it is a strongly Turkish-dominant register. Some 'obvious' Dutch words, mostly nouns and in any case lexical gaps, are the only elements that set it apart from informal 'monolingual' registers. An interesting aspect is the use of Turkish word-formation suffixes on Dutch words. In the idiolects of speakers at the next stage (intermediate generation) the mixed lect does not make use of this type of word formation anymore, presumably because the words that would be formed have now been conventionalised in their Dutch form. Where the first generation speaker uses *friet'çi*, the intermediate generation speaker uses *friettent* (cf. Ex. (6) and (9)). In general, the mixed lect of the intermediate generation shows a high amount of insertion-type codeswitching from a Turkish base, with patterns largely adhering to the patterns predicted by the Matrix Language Frame Model (Myers-Scotton, 1993). However, in the mixed lect used by the second generation, these patterns have become much rarer. Examples (16) and (17) show that they still exist (e.g. Dutch infinitives are still incorporated into Turkish matrix sentences through the use of the auxiliary *yapmak*, 'to do'), but they are far outnumbered by intersentential codeswitching.

Elsewhere (Backus, 1993), I have related the differences in CS behaviour to differences in Dutch proficiency: the more conventionalised elements in the Dutch register of the idiolect, the larger the Dutch chunks in the mixed lect of that same idiolect. This development can be traced from *frietçi* in (6) to *friettent* in (9), to *taal beheersen* and *op kamers wonen* in (10) and (11), and finally to *dan is het niet meer erg* in (19). Seen this way, the make-up of the mixed lect shifts along a continuum from lexical gap-insertion to regular code alternation, as the Dutch proficiency of the speaker shifts from that of a learner of Dutch as a second language towards that of a native speaker of Dutch.

However, a modification needs to be made. The examples cited in this paper show that patterns typical of the early versions of the mixed lect are still available to the second generation speaker. The '*yapmak*-rule' has been conventionalised, in much the same way as the word *friet* has been conventionalised, or the 'pragmatic rule' that the two languages can be juxtaposed to achieve certain effects.

Though they share certain features, the prototypes of the three versions are sufficiently different for us to be able to make a distinction between them. They can be perceived as three distinct varieties because their prototypes diverge enough (recall the *variation* problem discussed earlier). They can also be seen as different stages in the development of a single language, especially because the stages correlate with L2 proficiency of otherwise comparable speakers. The stages can be compared to each other by listing the effects of conventionalisation and attrition, the normal processes responsible for change. In this paper we have compared the type and amount of overt Dutch elements (i.e. codeswitching) in the mixed lect, but covert characteristics (e.g. word order) can of course also be compared.

It seems reasonable to expect that in immigration contexts proficiency in L2 is a better predictor of the structure of the mixed lect than in more stable bilingual communities. On the one hand, this is because the differences in L2 proficiency will decrease within the community as all people have had about the same amount of exposure to L2. On the other hand, it is because over the years the mixed lect will conventionalise many L2 elements, which speakers will learn as part of the mixed lect, not necessarily as part of L2. So it can happen that in the Malinche area in Mexico, Hill & Hill (1986) found that the amount of Spanish loan material in running speech was not a good measure to differentiate between monolingual Mexicano speakers and balanced Spanish-Mexicano bilinguals.

In this paper I have tried to argue that immigration provides a good context for studying the *emergence* of a mixed lect, with particular reference to the influence of L2 proficiency on the process. Later on in the life of the mixed lect, i.e. if social circumstances allow it to survive as the basic vernacular of the community, influence of proficiency decreases. The mixed lect has then really become a normal language, with a 'normal' range of variation and 'normal' rates of change.

References

Backus, A. (1992) *Patterns of Language Mixing. A Study in Turkish-Dutch Bilingualism.* Wiesbaden: Harrassowitz.
— (1993) Bilingual norms and linguistic change. Paper read at NWAVE XXII, Ottawa, October 1993.
Fife, J. (1992) On defining linguistic periods: Gradients and nuclei. *Word* 43, 1–14.
Gumperz, J. (1968) Types of linguistic community. In J. Fishman (ed.) *Readings in the Sociology of Language* (pp. 460–72). The Hague: Mouton.
Hill, J. and Hill, K. (1986) *Speaking Mexicano. Dynamics of Syncretic Language in Central Mexico.* Tucson: University of Arizona Press.
Johanson, L. (1993) Code-copying and immigrant Turkish. In G. Extra and L. Verhoeven (eds) *Immigrant Languages in Western Europe* (pp. 197–221). Clevedon: Multilingual Matters.
Langacker, R. (1987) *Foundations of Cognitive Grammar* Vol. 1. Stanford: Stanford University Press.
Myers-Scotton, C. (1993) *Duelling Languages. Grammatical Structure in Codeswitching.* Oxford: Clarendon.
Weinreich, U. (1968) Is a structural dialectology possible? In J. Fishman (ed.) *Readings in the Sociology of Language* (pp. 305–19). The Hague: Mouton.

14 Words and their Meaning – The Language Learner and The Translator

GUNILLA ANDERMAN

Introduction

In the changing world of Europe today the field of translation is attracting increasing attention. This in turn has resulted in linguists looking to translation studies in order to apply the findings emanating from current research in linguistic theory. Thus, *Discourse and the Translator* (Hatim & Mason, 1990) reflected recent interest in discourse analysis, while *Translation and Relevance. Cognition and Context* (Gutt, 1991) applied relevance theory (Sperber & Wilson, 1986) to translation.

The same holds true for prototype theory (cf. Rosch, 1973, 1975; Rosch & Lloyd, 1978). Since its emergence in the 1970s the role of prototype theory in the learning of the meaning of new words has attracted considerable attention. But while attempts have been made to apply prototype theory to translation (cf. Neubert & Shreve, 1993; Snell-Hornby, 1993), translation theorists seem to have paid limited attention to the linguistic insights already gained in the fields of L1 and L2 acquisition.

Characteristic of a changing world is the need to draw upon other subject areas, an increasing interdependence of disciplines. In this paper I suggest that the field of translation studies may further benefit from the observations made with respect to prototype theory and its relevance to L1 and L2 acquisition. The paper starts by briefly discussing the notion of prototype. This is followed by a discussion of 'prototypology', the attempts already made to apply prototype analysis to translation. The third and main section of the paper presents some observations made with respect to the role of prototype theory in L1 and L2 acquisition, showing their relevance to the field of translation studies.[1]

The Notion of Prototype

Rosch's research, which is now well known, has shown that certain representatives of a category are perceived as more 'typical' of that category than
others. It is equally well known that English speakers when tested felt that
some birds were 'better', or more typical, birds than others; the robin ranked
higher than the canary which in turn ranked higher than the penguin (Rosch,
1975).

Rosch has also shown that children tend to make more errors in relation
to more peripheral members of a category, which suggests that more typical
representatives of a category may be learnt first. Rosch refers to these central
instances as 'prototypes'. According to Rosch categories have 'internal
structure' with a prototype or central instance as a core and with less central
instances grouped around it.

Prototypology

Applying the notion of prototype to translation, Neubert & Shreve (1993)
are concerned with the prototypology of texts, the textual features most typical
of different kinds of text. In order to ensure that the textual features appropriate to a particular subject area in the target language (TL) have been
identified the translator is advised to collect and study relevant background
texts. This means that a translator commissioned to translate the *British
Highway Code* into French should make a point of examining the style,
grammar, and vocabulary of *La code de la route* (Neubert, 1981: 135). The
textual features resulting from such an analysis will then enable the translator
to 're-texture' the source language (SL) text into the TL text, ensuring conformity to the prototype.

Snell-Hornby (1993) makes use of the notion of prototype for translation
purposes somewhat differently, distinguishing between five basic groups of
prototypes, all with 'fuzzy edges'. The first group consists of terminological
concepts, such as 'oxygen', which are most likely to have a one-to-one correspondence in other languages. The second category comprises items such as
the days of the week which, if not globally known, at least may be common
to a large number of languages. The third category contains concrete objects,
basic level items such as 'chair', which often have an equivalent in other languages. In the case of category four, however, (words expressing perception
and evaluation such as English 'bleak' and German '*gemütlich*'), the concept
of equivalence becomes more difficult to apply. Prototype four, as well as
prototype five, (culture-bound items like English 'wicket' and German
'*Pumpernickel*'), represent items below the third, basic level category resulting
in even greater difficulties for the translator.

Thus, while Neubert and Shreve make use of the notion of prototype to ensure that the TL text contains prototypical textual features, Snell-Hornby groups words together into prototypes, categories where increasingly less prototypical instances veer towards the periphery. These attempts to relate prototype theory to translation, however, do not exhaust the possibilities for the translator to benefit from the concept of the prototype.

First Language Acquisition

With respect to L1 acquisition, prototype theory has been quoted as an explanation for the reasons why children may assign different meanings to words than adults as in the case of the young child who would use *bow-wow* for dogs and cats as well as for scarves and fluffy bedroom slippers (Clark & Clark, 1977:490). The failure to understand that everything hairy and fluffy does not necessarily belong to the same category is due, not surprisingly, to children focusing on different distinguishable characteristics from adults. After a while, however, children seem to decide on the prototype of a word as having certain characteristics. Bowerman (1978) has reported on 17-month-old Eva, using *kick* not only for herself kicking a stationary object but also for a number of other activities such as cartoon turtles on television throwing their legs up, a fluttering moth, and bumping a ball with her tricycle wheel, making it move. In the end, however, Eva seems to have settled for a proto-type for *kick* containing three main characteristics: a waving limb, sudden sharp contact between part of a body and an object, and propulsion forward of the object (Aitchison, 1987: 92).

Eva's problems in narrowing down the wide range of activities initially covered by *kick* may be linked to the status of this verb as a lexicalisation doublet in English. While in *I kicked the wall with my left foot* the object being kicked remains stationary, this is not the case in *I kicked the ball with my left foot* (Talmy, 1985: 65). But whereas in English there are a number of verbs like *kick* which may express motion as well as manner this does not hold true for French where manner is normally expressed through an independent constituent as noted by Vinay & Darbelnet (1958: 106) in their discussion of translation problems between English and French:

Elle	descendit	l'escalier	sur	la	pointe	des	pieds.
she	went down	the stairs	on	the	tips	of the	feet.

'She tiptoed down the stairs.'

Alternatively, manner may be omitted altogether (Vinay & Darbelnet, 1958: 106):

Les	cavaliers	sont	entrés	dans	la	cour.
the	horsemen	are	entered	in	the	yard.

'The horsemen rode into the yard.'

However, the typological feature that manner and motion cannot be conflated in the verb is not unique to French but is shared by all the Romance languages, as shown by the translation into Spanish of the sentence involving the English verb *float* (Talmy, 1985: 69):

El	globo	subió	por	la	chiminea	(flotando)
the	balloon	moved-up	through	the	chimney	(floating)

'The balloon floated up the chimney.'

Hence, for a Romance L1 speaker wishing to learn English belonging to a different Indo-European language family, part of the learning process would necessarily entail an analysis of verbs such as *kick* and *float* in order to ensure that this type of verb is assigned the appropriate prototypical characteristics. Then, having come to grips with the typological difference between the two languages, the Romance L1 speaker must also, in his/her capacity as a translator, learn to recognise when translating into, say, French or Spanish manner needs to be specified and when it may be left unstated, deducible from context. In this respect the translator is not unlike the child, learning, with time and experience, when distinctions need to be acknowledged explicitly and when they may be left implicit in the TL. There are thus a number of points of contact between the translator and the L1 learner. Let us now turn to research into L2 acquisition to see what this field has to offer to the translator.

Second Language Acquisition

In the case of L2 acquisition some interesting observations have been made with respect to 'prototype effect' (Viberg, 1985, 1988; Kotsinas, 1985). In general, the kind of prototype effect or 'asymmetry in a category where one member or subcategory is taken to be somehow more basic than the other (or others)' (Lakoff, 1987: 60–1) is referred to in linguistics as markedness.

Although the four open word classes – nouns, verbs, adjectives, and adverbs – seem to be found in all European languages, each with several thousand members, some words tend to occur more frequently than others. This tendency to favour a limited set of words appears to be most pronounced in the case of verbs (Viberg, 1990a: 397). Semantically, these core verbs show a number of similarities amongst the European languages, forming a nucleus inside the category to which they belong. They are also acquired early in L1 as well as L2 acquisition. With respect to L2 acquisition a number of studies of migrant L2 learners point to a tendency for speakers to rely heavily on these core verbs, leading to pronounced over-use of this set of lexical items. L2 learners, it appears, tend to select one or two of these verbs from each semantic field which they then use in place of verbs still unfamiliar to them. In the category formed by the verbs of motion two such 'nuclear' verbs (Viberg, 1990a, 1990b) are *go* and *come*.

Studies of the equivalents of these two verbs in a number of different languages have provided some interesting information about their use in the language acquisition process of L2 learners. In a study of L2 learners of Swedish, speakers of languages as far apart linguistically as Finnish and Spanish were found to use *gå* (*go, walk*) and *komma* (*come*) for any verbs of motion (Viberg, 1988: 227) although the preference for one over the other seemed to be different for different stages of proficiency. While *komma* first tends to function as the overall verb of motion, at a more advanced stage this position seems to be taken over by *gå* (Kotsinas, 1985: 35). This pattern has also been observed amongst L2 learners of German with a Romance language background with respect to the use of *kommen* (*come*) and *gehen* (*go*) (Viberg, 1985: 31–3) and amongst Swedish L1 speakers learning French, showing early preference for *venir* (*come*) later to be replaced by consistent use of *aller* (*go*) (Viberg, 1985: 37–8).

Reliance on a limited set of lexical items is also a characteristic feature of popular fiction with its language of everyday situations, where basic core words and non-specific references figure prominently. Although this genre of writing should be familiar to most non-technical translators, full awareness of its salient linguistic features, its reliance on prototypical rather than peripheral members of individual semantic categories, nevertheless seems to be lacking. In a comparative study of the vocabulary used in Swedish novels and in novels translated from English into Swedish, Gellerstam (1985) discusses the over-use of certain words in the translated Swedish texts. Gellerstam notes in particular the translation of the verb *arrive* into Swedish. While *arrive* may occur in a wide range of contexts in English, the use of *anlända*, its standard dictionary equivalent in Swedish, is normally restricted to the arrival of trains and aircraft. A typical example of a low frequency verb in Swedish, *anlända*, is nevertheless found with surprisingly high frequency in translation. What the translation calls for instead is a verb occurring in a wide range of contexts such as *komma fram*. Like other nuclear verbs in Swedish, *komma* (*come*) may acquire a different meaning through the addition of a particle, in this case *fram* (*along, forward*). Unfortunately, however, through the choice of *anlända* instead of *komma fram*, a peripheral as opposed to a prototypical member of the semantic category of motion verbs in Swedish, an element of 'translationese' was unwittingly added to the TL text. Translators, it appears, are not fully aware of the importance of the nuclear verbs in communication, a knowledge that may most easily be conveyed through a study of their use in L2 acquisition.

Conclusion

This paper has considered the relevance of the notion of prototype to the field of translation studies. It has been shown that in addition to earlier attempts to apply prototype theory to translation, the findings yielded by studies of L1 and L2 acquisition may also be of interest to the translator. Whether it is the acquisition of words in their own or in a foreign language, the experience of the language learner is likely to shed light on the difficulties confronting the translator, concerned with the transference of words and their meaning from one language to another.

Note

1. For a more detailed discussion of these issues, see G. Anderman and M. Rogers (eds) (forthcoming) *Words, Words, Words . . .* Clevedon: Multilingual Matters.

References

Aitchison, J. (1987) *Words in the Mind. An Introduction to the Mental Lexicon.* Oxford: Blackwell.

Bowerman, M. (1978) Systematising semantic knowledge: Changes over time in the child's organisation of meaning. *Child Development* 49, 977–87.

Clark, H.H. and Clark, E.V. (1977) *Psychology and Language. An Introduction to Psycholinguistics.* London: Harcourt Brace Jovanovic.

Gellerstam, M. (1985) Translationese in Swedish novels translated from English. In L. Wollin and H. Lindquist (eds) *Translation Studies in Scandinavia. Proceedings from the Scandinavian Symposium on Translation Theory* SSOTT II, 88–95, Lund 14–15 June 1985. Lund: CWK Gleerup.

Gutt, E-A. (1991) *Translation and Relevance. Cognition and Context.* Oxford: Blackwell.

Hatim, B and Mason, I. (1990) *Discourse and the Translator.* London: Longman.

Kotsinas, U-B. (1985) *Invandrare talar svenska.* Ord och stil. Malmö: Liber.

Lakoff, G. (1987) *Women, Fire and Dangerous Things. What Categories Reveal about the Mind.* Chicago, London: The University of Chicago Press.

Neubert, A. and Shreve, G.M. (1993) *Translation as Text.* Kent, Ohio; London, England: The Kent State University Press.

Neubert, A. (1981) Translation, interpreting and text linguistics. In B. Sigurd and J. Svartvik (eds) AILA 81 Proceedings: Lectures. *Studia Linguistica* 35, 130–45.

Rosch, E. (1973) Natural categories. *Cognitive Psychology* 4, 328–50.

— (1975) Cognitive representations of semantic categories. *Journal of Experimental Psychology: General* 104, 192–233.

Rosch, E. and Lloyd, B.B. (eds) (1978) *Cognition and Categorization*. Hillsdale, NJ: Erlbaum.

Snell-Hornby, M. (1993) Word against text: The role of semantics in translation. In G. Jäger and K. Gommlich (eds) *Text and Meaning*. Kent, Ohio; London, England: The Kent State University Press.

Sperber, D. and Wilson, D. (1986) *Relevance. Communication and Cognition*. Oxford: Blackwell.

Talmy, L. (1985) Lexicalization patterns: Semantic structure in lexical forms. In T. Shopen (ed.) *Language Typology and Syntactic Description* Vol. III. Grammatical Categories and the Lexicon. Cambridge: Cambridge University Press.

Viberg, Å. (1985) Lexikal andraspråksinlärning. Hur polsk-, spansk – och finsk – språkiga lär in svenskans placeraverb. In M. Axelsson and Å. Viberg (eds) *SUM – rapport 2*. Stockholm: Institute for Bilingual Research, University of Stockholm.

— (1988) Ordförråd och ordinlärning. Några utgångspunkter för en studie av hur ordförrådet lärs in. In K. Hyltenstam and I. Lindberg (eds) *Första Symposiet om Svenska som Andra Språk*. Centrum för tvåspråkighetsforskning, Stockholm University.

— (1990a) Svenskans lexikala profil. In E. Andersson and M. Sundman (eds) *Svenskans beskrivning 17* Turku. Åbo: Åbo Academy Press.

— (1990b) Språkinlärning och språkundervisning. In V. Adelswärd and N.F. Davies (eds) *På väg mot ett nytt språk. Rapport från ASLA:S höstsymposium.* Linköping, 9–10 November 1990.

Vinay, J.P. and Darbelnet, J. (1958/1969) *Stylistique comparée du français et de l'anglais*. Paris: Didier.

15 Translation Theory and Cognitive Linguistics

MAEVE OLOHAN and CHRISTOPH ZÄHNER

Introduction

This paper endeavours to approach translation and translation theory from a cognitive perspective. Translation is discussed in the light of new cognitive approaches to language and grammar. The paper illustrates how insights gained from cognitive linguistics are directly relevant to the formulation of a cognitive translation theory.

Traditionally, translation theory has been concerned with the translation product and has been largely prescriptive in its nature, having as its central aim the establishment of a set of rules – predominantly syntactic – which could be applied in order to achieve what was often assumed to be the only correct translation. Although it can be argued that this approach to translation was not inappropriate when used in conjunction with biblical translation and translation of the classics, its suitability with regard to modern-day translation is questionable. This normative approach focused on the form of the source text (ST), often aiming to adhere as closely to its surface syntactic form in the formulation of the target text (TT).

There was a perceptible shift in the approach to translation theory in the second half of this century when translation began to have importance as a means of communication, rather than as a scholarly or academic exercise. Technological advances brought an increased need for translation and it was felt that a closer examination and a deeper understanding of the translation activity were required. Influences from other areas of language studies and linguistics were also felt within the field of translation. The notion of equivalence underwent some change, with a gradual shift from the notion of one-to-one equivalence to the consideration of the text's situation and the aim of equivalent effect, i.e. the transferral of meaning rather than form with the aim of evoking from the TT reader the same or similar effect as that experienced by the ST reader. Structural semantics brought about a concentration on lexical equivalence through the use of componential analysis while text linguistics encouraged a more textual and intertextual approach to translation. There was thus a movement towards focusing on the extratextual and indeed extralinguistic aspects of translation, where significance and importance is attached to the culture of both source-language (SL) and target-language (TL) audiences, the function or purpose of the texts, the communicative situation (Nord, 1991) and the *skopos* or prospective target situation (Vermeer, 1991).

In spite of these developments, translation theory has remained largely normative, often criticised for advocating translation techniques, methods or, at best, approaches to translation. In the past decade, some translation theoreticians have attempted to investigate translation in terms of cognitive activities, seeking to isolate and identify the cognitive processes at work during translation and thus shifting emphasis from the product to the process of the translation activity.

These attempts have generally drawn on data from introspective studies, predominantly employing concurrent verbalisation (thinking aloud). Although interesting observations were made in these studies, there has, however, also been some opposition to them and some doubt as to the validity and accuracy of thinking-aloud protocols and the introspective research method (Ericsson & Simon, 1984). More importantly, however, this research has generally not been supported by a theoretical framework which would serve to confirm and elucidate the data supplied by introspective research. This perhaps highlights the need for a linguistic theory which unifies the accumulation of knowledge about language structure in a comprehensive way, a theory which tackles the issue of differences in conceptual structures and conceptual organisation between languages, and which considers the importance of these in the consideration of meaning and use of language(s). In view of the insights offered by cognitive linguistics with regard to the crucial nature of conceptualisation and cognitive processing for the study of meaning, this paper argues that the interaction of two languages in translation must also be approached from a cognitive linguistics perspective. In this respect, two aspects of cognitive linguistics merit discussion: cognitive grammar and categorisation based on prototype theory.

Cognitive Grammar

Cognitive grammar was developed by Ronald Langacker during the 1980s, in response to what he considered the fragmentary nature of linguistic theory (Langacker, 1987). In developing cognitive grammar, he re-examined fundamental assumptions of language and linguistic theory and rejected many of the basic notions traditionally held by linguists which had previously been accepted without question. It is not possible within the scope of this paper to give more than a very brief outline of some of the notions underlying cognitive grammar's 'radical conceptual reformulation'. It is this reformulation which causes it to differ so strikingly from traditional linguistic theories and which makes cognitive grammar relevant for translation theory.

Langacker rejects the trend within linguistics towards formalisation which can, in his opinion, result in inadequacies within linguistic theories, for example their inability to successfully deal with figurative language – metaphor, use of idioms and semantic extension – which, he insists, are to be tackled, not as examples of special cases and exceptions within language, but as a natural and an integral aspect of language use. He thus describes cognitive grammar as 'a usage-based theory' (Langacker, 1991), in strict opposition to the traditional, rule-based perspective. In terms of translation, this approach to language is contrary to the explanation of translation in terms of syntactic transfer rules.

The nature of meaning plays some part in any linguistic theory. In cognitive grammar, meaning is a central issue and is determined by conceptualisation. Conceptualisation, which encompasses context and experience, is, in turn, determined by cognitive processing. Meaning is therefore a cognitive phenomenon. Thus, it is not possible to characterise, describe and understand linguistic structure without placing it in the context of cognitive functioning. It is necessary to characterise conceptual structure and to consider mental experience and cognitive processing in order to be able to carry out semantic analysis. Similarly, if translation is concerned with the transferral of meaning from one language to another, cognitive processing must be considered. The meaning of an expression is determined by how the language user conceptualises the situation conveyed by that expression. In order to then translate that expression, it is useful to examine the conceptualisation of the user, conveyed through the linguistic structures employed.

It is generally accepted that language is symbolic, consisting of a set of linguistic signs which connect a phonological representation to a semantic representation. However, traditional theories confine this bipolarity to lexical items. Cognitive grammar, on the other hand, treats not just lexicon but also grammar (i.e. morphological and syntactic structures) as symbolic – as consisting of two poles, a phonological one and a semantic one, and the association between them. Therefore grammatical and semantic components cannot be considered separable, a notion which is far removed from many other linguistic theories. In fact, grammar actually embodies what Langacker terms 'imagery', i.e. grammar serves to emphasise certain facets or a particular perspective from which a scene is viewed. Two sentences may have the same truth value and may be interchanged but by virtue of their differing grammatical structure, they also differ semantically, presenting the same scene through different images. For example, in the two sentences,

(a) He sent a letter to Susan.
(b) He sent Susan a letter.

(a) emphasises the path traversed by the letter, and (b), on the other hand, emphasises the resulting state of Susan's possession of the letter. Thus the salience of these two aspects or perspectives differs as a result of the dative shift.

Apart from causing variation in the perspective from which a situation may be viewed, differences in images of the same situation can occur in other ways. For example, they may differ in the respect that different features of the same situation may be selected for attention. These features may differ in relative salience, or the image may differ in the degree of abstraction with which the situation is viewed. This means that the full value of a conceived situation is a function of both its content and of how we structure or construe this content. Therefore, expressions, although referring to the same experience, will differ semantically if they use different images. Since these different images are conveyed through both grammar and lexicon, the expressions will differ semantically if different grammatical structures are used to describe the experience.

Langacker discusses the symbolic nature of grammar from a monolingual point of view, but this discussion can be extended to deal with the translation activity. While it is possible to transfer truth conditions from one language to another, it is necessary to examine the syntactic constructions by means of which these truth conditions are transferred. According to cognitive grammar, different aspects are emphasised if differing syntactic constructions are used and an awareness of this is required when translating. To illustrate this with regard to English and German we can take the phenomenon of nominalisation in German. When translating into English, the syntactic guideline prevails that English prefers verbalisation and that therefore nominalisations in German can best be rendered by verbal constructions in English. While not disputing that this is often true, we cannot ignore the differing conceptualisations which underlie the differing syntactic constructions. As already mentioned, different images imposed upon a scene, and designated by linguistic expressions, constitute different mental experiences. Mental experience is, according to Langacker, the flow of cognitive events, where an event is a cognitive occurrence of any degree of complexity.

Through complex sequences of mental operations we build up our conception of reality. Therefore, in order to have full awareness of the translation activity we need to place emphasis on the mental experience of both ST and TT readers.

Prototype Theory

One of the principles pervading much of Langacker's work is the notion of prototypicality, which does not feature in traditional rule-oriented, prediction-based or generative grammars, but must be fundamental to any discussion of cognitive activity and linguistic semantics. Prototype theory has played a crucial part in the revitalising of classical theories of categorisation, as achieved by Rosch (1978), Lakoff (1987) and others. In parallel with Langacker's rejection of hitherto seldom questioned assumptions about language, Rosch and Lakoff deviate from the principles of classical categorisation, in which set membership is characterised either by prediction (by conditions or rules) or by listing, and is thus either predictable or arbitrary. Instead, they employ the idea of prototypes – best examples – which are seen as cognitive reference points. They have a special cognitive status in that prototypes are central members of a category, and membership of non-prototypes to that category is determined by sufficient similarity or matching with the prototype, and thus occurs in varying degrees or gradations. This allows for 'fuzzy' categories, in contrast to classical categorisation in which class membership is 'black-or-white'. Thus, instead of accepting that language determines our conceptual system (the classical view), cognitive linguists see categorisation as fundamental to cognitive activity. Lakoff claims that prototype effects result from the nature of cognitive models which structure thought and are used in forming categories and in reasoning. In contrast to the classical model, a cognitive approach to categorisation accepts that categories can have fuzzy boundaries and that categories, systems of categories and the meaning which people attach to a category are determined by people's experience.

A Cognitive Theory of Translation

The approaches of Langacker, Lakoff and cognitive linguists have focused on language in general, but these approaches have many implications for studies of activities involving the interaction of two languages, such as translation or interpreting. Langacker asserts that it is not possible to assume universality of semantic structure even if one feels that cognitive ability and experience are comparable across cultures. It is clear from the above overview of some aspects of cognitive grammar that meaning is not an objective quality but is constructed by cognitive processing and conceptualisations. Our conception of reality, according to Langacker, is formed from experience and mental operations, and, in terms of meaning and linguistic semantics, it is not the objective reality of the real world which is of importance but, in fact, our conception of reality. Inherent in this conception is our realisation that it is just that – a conception, and our knowledge that, as such, it differs from the real world and from other people's conception of reality.

Lakoff questions whether, given two languages with radically different conceptual systems, it may not be possible to translate from one language to another, and indeed whether different conceptual systems may hinder the understanding or learning of the foreign language. However, the fact that it is possible to learn very different languages, despite the existence of different conceptual systems for those languages can be accounted for by our conceptualising capabilities. We are capable of conceptualising a domain in different ways, within one conceptual system and one language. Consequently, Lakoff sees the learning and understanding of another language, given similar basic experience and similar conceptualisation of domains, to be possible, because of our ability to construct the other conceptual system. Understanding and learning may also be possible in the case of vastly different conceptual capabilities if, for example, one lives in the country in which the foreign language in question is spoken. This does not necessarily imply, however, that translation, requiring a mapping from one language to another, is also possible. Some basic experiences are considered by Lakoff to be universal (e.g. basic-level perception of physical objects) and in relation to these, understanding and translation pose little difficulty. Of course, many concepts are not shared (e.g. culturally- or metaphorically-defined concepts). It is possible to transfer truth conditions of sentences from one language to another one which has a very different way of conceptualising, but in doing this, there is not always consideration given to how concepts are organised and sentences understood.

This approach implies that use of language is inextricably linked to conceptualisation and conceptual structure, a fact which certainly supports the view that focusing on lexical items, syntactic structures, textual features, and translation skopos is not necessarily sufficient in order to successfully carry out the activity of translation. We also need to concentrate on the conceptual organisation reflected in the two languages, identifying differences and compensating for them if necessary. This is an approach which has been applied in monolingual and multilingual terminology work within specialised fields, but is not normally extended to the study of translation.

With regard to the concrete implications of these ideas, translation theory must aim to convey the awareness that a matching or mapping of lexical items and syntactic structures of SL and TL is not always sufficient. There must be a realisation that the way in which the SL is used *may* reflect a different conceptualisation organisation, and thus different concepts or different aspects of concepts than the seemingly equivalent structures in the TL. It should encourage awareness of the need to construct the conceptual structures of the SL (usually the foreign language). Instead of matching two phonological representations (a TL and an SL one) to one concept which is essentially the concept designated by the TL (usually native language) phonological representation, there must be the realisation that the SL concept can differ from the TL one. This certainly occurs with regard to highly culture-specific notions, e.g. students of German will be aware of the difference between the English *seminar* and the German *Seminar* or the English *sausage* and the German *Wurst*. This is not always the case with grammatical structures however. Consider the following two constructions:

(a) Ich wohne seit 1992 in Manchester.
(b) I have been living in Manchester since 1992.

Students would not hesitate to deem the two constructions equivalent, in spite of the syntactic differences. However, they would probably not reflect on the conceptual differences between the constructions. (a) emphasises the two temporal points, 1992 and today, whereas (b), by means of the continuous verb form, focuses more on the time which has elapsed between the two points. This could be explained as an example of a mapping between differing syntactic structures in the two languages, but such an explanation cannot account for the fact that (a), for example, could be followed by:

(a2) Damals wollte ich nach Italien ziehen aber eigentlich ist Manchester viel schöner.

whereas it would be unusual to follow (b) with the equivalent:

(b2) At that time I wanted to move to Italy but actually Manchester is much nicer.

The *damals* linked to (a) obviously means in 1992 but linked to (b), *at that time* cannot have the same anaphoric function, since (b) emphasised the time elapsed rather than any specific point in time. This phenomenon can best be explained with reference to the different conceptualisation of time and elapsed time reflected in the structures in the two languages.

Conclusion

It may be argued that it is not possible to teach different conceptual organisations to language or translation students, and that this is what they learn by spending time in the foreign-language speaking environment. There is, however, no doubt that students should realise that these differences exist. The type of introspective studies mentioned above can play a part in determining to what extent students are aware (or unaware) of the conceptual ordering and organisation of the two languages with which they are working. When exposed to such differences as reflected in linguistic structures, they can then learn to recognise them and thus to translate in a more conceptual and cognitive way.

References

Ericsson, A. and Simon, H.A. (1984) *Protocol Analysis: Verbal Reports as Data.* Cambridge, MA: MIT Press.

Lakoff, G. (1987) *Women, Fire, and Dangerous Things: What Categories Reveal about the Mind.* Chicago: Chicago University Press.

Langacker, R.W. (1987) *Foundations of Cognitive Grammar Vol. 1: Theoretical Prerequisites.* Stanford: Stanford University Press.

— (1991) *Concept, Image, and Symbol: The Cognitive Basis of Grammar.* Berlin, New York: Mouton de Gruyter.

Nord, C. (1991) *Text Analysis in Translation: Theory, Methodology and Didactic Application of a Model of Translation-Oriented Text Analysis.* Amsterdam: Rodopi.

Rosch, E. (1978) Principles of categorisation. In E. Rosch and B.B. Lloyd (eds) *Cognition and Categorisation* (pp. 27–48). New York: Erlbaum.

Vermeer, H.J. (1991) *Skopos und Translationsauftrag.* Heidelberg: Heidelberg Unidruckerei.

16 Media Translation and Translation Studies

EITHNE O'CONNELL

Introduction

Until quite recently, translation studies tended to concentrate on difficulties associated with the translation of the written word, whether in a technical or literary context, and the translation of the spoken word, in the form of either consecutive or simultaneous interpreting. However, as our culture places increasing emphasis on oral, aural and visual communication, it seems appropriate that translation studies should devote more attention to the variety of ways in which audiovisual material can be rendered in another language. The fact that in the past media translation did not attract much scholarly interest is at once understandable and shocking. Understandable, because as Delabastita (1990: 97) points out:

> The social sciences tend to select their objects of study on the basis of cultural prestige rather than intrinsic value. It is often thought more prestigious to study Shakespeare than to study popular literature or, for that matter, derivative phenomena such as translations.

But the lack of interest is shocking because of the amazingly powerful role of television in modern society. According to Gottlieb (1992: 169), for example, in 1987 the Danish adult and teenage population spent an average 280 minutes per week reading books, magazines, etc. while they spent 134 minutes watching subtitled programmes, i.e. 'reading' audiovisual material. Clearly, therefore, there is a need to look closely at the phenomenon of media or screen translation so as to understand better the technical, linguistic, cultural and political implications of this kind of transfer.

Media translation is generally taken to mean dubbing and/or subtitling but there are other forms of language transfer or versioning currently used by the audiovisual industry, many of which are cheaper and less complicated, e.g. free commentary, narration, voice-over, captioning. Any one of these methods could be used in certain cases on its own or, as is often the case, they can be combined. An example of the latter is the German TV cartoon series 'Janosch Geschichten' rendered into Irish as 'Scéalaíocht Janosch' which uses both narration and full dubbing for all the cartoon characters.

Dubbing and Subtitling

Generally, however, a film or TV programme is either exclusively dubbed or subtitled depending on a number of factors which, in theory at least, include local conventions, cost, programme genre, time, etc. In practice, the established tradition or convention in the country or region where a programme is to be broadcast is often by far the most significant determining factor in terms of language transfer method. It has been pointed out by many commentators including Gambier (1994: 243) that Europe can be subdivided into dubbing countries such as France, Germany, Spain, Italy, etc. and subtitling countries such as Portugal, Wales, The Netherlands, Scandinavian countries, etc. The usual explanation offered for this division is that as dubbing is more costly, it is financed by larger wealthier countries with large potential audiences, while smaller countries with their speakers of 'lesser-used' languages have to be content with subtitles. While there is much truth in this, the fact that the Basque country only uses dubbing on its main Basque language channel shows that this analysis is simplistic. The reasons why minority broadcasting opts for dubbed programmes in spite of many associated disadvantages including greater expense are complex, but certainly include cultural and language planning considerations which are of the utmost importance to threatened linguistic minorities. As O'Connell (1994: 371) has demonstrated, programmes aimed, for example, at native Irish speakers and broadcast in Irish with English subtitles serve, in practice, to undermine further the linguistic competence of the main group supposedly being served. This is due to the fact that if subtitles are broadcast they will be read regardless of whether or not they are needed. According to Delabastita (1989: 198):

> The whole process of subtitle perception tends to be largely automatized, so much so that viewers who have no need of subtitles find it hard to avoid reading them.

Dubbing and subtitling have their origins in the early days of silent film. The original intertitles bearing captions such as 'Meanwhile back at the ranch . . .' were the precursors of modern subtitles, while the piano player playing his heart out at the earliest film showings was preparing the way for simple soundtracks. By about 1927, with the advent of sound, intertitles began to disappear and film-makers came up with the idea of recording the original soundtrack in several languages (Ivarsson, 1992: 15). In the 1930s, some US films were available in up to 15 different language versions! In Germany and Italy, in particular, the political situation and the significance of the national film industry dictated that all foreign films should be dubbed before being shown. This reinforced the national language and culture and provided scope for subtle script changes which suited the prevailing ideology. Since then, however, it seems that we may have lost sight somewhat of the significant cultural and political dimension to language transfer.

In Europe of the 1990s, however, the need to provide EU (European Union) member states with a transnational European identity, while simultaneously respecting and developing the linguistic and cultural diversity which is Europe, once again throws the spotlight on the audiovisual industry in general and media translation in particular. At an EU level, there is a strong commitment to strengthening the audio-visual industry within Europe and fighting off cheap imports from the US in an effort to protect and develop jobs within the EU. Consequently, the cost factor in the dubbing v. subtitling debate is of paramount importance, and current policy is to encourage much more sub-titling even in countries not traditionally associated with this transfer method.

Apart from financial considerations, there are other reasons why subtitling is finding increasing favour at this time. For one thing, it enables viewers to enjoy the full original soundtrack and enter into the cultural spirit or mood of the programme or film. For those who are interested in improving foreign language skills, subtitles can be a painless aid and, of course, they find parti-cular favour amongst the elderly with impaired hearing and the growing number of young people suffering the ill effects of 'Walkman and disco abuse'.

Dubbing, on the other hand, while generally more expensive, has the advantage of not interfering with the visual integrity of the framed shot and is ideal (as a recent Channel 4 survey in the UK revealed) for women, in particular, who often do not get a chance to simply watch TV but rather combine that activity with other activities, e.g. ironing, knitting, etc. Not surprisingly, dubbed films find particular favour in countries with a high level of illiteracy in the population.

The Constraints on Media Translation

In many ways, media translation is by definition much more constrained than most other types of translation. In addition to the usual L1/L2, Culture 1/ Culture 2 tensions, translators preparing a translation of a dubbing script are severely curtailed by the requirements of lip-synch, at least in sentence initial positions. Lip-synch as explained by Luyken (1991: 73) is:

> The replacement of the original speech by a voice track which is a faithful translation of the original speech and which attempts to reproduce the timing, phrasing and lip movements of the original . . . The aim is to create the illusion that the on-screen characters are speaking in the target language, i.e. the language of the audience.

The subtitler, on the other hand, operates in the clear knowledge that we all read more slowly than we speak, so in most cases a subtitled text will have to be a summary of the original script and much is inevitably lost as a result.

But there are other broader problems associated with media translation which have to do with the nature of the 'text' involved. As Delabastita (1989: 196) points out:

> Film establishes a multi-channel and multicode type of communication. As opposed to radio communication or communication through books, for instance, film communication takes place through two channels rather than one: both the visual channel . . . and the acoustic channel are simultaneously utilised.

This becomes further complicated once the element of translation is introduced because this necessitates code-switching. In the case of dubbing the shift is from L1 to L2 but in subtitling there is the added shift from the oral to written code. It is clear, therefore, that dubbing and subtitling both differ substantially from other types of translation, e.g. literary, technical, commercial and the problems posed by them go beyond the merely technical ones focused on by programme/film makers and crews. Consequently, it is important that these be included in the field of translation studies.

Dubbing is very much a team effort involving the translator, actors, director and dubbing studio crew and consequently it poses problems for those who only want to investigate the linguistic/translation aspects of the process. Subtitling, on the other hand, is essentially the responsibility of a single translator or group of translators and can more easily become the object of investigation of those interested in translation theory and practice. As already mentioned, subtitling is governed in the first instance by certain formal or technical constraints (Gottlieb, 1992: 164), namely space and time. The former constraint arises as subtitles are usually limited to two or three lines of about 35 characters each so as not to impinge unduly on the visual image. The time factor is significant as research (Hanson, 1974: 102) has shown that the average viewer requires approximately six seconds to read a two-line subtitle.

In addition to the formal considerations, there are textual constraints to be remembered. For example, subtitles should be drafted and imposed in such a way that they provide maximum information while causing the minimum of distraction from the main on-screen activity and should, where possible, not be used across cuts or exposed for longer or shorter durations than appropriate as this can prove irritating in the extreme (O'Connell, 1994: 369).

The actual linguistic/translation strategies used within the context of constraints mentioned above constitute a subset of the total number of translation strategies outlined by Newmark (1982: 30). In a study based on an analysis of Mel Brook's 'Young Frankenstein', Gottlieb (1992: 167) found that 10 strategies were used, of which transfer (44.9%), paraphrase (14.5%), condensation (12.9%), decimation (8.1%) and deletion (7.4%) were the most common.

Of course, just as the decision on whether to dub or subtitle must be based on a variety of factors including programme genre and potential audience, the subtitling strategies used and their relative frequency is also dependent to a considerable extent on such considerations. Feature films, documentaries, news programmes and children's programmes represent 'text types' as various as novels, sales brochures and fairy stories and consequently require that the translator adopt differentiated approaches when drafting subtitles for them.

Conclusion

In conclusion, it should be pointed out that, as the shift in interest from books and magazines to TV, film and video screens continues, the audiovisual media and industry will grow in size and importance. It is vital that those who are involved as screen translators in the process of mediating between languages and cultures should have a full theoretical and practical understanding of the implications and complexities of their work and of the responsibilities that go with it. This can best be achieved by increasing the amount of attention devoted to media translation within the broad framework of translation, cultural and communication studies.

References

Delabastita, D. (1989) Translation and mass communication. *BABEL XXXV*, Vol. 4, 193–218.
— (1990) Translation and the mass media. In S. Bassnett and A. Lefevere (eds) *Translation, History and Culture* (pp. 97–109). London: Pinter Publishers.
Gambier, Y. (1994) Subtitling: A type of transfer. In F. Eguiluz *et al.* (eds) *Transvases Culturales: Literatura, Cine, Traduccion* (pp. 243–51). Vitoria: Facultad de Filologia.

Gottlieb, H. (1992) Subtitling – a new university discipline. In C. Dollerup and A. Loddegaard (eds) *Teaching Translation and Interpreting* (pp. 161–70). Amsterdam: John Benjamins.

Hanson, G. (1974) *Läsning av text i tv*. Stockholm: SR/PUB.

Ivarsson, J. (1992) *Subtitling for the Media*. Stockholm: Transedit HB.

Luyken, G. (1991) *Overcoming Language Barriers in Television*. Manchester: EIM Media Monograph No. 13.

Newmark, P. (1982) *Approaches to Translation*. Oxford: Pergamon.

O'Connell, E. (1994) Media translation and lesser-used languages. In F. Eguiluz *et al.* (eds) *Transvases Culturales: Literatura, Cine, Traduccion* (pp. 367–73). Vitoria: Facultad de Filologia.

17 Text, Discourse Community and Culture: A Social Constructive View of Texts from Different Cultures

BRITT-LOUISE GUNNARSSON

Introduction

European writing communities are becoming increasingly international with every passing decade. In countries with mother tongues other than English, we are reading more and more books and producing more and more texts in other languages than our own. For much of the business world and for the academic community, communication in foreign languages plays a central and important role. It is of course English that is replacing native languages as the main medium of communication, but in a growing European community we can expect German, French, Spanish and maybe also Russian gradually to assume greater significance.

The internationalisation of Europe, however, is not without its complications. It requires knowledge and skills on the part of those who want to compose texts in foreign languages – a knowledge relating to the textual as well as to the word and sentence levels. Language is an important part of the national culture and identity, and language patterns at different levels are closely related to cultural patterns and to societal conditions. It has long been known that vocabulary reflects society. Less well-known is the fact that textual patterns are culture-specific. Contrastive studies which have focused on these levels, however, have been able to point to clear differences between texts produced within different language communities, differences which could be related to differences in cultural background and context.

Textual patterns are acquired rather than consciously learnt. They are intertwined in the socialisation process as part of the formation of a social and societal reality and identity, and also of a national identity. Contrastive studies have brought to light clear differences between texts produced in different cultures and subcultures with regard to their content structure and patterns at the thematic, pragmatic and rhetorical levels. They have also shown how our knowledge of native text patterns is unconsciously transferred to texts written in a foreign language. Studies have also shown how culture-bound our text expectations and interpretations are, that is, how readers interpret texts differently depending on whether or not they are familiar with the text patterns which they contain. Unfamiliarity with the patterns of a text often leads to underestimation and misinterpretation of the text on the part of the reader.

The internationalisation of European writing communities can also be viewed from another standpoint. When different cultures meet and merge, it is often the weaker one that is threatened. If the smaller nations adapt too much to foreign patterns, they run the risk of losing their national text identities. They risk ending up in a diglossic situation, in which the national language is used for certain purposes, and foreign languages like English for others. If this were to happen, complete knowledge of these smaller languages could in the long run be eroded. The national language would eventually not be fully represented across the entire spectrum of different functions.

If we consider the situation in Sweden, for instance, we find that the Swedish academic community is threatened by a diglossic situation of this kind. In many contexts English is most certainly replacing Swedish as the main scientific language. The question is what consequences this will have for the Swedish scientific language and for Swedes' competence in their national language. Will Sweden end up with a diglossic academic language community, with English used for scientific purposes and Swedish for teaching at lower levels and for popular purposes? Will Swedes end up with a new set of textual patterns adapted to a new language situation? Will new academic genres evolve? Will Swedes eventually forget how to use Swedish for scientific discourse?

This article will discuss the relationship between text, discourse community and culture. Following a theoretical discussion of a sociolinguistic framework for contrastive text analysis, I will go on to present a number of studies relating to the European discourse situation.

The Origins of Textual Patterns

Central to our understanding of text patterns in the contrastive perspective involved here is the question of how these patterns have emerged and developed. A fuller presentation of the theoretical framework can be found in Gunnarsson 1995, of which a summary will be given here.

Textual patterns are the result of a process of construction in which cognitive, social and societal factors interact. In every strand of human communication, language plays a role in the formation of a social and societal reality and identity. We construct ourselves and our roles within the group and within society via communicative interplay with others, and we are also perceived by others through their interpretation of our communicative behaviour. This is true of both oral and written communication. It is true of both individuals and groups.

Textual patterns are thus formed by processes in which individuals and groups are actors and creators of meaning. In this dynamic process, three main constituents will be distinguished: one relating to *cognitive* types of activities, one to *societal* and one to *social*. My discussion here will focus on the construction of academic and other forms of professional discourse.

If we begin by considering the cognitive layer, we find that each profession has a certain way of viewing reality, a certain way of highlighting different aspects of the world around it. Socialisation into a profession means learning how to discern the relevant facts, how to view the relationships between different factors. We are taught how to construct and use a grid or a lens to view reality in a professionally relevant way. Language, texts and spoken discourse help us in this construction process. We use language in the construction of professional knowledge. And if we now look at a professional group as a whole, we see that its professional language has developed as a means of expressing this professional view of reality.

Secondly, as regards the societal layer, each professional group also stands in a particular relationship to the society in which it operates; it performs certain functions and is given a certain place within that society. The members of a profession play a role in relation to other actors in society, and the professional group acts in relation to other groups. They play – or do not play – a role on the political scene, within the business world, the education system, in relation to the media, etc. And this cluster of societal functions is essential for language. It is through language that professional groups perform their societal function. If they are going to play a role on the political scene, they have to construct their communicative behaviour in a way that is adequate for that purpose. Their relationship to written texts and spoken discourse and to different genres is also important. Professionals adapt to established genres, but are also involved in forming new genres. The societal layer is of course related to economic and political factors. It is related to power and status patterns in society.

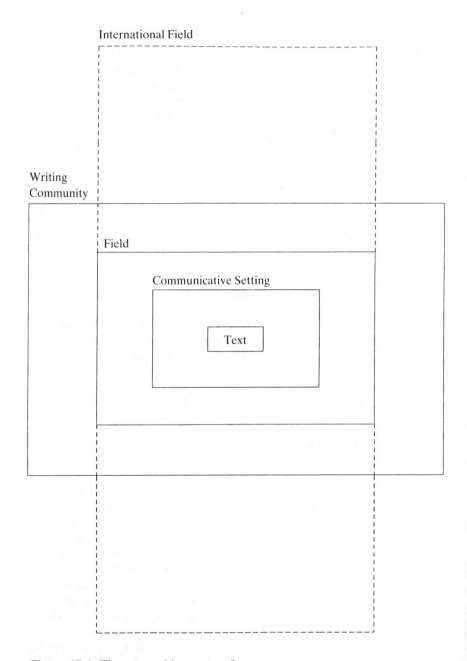

Figure 17.1 The text and its context frames

Thirdly, regarding the social layer, every professional group, like other social groups, is also formed by the establishment of an internal role structure, group identity, group attitudes and group norms. The need for a professional identity, for a professional sense of 'us-ness', for separation from the out-group, has of course played an important role in the construction of professional group language and constantly motivates people to adapt and be socialised into professional group behaviour. Socialisation into a group also means establishing distance from people outside the group.

These three layers are strongly related to the emergence and continuous re-creation of professional language, and they are a part of the construction of professional communication, both written and spoken.

Textual patterns are thus formed in a dynamic process, as a result of the interplay between these three layers. The formation of text patterns takes place at different levels. It is related to the text content, the referential structure, the pragmatic structure, and to the thematic and rhetorical structure.

The construction of textual patterns can also be analysed in relation to the different context frames within which the text is produced: the *communicative setting*, the *field*, the *national writing community*. The production of the text is related to the *communicative group*, to the *subculture* and to the *national culture*. Figure 17.1 illustrates the relationship between the text and its context frames.

A question of interest is of course also whether we can talk about an *international field*. That would mean that texts within a certain field, e.g. medicine, are formed according to similar patterns over national and language borders. For example, Swedish, English and German medical texts of a certain type are formed in the same way (cf. Figure 17.1).

Textual Diversification Within a Writing Community

Before going into the issue of universality in more depth, our focus will turn towards the findings of studies of textual diversification within the writing community, that is, studies of the relationship between *text genre* on the one hand and *field* and *national writing community* on the other.[1]

The assumption behind these studies is that text and discourse patterns reflect the cultural and subcultural contexts, and that socialisation into a culture, or a subculture, among other things means learning patterns for texts and discourse.

Many studies within sociology, sociolinguistics, rhetoric, ethnology and communication have shown and discussed differences between texts produced within different fields within a writing community[2] (cf. Swales, 1981, 1990; Bazerman, 1988; Myers, 1990; Bazerman & Paradis, 1991; Berkenkotter & Huckin, 1995).

Of particular interest from the point of view of the smaller European languages are studies of texts in languages other than English. At Uppsala University, for example, a research project entitled *LSP texts in the 20th century* has studied the historical development of two Swedish genres – the scientific article and the popular article. These studies have clearly highlighted differences between texts from different fields. Texts on economics, medicine and technology from three periods of this century, around 1900, 1940 and 1980, were analysed.

These analyses were related to four different text levels: a cognitive, a pragmatic, a microsemantic and a macrothematic level (Gunnarsson, 1989). The results clearly show that Swedish text patterns during the period studied, from 1895 to 1985, have undergone radical changes with regard to all levels studied (cf. Gunnarsson, 1992a, 1992b, 1993, Melander, 1991; Näslund, 1991; Skolander, 1992; Melander & Näslund, 1993; Gunnarsson, Melander & Näslund, 1994). It is also of interest to note here that, according to our results, each field has in many respects followed a unique course of development. Scientific economics articles follow their own course, different from that of either medical or technical articles. Each field has undergone a unique development, which is related not only to the cognitive level but also to the pragmatic, microsemantic and rhetorical levels. The results of these studies show that the *field* is a reality for the forming of genre variants. In other terms, these results point to similarities in the way these genres have developed, reflecting the relationship between the genres and Swedish society as a whole. Swedish society has undergone changes since the beginning of this century, and these are reflected in texts from different fields. Our results can thus be interpreted as illuminating the relationship both between *text* and *field* and between *text* and *national writing community*.

Unity and Diversity in Patterns of Texts from Different Writing Communities

In these studies, the Uppsala group analysed and compared texts produced within the same national writing community, i.e. that of Sweden. A different though associated research problem is that of the relationship between the *national field and writing community* and the *international field*. As far as this latter question is concerned, we all know that a quite widely held view among scientists is that scientific language is international in character. Those who share this view stress the similarities between texts from different cultures, similarities which they argue are due to a common knowledge base – as the same reality is being studied – and a common function base – as science has the same aims in different cultures.

Contrastive studies, however, have come up with results that can be seen as running counter to this hypothesis of an international scientific language. A large proportion of these studies have been carried out on the basis of the English language, and often the explanatory perspective has been Anglo-centric (Kaplan, 1966, 1987, 1988). Texts produced in Britain or in the US have been compared with texts produced within distant cultures such as India, Korea, Thailand, China and Japan (Hinds, 1987), and also within closer cultures such as Germany (Clyne, 1987; 1991), Finland (Tirkkonen-Condit & Liefländer-Koistinen, 1989; Mauranen, 1993) and Greece (Tannen, 1979). Michael Clyne, for instance, was able in his studies to demonstrate clear differences in textual patterns between academic articles produced in England, Australia and the US on the one hand and those produced in Germany on the other. Anna Mauranen's research points to remarkable differences between Finnish and English academic articles. Both researchers attributed these textual divergences to differences in academic culture and national text tradition. Clyne and Mauranen have also studied what happens when Germans and Finns write in English, and found that in both these cases writers follow to a large extent the textual patterns characterising their native language when writing in a foreign language.

Contrastive text-linguistic studies covering the Nordic languages – Swedish, Danish and Norwegian – have until recently been something of a rarity. There is, however, a growing interest in these issues, and in Sweden at least several studies have recently been completed, are in progress or have just started. *The Research Group on Discourse in the Professions*, which I am directing at Uppsala University, is the focal point of these studies. All these contrastive studies involving Swedish texts have pointed to clear and quite remarkable differences between, on the one hand, Swedish text patterns and, on the other hand, those of German, English and American texts.

Kirstin Fredrickson, in a joint Swedish-American research venture, has compared Swedish and American court documents at different textual levels, cognitive, pragmatic and macrothematic, using the methods elaborated for the Uppsala LSP study (see above). Fredrickson discusses the differences observed between the documents in a juridico-sociolinguistic framework (Fredrickson, 1992, 1995). Another study is presented in Andersson & Gunnarsson, 1993. The argumentative structures of Swedish and German editorials were compared, revealing quite remarkable differences between their text patterns. Similarly, Melander, Swales & Fredrickson (1994) found differences between Swedish and American medical article abstracts.

More indirect comparisons of Swedish and Anglo-American text patterns have also been carried out. The rhetorical structure of Swedish academic articles has, for instance, been analysed in relation to the prototype of the Anglo-American academic article. From a historical point of view, the Swedish medical article pattern has been found to have gradually approached that of the Anglo-American one (Gunnarsson, 1990). In the fields of linguistics, economics and technology, however, the rhetorical structure of Swedish articles is still remarkably different from the Anglo-American pattern (Skolander, 1992; Fredrickson & Swales, 1994).

Finally, mention should be made of a recently launched major research project based in Uppsala, entitled *Texter i Europeiska skrivsamhällen. En kontrastiv studie av svenska, engelska och tyska textmönster* [Texts in European writing communities. A contrastive study of Swedish, English and German text patterns]. The aim of this contrastive project is to compare texts produced in four different communicative settings – a bank, a construction firm, a history department and an occupational medicine department – within three different national writing communities, those of Sweden, Britain and Germany. The organisational structure and communicative setting of a Swedish, a German and a British bank, construction firm, etc. will be described from a sociolinguistic viewpoint. We will then collect central texts for each organisation, and these texts will be analysed using the socio-text-linguistic model developed for the earlier mentioned Uppsala study of Swedish LSP texts. Our analyses will focus on the cognitive, the pragmatic and the text-structural levels (Gunnarsson, 1989). The results will be discussed in relation to the communicative setting, the field, the national writing community and the international field (Gunnarsson, 1994).

During the planning of this major project we decided to undertake a pilot study. We wanted to try our methods of analysis on a small corpus. We decided to begin with articles published in medical journals in Sweden, Britain and Germany. Our aim was to compare the text patterns of articles of a similar kind published in what could be considered the main medical journals in the three countries: *British Medical Journal*, *Deutsche Medizinische Wochenshrift* and *Läkartidningen*. We went through a number of issues of each journal, roughly analysing the articles therein to get a picture of what was typical. We then chose one article from each journal that could be said to be typical of the journal in its general style and pattern. The three chosen articles were as similar as possible in content.

Our analysis comprised the cognitive, the pragmatic and the macrothematic levels, following the methods elaborated for the earlier mentioned study of *LSP texts in the 20th century* (Gunnarsson, 1989). At the cognitive level, we analysed the content of the texts using an abstract model for content categorisation, involving the concept of 'cognitive world'. At the pragmatic level we studied illocution types, and at the macrothematic level we examined the global structuring of the texts. We categorised each macro-syntagm of the articles and calculated the relative frequencies of the different text variables.

Gunnarsson, Bäcklund & Andersson (1995) present the results in detail. My aim here, however, is mainly to give a brief summary of some of our findings. I must add that our corpus is small, which means that the results have to be regarded as tentative.

A comparison of our analyses of the German and English articles revealed remarkable similarities. They were structured in a similar way at all three of the levels focused on in our analysis. Both the German and English texts followed a strict scientific text pattern of an 'Introduction' – 'Method' – 'Result' – 'Discussion' type. Both articles devoted a similar proportion of the text to our different cognitive categories, more than two thirds of the content was classified as belonging to the scientific world and a large part was devoted to describing processes and results. The illocution patterns were also similar; two thirds of the macro syntagms were descriptive and one third explanatory.

This similarity between the English and German articles was not expected, however. As was mentioned above, Michael Clyne found striking differences between the German and English text patterns in the articles he studied. One explanation for the difference between Clyne's results and ours, could be that we were studying different fields: Clyne studied articles within the social sciences, while we examined medical articles. Another possible explanation is that German text patterns have changed towards greater similarity with those of English. Clyne's articles are 10 to 20 years older than ours. The medical scientific language of German seems to have moved closer to that of the English.

The most striking result of our study, however, was the considerable difference between the Swedish article on the one hand and the German and English on the other. The Swedish article differed from both the English and the German. Here we did not find a specific scientific paper structure; rather, the structure resembled that of a newspaper article. It contained a two-part introduction, the first part of which – set in boldface – functioned like the opening paragraph in a newspaper. The rest of the article was structured in a cyclic manner rather than a straight line. The main point was repeated several times. The subheadings also had a different character and function. They did not reflect the text structure, as they did in the German and English article. Instead they related to the content.

At the pragmatic level, the Swedish article was strikingly more explanatory and less descriptive, and at the cognitive level it was less scientific and more concerned with object description. In terms of content, moreover, it was more concerned with describing background and causes and less with describing processes and results than the German and English articles were.

On the whole, we found that the Swedish article exhibited certain traits which are usually found in more popular articles and others that clearly belong to the scientific genre. The Swedish article can thus be said to represent a different genre to the German and English medical articles. When we compared these results with those found for medical articles in the earlier mentioned historical study of LSP texts 1895–1985, our conclusion was that something radical had happened to the Swedish medical article in the last decade. Compared with Swedish medical articles from the third period, 1975–85, the articles from 1994 could be said to represent a partly new, more popular genre.

As my interview with the editor of *Läkartidningen* revealed, the Swedish journal has indeed come to define such a popular role for itself during the last decade. A factor behind this development, according to the editor, is the merit system practised at universities. This system brings about a situation in which scientists are forced to present their original results in international journals. Presentations aimed at a Swedish audience serve different purposes. Writing in Swedish is nowadays reserved for popular purposes. Articles published in *Läkartidningen* in the 1990s are intended to provide overviews and introductions to interesting findings, rather than to present original research results. This can be contrasted to the situation in the 1980s, the last period covered by our historical LSP corpus. We had no problem finding Swedish medical articles during that period which presented original research results, so the change seems to have taken place quite recently.

When Swedish medical scholars present their research results, they do so in English in international journals. They write for the international field. A question of great interest, of course, is what happens when Swedish scientists write in English. Do they, as Michael Clyne and Anna Mauranen found in their studies, follow their native Swedish text patterns, or do they write in an English way?

In this case the two authors of the Swedish medical article had presented the same investigation in an English article. We also examined this English article by the Swedish authors. This article, too, was thus analysed at the macrothematic, cognitive and pragmatic levels. What we found was that, with regard to the global structuring of the text and its cognitive content, the Swedes seemed to have adapted to the English patterns. In terms of its pragmatic pattern, however, their English article differed from the English and German articles and showed a considerable resemblance to their Swedish article. A possible explanation for this finding is that pragmatic patterns are unconsciously acquired and belong to an area of our communicative competence of which we are less aware.

Conclusions

In my introduction I mentioned the risk which non-English-speaking countries in Europe, like Sweden, are running of ending up in a diglossic situation, with the native language used for certain purposes and English for other purposes. Our results can most certainly be discussed in this light. In the medical field at least, Sweden seems to be faced with a diglossic situation in which the English language is used for scientific purposes and the Swedish language for semi-popular purposes. It is obvious that many other nations in Europe are facing a similar situation. Not only small countries such as Finland, Norway, Denmark, Austria, Belgium, The Netherlands, the Czech Republic and Hungary, but also larger ones like Germany, France, Italy and Spain are approaching a diglossic situation in which English is taking over some of the functions of the national language. Whether this is a good thing or a bad thing depends, of course, on the value we attach to the internationalisation of Europe, as compared to the independence of national cultures and national text identities.

Notes

1. I should perhaps clarify what I mean here by 'genre'. Like Miller (1984), Martin (1992), Swales (1990), Mauranen (1993) and many others, I give 'genre' a social meaning. Genre is thus used in the sense of 'social activity of a typical and recognizable kind in a society which is realized through language'. This definition means that 'genre' is better distinguished by social than by linguistic parameters. Genres like the scientific article, the research report or the plenary talk can thus better be described with reference to their social aims and conditions than with reference to their linguistic traits.
2. The concept of 'discourse community' (Faigley, 1995; Swales, 1990) and 'communicative community' (Gunnarsson 1992c, 1996) have been introduced as terms of broader scope than 'speech community'.

References

Andersson, B. and Gunnarsson, B.-L. (1993) Comparative text research: Swedish and German editorials. Paper presented at the Symposium 'Persuasive Texte in der Presse', Germanistisches Institut, Helsinki University, May 17–18, 1993.

Bazerman, C. (1988) *Shaping Written Knowledge. The Genre and Activity of the Experimental Article in Science.* Madison, WI: The University Wisconsin Press.
Bazerman, C. and Paradis, J. (eds) (1991) *Textual Dynamics of the Professions. Historical and Contemporary Studies of Writing in Professional Communities.* Madison, WI: University of Wisconsin Press.
Berkenkotter, C. and Huckin, T. N. (1995) *Genre Knowledge in Disciplinary Communication. Cognitive/Culture/Power.* Hillsdale, New Jersey: Lawrence Erlbaum.
Clyne, M. (1987) Cultural differences in the organisation of academic texts. English and German. *Journal of Pragmatics* 11, 211–47.
— (1991) The sociocultural dimension: The dilemma of the German-speaking scholar. In H. Schröder (ed.) *Subject-oriented Texts. Languages for Special Purposes and Text Theory.* Berlin; New York: Walter de Gruyter.
— Faigley, L. (1985) Nonacademic writing: The social perspective. In L. Odell and D. Goswani (eds) *Writing in Nonacademic Settings.* New York; London: The Guildford Press.
— Fredrickson, K.M. (1992) *The Case of Swedish Court Documents.* TeFa nr 4 (= FUMS Rapport nr 165.) Uppsala: Uppsala University.
— (1995) American and Swedish Written Legal Discourse: The Case of Court Documents. PhD dissertation, University of Michigan.
Fredrickson, K.M. and Swales, J. (1994) Competition and discourse community: Introductions from Nysvenska studies. In B.-L. Gunnarsson, P. Linell and B. Nordberg (eds) *Text and Talk in Professional Contexts. Selected Papers from the International Conference 'Discourse and the Professions'.* ASLA 6. Uppsala: Uppsala University.
Gunnarsson, B.-L. (1989) *Facktexter under 1900-talet 2. Metoder för textanalys på makro- och mikronivå.* FUMS rapport nr 145. Uppsala: Uppsala University.
— (1990) Makrotematiska och pragmatiska mönster i medicinska artiklar. *Svenskans Beskrivning 17* (pp. 97–114). Åbo: Åbo Academy Press.
— (1992a) Linguistic change within cognitive worlds. In G. Kellermann and M.D. Morrissey (eds) *Diachrony within Synchrony: Language History and Cognition* (pp. 205–28). Frankfurt am Main: Verlag Peter Lang.
— (1992b) Pragmatic structure of LSP-articles from a diachronic viewpoint. In A. Grindsted and J. Wagner (eds) *Communication for Specific Purposes/ Fachsprachliche Kommunikation* (pp. 72–92). Kommunikation und Institution 21. Tübingen: Gunter Narr Verlag.
— (1992c) *Skrivande i yrkeslivet. En sociolingvistisk studie.* Lund: Studentlitteratur.
— (1993) Pragmatic and macrothematic patterns in science and popular science: A diachronic study of articles from three fields. In M. Ghadessy (ed.) *Register Analysis: Theory and Practice* (pp. 165–79). London: Pinter.
— (1994) *Texter i Europeiska skrivsamhällen. En kontrastiv studie av svenska, engelska och tyska textmönster.* Forskningsprogram [Research Programme]. Uppsala: FUMS, Uppsala University.
— (1995) Studies of language for specific purposes – a biased view of a rich reality. *International Journal of Applied Linguistics* 5, 1, 11–134.
— (1996) The writing process from a sociolinguistic viewpoint. *Written Communication* 13.
Gunnarsson, B.-L., Bäcklund, I. and Andersson, B. (1995) Texts in European writing communities. In B.-L. Gunnarsson and I. Bäcklund (eds) *Writing in Academic Contexts. TeFa nr 11* (pp. 30–53). Uppsala: Uppsala University.

Gunnarsson, B.-L., Melander, B. and Näslund, H. (1994) LSP in a historical perspective. In M. Brekke, Ö Andersen, T. Dahl and J. Myking (eds) *Applications and Implications of Current LSP Research* (pp. 877–918) Vol. II. Bergen: Fagforlaget.

Hinds, J. (1987) Reader versus writer responsibility: A new typology. In U. Connor and R.B. Kaplan (eds) *Writing Across Languages: Analysis of L2 Text* (pp. 141–52). Reading, MA: Addison-Wesley.

Kaplan, R. (1966) Cultural thought patterns in intercultural education. *Language Learning* 16, 1–20.

— (1987) Cultural thought patterns revisited. In U. Connor and R.B. Kaplan (eds) *Writing Across Languages: Analyzing L2 texts* (pp. 9–22). Boston: Addison Wesley.

— (1988) Contrastive rhetoric and second language learning: Notes towards a theory of contrastive rhetoric. In A.C. Purves (ed.) *Writing Across Languages and Cultures: Issues in Contrastive Rhetoric.* Written Communication Annual. An International Survey of Research and Theory, Vol. 2. London: Sage Publications.

Martin, J.E. (1992) *Towards a Theory of Text for Contrastive Rhetoric. An Introduction to Issues of Text for Students and Practitioners of Contrastive Rhetoric.* New York: Peter Lang.

Mauranen, A. (1993) *Cultural Differences in Academic Rhetoric. A Textlinguistic Study.* Frankfurt am Main: Peter Lang.

Melander, B. (1991) Innehållsmönster i svenska facktexter. PhD dissertation. *Skrifter Utgivna av Inst. för Nord. Språk vid Uppsala Universitet* 28. Uppsala: Uppsala University.

Melander, B. and Näslund, H. (1993) Diachronic developments in Swedish LSP texts: A presentation of some of the results from the research project 'LSP Texts in the 20th Century'. In *FINLANCE/A Finnish Journal of Applied Linguistics,* Vol. XII, 1993, 63–94.

Melander, B., Swales, J. and Fredrickson, K. (1994) Journal abstracts from three academic fields in the United States and Sweden: National or disciplinary Proclivities? Manuscript.

Miller, C.R. (1984) Genre as social action. *Quarterly Journal of Speech* 70, 151–67.

Myers, G. (1990) *Writing Biology. Texts in the Social Construction of Scientific Knowledge.* Madison, WI: University of Wisconsin Press.

Näslund, H. (1991) Referens och koherens i svenska facktexter. PhD dissertation. *Skrifter Utgivna av Inst. för Nord. Språk vid Uppsala Universitet 29.* Uppsala: Uppsala University.

Skolander, B. (1992) *Facktexter under 1900-talet 5. Innehållsstrukturella mönster.* TeFa nr 6 (FUMS Rapport nr 168). Uppsala: Uppsala University.

Swales, J. (1981) *Aspects of Article Introductions.* Birmingham, England: University of Aston.

— (1990) *Genre analysis. English in academic and research settings.* Cambridge: Cambridge University Press.

Tannen, D. (1979) What's in a frame? Surface evidence for underlying expectations. In R.O. Freedle (ed.) *New Directions in Discourse Processing* (pp. 137–81). New Jersey: Norwood.

Tirkkonen-Condit, S. and Lieflander-Koistinen, L. (1989) Argumentation in Finnish versus English and German editorials. In M. Kusch and H. Schröder (eds) *Text, Interpretation, Argumentation* (pp. 173–81). Hamburg: Helmut Buske Verlag.

18 The Discourses of Infertility Treatment: A French–English Comparison

MARGARET GIBBON

Aims

The chief aim of this paper is to study and reflect upon the connections between language and social reality. The research upon which it is based focuses on the written language of guidelines for potential patients of doctors practising *in vitro* fertilisation (IVF). The language of these documents reflects, reinforces, and possibly even creates, the social relations between doctors in a high-technology field of medicine and their patients.

The corpus is derived from four countries (Ireland, France, Belgium and Britain) and is made up of patient guidelines in French and English. The documents were obtained by contacting IVF specialists in their public or private practices. Each was asked to provide copies of any explanatory or instructional documents they distributed to their patients, actual or potential. The guidelines are written by one or several members of the team of doctors and biologists involved in IVF procedures. They vary in length from five to 30 A4 pages, but I chose documents of similar length for the comparison presented here.

The texts display many similarities, as one would expect in any sub-language (Kittredge, 1982), but also a number of differences in both content and style. A further aim of this paper is then to account for these, but space limitations permit only a cursory explanation. The differences in text content, at least, do seem to derive from economic, political, social, and cultural variations

between the countries under consideration. Cultural differences – in particular regarding the status of science and of medicine – account for those
stylistic differences which cannot be explained purely by the different
possibilities inherent in the two languages as I shall show.

Context

A certain elementary knowledge of the IVF technique is a pre-requisite,
since if we know nothing about the procedures involved in IVF, we will be
unable to judge how thorough, relevant and balanced a set of guidelines
is. More crucially, we will be unable to spot omissions, distortions, misrepresentations and contradictions.

In vitro fertilisation – what the media erroneously term the 'test-tube
baby' technique – is a series of medical and surgical procedures designed to
permit couples without children to procreate. It is important to stress 'couples'
for a variety of reasons. Chief among these are the social criteria obtaining
in most countries: usually only married couples can avail of the technique.
A second reason to emphasise 'couples' is that, although the techniques
were designed to circumvent the infertility of women with damaged or absent
Fallopian tubes, IVF is now routinely used where sub- or infertility is due to
male factors. In other words, in up to 40% of cases fertile, healthy women
are being 'treated' because their partner is infertile (Laborie, 1990). These
two facts are sufficient to question the terms 'cure', 'treatment', and 'therapy'
used throughout the corpus. If IVF is a 'treatment', why can single women
not be 'treated'? If IVF is a 'treatment', why are healthy women undergoing it?

Those women who are genuinely infertile will remain so following IVF
since, by definition, it effects no cure. However such women will not be sick.
They will be women without (biological) children. In this sense, also, IVF is
not a treatment. Even if one considers such objections to be sophistry, one
cannot but be convinced by the statistics: a putative success rate of 23% at
best (Ireland) and more generally of between 5% to 14% (Mandelbaum &
Plachot, 1991: 103–8). Even if the Irish hospital figure *is* accurate, I would
contend it could be more accurately termed a failure rate of 77%. The 'treatment' should be described as a failed technology, or, at most, an experimental
procedure.

It is popularly believed that IVF is safe, and certainly the texts in this corpus
make only minimal references to complications or dangers. However, research
published in established medical journals outlines serious side-effects of the
drug regimen, especially of the medication prescribed to hyperstimulate the

ovaries. A number of women have died trying to conceive with this method. IVF is a highly invasive, gruelling procedure with little guarantee of success. Many doctors also fear long-term effects upon patients and any offspring since the drugs have been inadequately tested. They are also frequently given in higher doses than recommended by the manufacturers and over longer periods than specified. They remain in the bloodstream for up to six weeks, affecting the early development of the foetus, should a pregnancy ensue.

Hypotheses

Since doctors continue, in Western Europe, to enjoy high social status and, compared to other professionals, to be relatively unaccountable to clients, I hypothesised that textual evidence of a definite claim to truth, knowledge and authority, coupled with an assertion of objectivity, competence and success, would be found. Given the less favourable aspects of IVF practice, I hypothesised that contradictions, misrepresentations or distortions, omissions, and an attempt to eschew responsibility, would be present. Finally, I expected that occasional admissions of ignorance, mitigated perhaps by modal structures or hedges, would be present. A close, critical reading was necessary to identify such features.

Results

Once considered as an art, medicine is now widely considered a science. Enlightenment science has become so successful that it is generally accepted that if knowledge is not 'scientific', then it is not knowledge. Contemporary high-tech medicine partakes in Enlightenment science's fetishisation of method, certainty and objectivity. These values are reflected linguistically in the corpus under consideration.

The findings of this analysis are organised under the following headings:

- Objectivity/Impersonality
- Authority/Truth/Competence
- Omissions/Distortions/Contradictions

In what follows the relevant linguistic features are identified and discussed, with examples in both languages. Unfortunately, given space limitations, it is not possible to provide lengthy fragments of text. It is in looking at entire paragraphs that the flavour of the texts can best be appreciated, but short examples will have to suffice.

Objectivity/impersonality

In order to claim objectivity, doctors write in such a way that it is difficult, if not impossible, to identify them. Thus, the majority of the texts are unsigned or signed in an impersonal way, e.g. *l'équipe FIV* (the IVF team). By far the most common features, however, are syntactic structures which permit agent deletion. The use or over-use of the passive is the most noteworthy. In the first 150 lines of the guidelines from one French clinic, there were only five active sentences. The remainder were passive sentences or else sentences formed using metaphorical grammar, with inanimate subjects often derived by nominalisation. As Kress & Hodge have pointed out (1979: 25), the causes or agents of processes may be impossible to recover from the surface of a text in sentences of this type. Where in English we find substantives with passive verb forms, we often find in French similar nominalisations associated with reflexive verbs. In both cases agents are deleted, as the following examples show:

A decision may have to be made . . .
Oocyte retrieval will be scheduled for mornings.

Le prélèvement se fait . . .
. . . à une heure qui sera déterminée d'avance
la surveillance s'effectue à des jours précis

We also find totally impersonal structures such as:

It is anticipated that . . .
Il se pose le problème de savoir si . . .

and extremely common use of metaphorical grammar:

Therapies have shown a poor response
Une échographie apprécie le nombre et la taille des ovocytes.

Other common features are the use of dummy subjects in French:

on cherche à en obtenir plusieurs

and, in both languages, the use of gerundives, infinitive and participial constructions. These may also be associated with features such as passive adjectives, which further reinforce the agent deletion.

Typical examples in English would be:

To assess suitability . . .
Whether it is advisable or not
Suitable couples may be advised . . .
Postponement will be considered if . . .

In analysing such features we need to ask who 'disappears' from the surface of the text; and why; what is the effect of such impersonal structures; what do they require of the addressee? Certainly the effect of nominalisation is to permit them to take up theme position, thus elevating arbitrary data such as opinion to the status of given or world-knowledge. The same occurs with passive adjectives. We are unable to question the criteria which determine who would be, for example, a 'suitable' couple. Furthermore, passivisation is a linguistic resource which has a mystificatory effect, because causal connections are looser or deleted. For Kress & Hodge (1979: 25–8), it also has a mystificatory purpose.

Authority/truth/competence

Claims to authority, truth and competence are realised linguistically in a variety of ways. Whereas impersonality in texts depends largely on *syntax*, claims to knowledge are often realised by means of distinctive *lexical* features. However, we do also find syntactic features similar to those noted under the previous heading such as theme/rheme manipulation and a lack of transactional verbs. The verb *to be/être* and other relationals, often in collocations with passive adjectives, create an impression of definite, non-negotiable meaning. The effect is similar to that of substantivation of processes. Moreover, the use of the simple present tense conveys a sense of absolute or eternal truths, as these examples show:

> Ultrasound scanning is safe, simple and painless.
> This uncommon condition is self-limiting.
> After embryo transfer 20–30% of patients become pregnant.
>
> *Il existe deux possibilités . . .*
> *Cette étape est la plus simple.*
> *Une grossesse FIV a le même devenir qu'une grossesse naturelle.*

Finally, on syntactic features, certainty can be conveyed by repeated use of causal conjunctions of purpose and result, associated with the future tense. In English the 'will + infinitive' form is preferred. This form also conveys the mood of intentionality, and is the most definite and confident of those available.

Turning now to lexical resources conveying authority, truth and competence, we find a variety of features recurring. Chief among these is the preference for a denotative lexicon, producing a one-to-one representational correspondence between the term and the object, process or datum referred to. This type of lexicon is a common feature of sub-languages. Words and expressions such as 'recombinant follicle stimulating hormone' or '*une coelioscopie*', to name but two, could be considered typical examples.

Connotation is even less likely when obscure or foreign words are introduced. In medicine, these are often of Latin or Greek origin, although in IVF, a medical speciality developed in Australia and Britain primarily, the lexis is often derived from English terms, including acronyms and abbreviations. French patients are thus faced with '*le GIFT*', '*le ZIFT*' (*g*amete and *z*ygote *i*ntra-*f*allopian *t*ransfer, respectively), while Irish and British patients must decipher such terms as 'zona pellucida', 'corpus luteum' and 'down-regulation', frequent and yet unexplained terms in their guidelines.

This area – unexplained lexis – is one where clear differences between French and English texts arise, with a far greater tendency to find unexplained terms in the French documents than in the English ones. One text in English displays intralingual translation, but only at the very start of the document. Finding perhaps that such translation is tedious and breaks the flow, the author gives up after one paragraph. Not, however, before providing the reader with the following gem:

> IVF stands for *in-vitro* fertilisation, alternatively called 'test-tube baby'. It involves the removal of mature oocytes (ripe eggs) from the ovary and their fertilisation in the laboratory by the husband's spermatozoa (seed).

Contrastive stylistics of English and French do suggest a preference in French for erudite rather than prosaic terms, but, in a specialised field such as IVF, erudite terms are the norm in both languages. The net effect is contradictory. The patient may well be confused and intimidated by the jargon but equally and paradoxically may thus feel confidence in the medical personnel who produce it.

Omissions/distortions/contradictions

It is impossible to quote from the documents to give examples of omissions, since what is unsaid is, by definition, absent. However, they can be detected by reference to knowledge of IVF culled from other sources and also by comparing the texts. What appears in one may not figure in others. For example, whereas Irish and British texts give details of the costs of IVF, French texts do not. The reason for such an omission is simple: in France, the country with the greatest number of IVF centres per inhabitant in the world, IVF is centrally funded, and costs for four IVF cycles are reimbursed by the national health insurance system.

What is less acceptable in the French texts is the omission of any serious treatment of risks and side-effects associated with IVF. One Belgian text goes further by explicitly denying such risks:

Certaines patientes appréhendent des traitements hormonaux car des informations fantaisistes ont été publiées dans une certaine presse: risque de cancer de l'ovaire, de ménopause précoce par épuisement ovarien etc. etc. Ces données sont du domaine de la fantaisie absurde!

The British and Irish texts, by contrast, do make a small number of references to risks, complications and contraindications. However, these are couched in minimising terms. Modals and qualifiers soften the effect of such warnings. Typically, pain does not exist. Instead 'slight' or 'mild' discomfort 'may' occur for 'certain' patients. The established medical journals and specialist reviews are more explicit and mention a long list of sequellae, as Klein & Rowland point out (1988: 264–8). These include the precise conditions denied in the Belgian text. What the texts in this corpus call 'slight side-effects', or *'effets secondaires légers négligeables'*, due to the drug Clomiphene Citrate turn out, in specialised obstetrics/gynaecology journals, to include ovarian cancer, breast cancer, pulmonary effluvia and even death.

Similar comparisons can be made regarding distortions. Once again, the Belgian and French texts contain more distortions and a number of claims made in them are contradicted by the Irish and British texts. Regarding pregnancy outcome, for example, we read:

La qualité des grossesses obtenues et des enfants nés par ces techniques de pointe offrent des garanties absolues quant à leur innocuité. (Belgian text)

La grossesse a le même devenir que celui d'une grossesse naturelle. (French text)

However, a number of British and Irish texts contradict this optimism and point to increased risks of multiple pregnancy leading to premature, low birth-weight babies who may carry this initial disadvantage well into their third year. There is also a greatly increased rate of spontaneous abortion (miscarriage). One Irish text claims this to be in the region of 26%, and points out that up to 5% of IVF pregnancies are ectopic (tubal pregnancies). This is extremely dangerous and requires the removal of both tube and developing foetus. When we remember that up to 40% of women undergo IVF to counteract male factor infertility, the risk of ectopics looms particularly large. It is possible that the IVF procedure could induce infertility in fertile women.

It is in the sections dealing with drugs, outcomes and success rates that we find a lexis connoting uncertainty, coupled with frequent use of modal constructions. Once again, we encounter cultural differences. The French texts are universally more confident and employ far fewer modals, hedges and qualifiers than their English equivalents. Typically, modals are combined with impersonal forms, e.g. It would appear that . . ., *Il se peut que* . . . The lexis of uncertainty extends to adjectives and adverbs, e.g. possibly, maybe, a possible effect, a potential risk and, in French, *apparemment, théoriquement, le cas échéant*; and qualifiers, e.g. minor discomfort, *certaines patientes*.

Two longer quotations on psychological aspects of IVF illustrate the differences well:

> Couples embarking on IVF should be aware that although life, marriage and infertility may cause psychological trauma, Assisted Reproduction programmes can appear to make matters worse apparently giving rise to or accentuating underlying excessive stress reactions, marital problems, sexual problems and increase the difficulties in coming to terms with childlessness. (Irish text)
>
> *Nous ferons tout pour vous aider à vivre dans le calme et la bonne humeur ce qui a été qualifié d'un 'parcours du combattant'.*

The Irish text clearly portrays a more caring attitude, while the French one seems cavalier with regard to the difficulties associated with the technique. However, even in the Irish text, it should be noted that many formulations (may cause, can appear, apparently, excessive stress) have the effect of mitigating the responsibility of the medical team and of suggesting that psychological problems arise outside and prior to the IVF procedures.

Similarly, when the technology fails, as it does in the vast majority of cases, responsibility is eschewed. 'Therapies show a poor response', a woman may be a 'poor responder', as may her ovaries. Worse, the normal, healthy functioning of a woman's pelvic organs may 'interfere with the drug treatment', thus increasing the required dose of drugs. Similar terms are found in French, although it should be said that much less space is devoted to failure in general.

Conclusion

This paper has shown that functionally equivalent texts within a specialised field display little lexical or syntactic variation in lexis or syntax. The diverging content can only be explained by reference to cultural factors. My general conclusion, supported by a European Parliament report (1992: 70–9), is that IVF and its practitioners enjoy greater acceptance and prestige in France and Belgium than in Britain and Ireland. This is reflected in the textual content of my corpus. The inclusion in British and Irish documents of sections on risks, contraindications and side-effects effectively means that they display higher incidence of modality, qualifiers and a lexis of uncertainty. However, I would argue that this phenomenon is clearly socially and culturally, not linguistically, driven.

References

European Parliament (1992) *Bioethics in Europe*. (STOA report PE 158. 453). Luxembourg: Directorate General for Research.

Kittredge, R. (1982) Variation and homogeneity of sublanguages. In R. Kittredge and J. Lehrberger (eds) *Sublanguage: Studies of Language in Restricted Semantic Domains* (pp. 107–37). New York: Walter De Gruyter.

Klein, R. and Rowland, R. (1988) Women as test-sites for fertility drugs: Clomiphene citrate and hormonal cocktails. *Reproductive and Genetic Engineering* 1(3), 251–73.

Kress, G. and Hodge. R. (1979) *Language as Ideology*. London: Routledge and Kegan Paul.

Laborie, F. (1990) D'une banalisation sans evaluation et de ce qui peut s'ensuivre. In J. Testart (ed.) *Le Magasin des Enfants* (pp. 107–13). Paris: Editions François Bourin.

Mandelbaum, J. and Plachot, M. (1991) *Génération Eprouvette*. Paris: Flammarion.

19 Integrating Language and Cultural Awareness Components in Irish-Language Teaching Programmes

LIAM MAC MATHÚNA

Introduction

Once island-wide, Irish is nowadays restricted as a traditionally spoken community language to some 58,451 people (Central Statistics Office, 1993: 14, 18) living, for the most part, on the western sea-board. Elsewhere, the native language is spoken regularly by about 5–10% of the population (Ó Riagáin & Ó Gliasáin, 1994: 11, 13–4, 42–3). Otherwise and in general, English is dominant. However, the ideology of language promotion stresses that, potentially at least, Irish belongs to all the inhabitants of Ireland, north and south. There is also a strong tendency not to restrict the relevance of the Irish language to the more or less traditional way of living common in the small farm holdings of the west. One of the consequences of this attitude is that the affective motivation whereby learners have a greater or lesser wish to be assimilated into the community of the target language is essentially lacking with regard to Irish. For the vast majority of learners Irish is an additive dimension to their current group living, not primarily a means of socialising in the *Gaeltacht* or Irish-speaking areas (compare, for example, Gardner, MacIntyre & Lysynchuk, 1990). *De facto*, the culture of Ireland is treated as a continuum, reflected with varying emphases through both of the country's languages, a culture which is not sharply divided into discrete Irish-medium and English-medium sets.

Nonetheless, much of the societal support for the position of Irish in the country's schools is based on the importance attached to Ireland's traditions of literature and folklore, song, music and dance. The desire to have access to the rich cultural heritage embodied in the Irish-speaking *Gaeltacht* areas complements aspirations for an increasing role for the Irish language throughout the country. Irish is regarded as being at once a reservoir of cultural heritage, a window on the past as it were, and an empowering force, capable of promoting dynamic, independent-minded and forward-looking communities.

Thus the major national surveys on language attitude and usage conducted in 1973, 1983, and 1993 indicate widespread positive – if somewhat slackening – appreciation of Irish as 'a focus of ethnic or national identity' (Ó Riagáin & Ó Gliasáin, 1994: 19, 43), and of the value of its maintenance in the *Gaeltacht* (Ó Riagáin & Ó Gliasáin, 1994: 30, 45). Set beside this is the increasing public support for proactive government policies favouring language extension (Ó Riagáin & Ó Gliasáin, 1994: 22–3, 30–1, 44).

Cultural Awareness

Internationally, cognisance is increasingly being taken of the cultural dimension in foreign language learning. It is generally appreciated that there are greater or lesser extra-linguistic differences between the target community and that of the learner, as 'languages are neither neutral carriers of information nor unique views of the world' (Neubert, 1984: 29). Thus, the cross-cultural aspects of the education of immigrant groups in Western Europe and North America have attracted considerable attention over the past few decades, the former evolving into Council of Europe 'intercultural' educational programmes, the latter into a 'cultural pluralism' approach within a unitary framework (Blanche, 1992). Similar theoretical constructs could be applied to the situation of regional and minority languages *vis-à-vis* their dominant neighbour(s). However, the case of a national, official, indigenous and minority language such as Irish, spoken alongside a *lingua franca* such as English, would appear to be rather more complex.

Schooling

Symptomatic of the general attitude to Irish is the fact that school syllabuses offer the same programmes for all pupils, irrespective of their varied backgrounds as first and second language speakers of Irish and English. There is a relative paucity of specific culture-awareness components in Irish-language teaching programmes. However, it is worth noting that the content-neutral nature of the audio-visual conversational courses for teaching Irish, which have been the regular programmes in the Republic of Ireland's primary schools since about 1970, is a feature shared with the generality of audio-visual courses (Murphy, 1988). Murphy holds that the position is little better in courses based on the communicative approach. She argues that the civilisation module divorces culture from language, and calls for an integrated, holistic 'intercultural' approach (Murphy, 1988).

At any rate, it is clear that the practice in the educational system fails to encapsulate the importance which the public consistently accords Irish, precisely on foot of its cultural embodiment: 'By far the most frequently given reason for wanting to know Irish better is the importance of the language as part of subjects' cultural heritage' (Little, Singleton & Silvius, 1984: 158). This paper argues that the situation should be redressed by incorporating appropriate cultural resources into the new language syllabuses, which are currently being drawn up in conformity with the general communicative approach. This is actually in line with the *Report of the Review Body on the Primary Curriculum* (1990). While recommending 'that the general aim of the teaching of Irish in *Galltacht* [i.e. non-Irish-speaking districts] schools is to develop systematically the communication skills of pupils [during their schooling] at a level appropriate to their ability and environment', the Report formulates two of its general objectives as follows: 'That pupils should understand and appreciate Irish culture and their heritage as Irish people', and 'That pupils should be able to be involved in a meaningful way with whatever Irish is in their environment' (*Report*, 1990: 39–40). At second level, the importance of the cultural dimension has already been set out in the Introduction to the official syllabus for Irish in the Junior Certificate examination:

> As well as the language course itself other aspects of culture are recognised which pupils should have become accustomed to during the course. Among these are music and song, traditional lore, place-names and place-name lore, and social life. The pupil's environment is the starting point for this part of the course and every pupil will have to study through Irish some aspect of the culture of his own district, in accordance with his own ability. (An Roinn Oideachais, n.d.a.: 2; author's translation.)

However, neither this publication, nor its companion volume, *Gaeilge don Teastas Sóisearach: Treoirlínte do Mhúinteoirí* (An Roinn Oideachais, n.d.b.) provide any specific guidance for teachers, not even by way of a select bibliography.

Other Cultural Aspects

In fact, there are many cultural areas which are potentially of great interest to pupils. These include personal names, surnames, local place-names – be they of fields, country roads and townlands, or of streets, housing estates and suburbs. Indeed, the study of Ireland's place-names, whether they be rural or urban, offers wide-ranging interdisciplinary possibilities. Ireland's bilingual urban place-name matrix presents a microcosm of the interaction of human beings and their environment over the ages. The name types are diverse, being both administrative (county, barony, parish, townland, district, road and street) and topographical (including elevations, rivers, coastal features).

Linguistically, in Dublin the name forms link Norse and English with the various stages of Irish, culminating in the extended bilingual interplay of Irish and English on the city's place-names over the past 400 years. Apart from *Dublin/Duibhlinn* and *Baile Átha Cliath* and current suburb names such as *Cluain Dolcáin/Clondalkin, Glas Naíon/Glasnevin, Deilginis/ Dalkey, Oxmantown, Irishtown, Baile Phámar/Palmerstown, Portobello, Marino*, one notes the resonances of *Bóthar na gCloch/Stoneybatter, Sráid San Tomás/Thomas Street, Sráid na gCócairí/Cook Street*, not to mention former exotica such as *Hangman Lane, Cutthroat Lane, Rapparee Alley, Hell* and *Paradise Row*. These latter find their match in recent coinings such as *Cosán Aildrin/Aldrin Walk, Bealach Apollo/Apollo Way* and *Garrán an tSuaimhnis/Tranquillity Grove* (de hÓir, 1975; Mac Mathúna, 1992).

The visual environment of bilingual road-signs, name-plates, and bus-scrolls could be readily used to form the basis of resource kits, facilitating the integration of aspects of history, geography and environmental studies, folklore and literature into language teaching.

Language Awareness

As in the case of culture, so in the case of language. One may fairly claim that the international attention paid to language awareness in school sylla-buses has not yet impinged explicitly on the Irish language class, not even in the guise of 'knowledge about language', as in the UK context (see Hawkins, 1984; Fairclough, 1992; Farren, 1992; Hawkins, 1992). But in many ways this is where Irish might well come into its own (Singleton, 1992). With the eschewing of traditional grammar lessons, pupils have increasingly been left to their own devices, left to grasp internal language structure and inter-language similarities by means of some unaided 'discovery' method. The conscious attention to the structure and functions of language as an element of language education, which language awareness promotes, seems ideally suited to Irish, where the structural contrasts between Irish and English serve to heighten metalinguistic sensibilities. The sociolinguistic interplay between school learning and societal usage suggests that investigation of functional aspects would be of particular relevance.

Restricting the discussion here to structural contrasts, I should like to draw attention to a few representative features which are new to learners of Irish who come from an English-speaking background. This is not to say that there are not very many linguistic and cultural similarities involved. There are, just as there are with other language pairs such as English and French or English and German.

Language and Culture

One can cogently contend that the major Western European languages have been such close neighbours that they may well have been converging since the Renaissance in ways that facilitate our latter-day translators and interpreters. Not so with Irish, which socio-political forces pushed from the mainstream in the early 17th century. For instance, the replacement of the original second person singular vs second person plural opposition [one person vs more than one person] by a polite use of the second plural to refer to one person is – or was until recently – the norm in German and French on the European mainland, and continues to be the position in Britain with regard to Welsh and Scottish Gaelic. English of course has extended the second plural form to all instances. Irish actually did have the polite second plural in the early 17th century, but lost it again. Nowadays, then, Irish differs from English quite radically in this respect. And it is more than likely that Irish has been instrumental in bolstering Hiberno-English's use of *oo* vs *ee* and *ya* vs *yis* as substitute singular vs plural markers in both rural and Dublin city varieties of Hiberno-English.

As to word order, Irish, in common with only an estimated 40 or so languages worldwide, starts most of its unmarked, affirmative sentences with a verb. Like Scottish Gaelic, Welsh and the other Celtic languages, Irish has a normal word order of Verb–Subject–Object, e.g. *Bhuail Éire an Iodáil,* whereas English has the order Subject–Verb–Object, *Ireland beat Italy*. It is interesting that few if any learners of Irish in the educational system take *Tá sé* (is he) 'he is' to be a question, rather than a statement, no matter how minuscule an amount of Irish they may profess to have acquired at school. In fact, even those who would rib the pioneer Gaelic Leaguers used to do so by dubbing them *'tá sé*'s. In other words, they incorporated into their very banter this verb-first order. This example of language awareness was often extended to the rudimentary, but similarly significant phrase *Tá sé mahogany gaspipe*.

Questions and Answers

Another characteristic feature of Irish acquired very early on in the learning process is the understanding that questions are regularly formulated, not by inverting the word order, but by prefixing interrogative particles such as *an* and *ar* to the verbal form. So, where English may frame a question by transforming *He is coming* into *Is he coming?*, and French may make *Parlez-vous?* of *Vous parlez*, Irish changes *Ceannaíonn siad* to *An gceannaíonn siad?* And then, what of the answer? Well, if one enquires *An bhfaca tú mo Shéamaisín?* 'Have you seen my Séamaisín?', the answer would usually be either *Chonaic* or *Ní fhaca*. In English, one expects either standard 'Yes' or 'No', or a Hiberno-English hybrid, 'Yes, I did', 'No, I didn't'. In fact, in Irish replies to questions echo the tense, e.g. *An dtiocfaidh?* elicits *Tiocfaidh, Ar tháinig? Tháinig* and so on. Thus, whereas asking questions is perhaps structurally simpler in Irish than in English, answering them is not. The English speaker will get by fine with just *Yes* and *No* (perhaps with *Maybe* as back-up, just in case), whereas the Irish speaker really needs to be able to manipulate the verbal forms across the entire gamut of tenses and moods. It is small wonder then that this fundamental difference between the two languages generated considerable interest among the Irish-speaking community, as they increasingly came into contact with English. In the Baile Bhuirne district of the Co. Cork *Gaeltacht*, they were moved to compose and recite with relish the pithy little verse:

> *Yis agus No,*
> *an chuid is mó*
> *den Bhéarla.*

> 'Yes and No
> (are) the greater part
> of the English'.

Phonology and Morphology

With regard to consonantal sounds Irish has a palatal vs velar opposition, which turns on whether the front of the tongue is raised towards the hard palate or the back towards the soft palate. This difference can affect the sense. Thus, the singular *capall*, ending in a velar *ll*, is quite distinct from the plural *capaill*, which ends in a palatal *ll*. Irish has both velar and palatal realisations of the voiced and voiceless fricatives *gh* and *ch*, sounds no longer to be met with in Standard English. In fact, Irish abounds in fascinating linguistic features, some of which seemed to diverge so much from Standard Average European – as Whorf (1956) termed this norm – that 150 years ago they even raised doubts as to whether or not the Celtic group of languages belonged to the Indo-European family at all. Probably the most striking claim of Irish to linguistic structural note is its developed systems of initial mutations or regular sound changes at the beginning of words, which affect the sense: e.g. *a cat, a chat* and *a gcat* all bear different meanings, namely 'her cat', 'his cat' and 'their cat'.

Prepositions and pronouns regularly coalesce in Irish giving the hybrid category of prepositional pronouns. So, where in English one has 'with me, with you, with him, with her', in Irish one has *liom, leat, leis, léi*, and the like.

Vocabulary

At the level of vocabulary the Irish language offers many surface contrasts to English. Like German and Swedish, Irish lexically marks adverbs of direction, depending on whether movement is towards or away from a point of reference. It also distinguishes both of these from the stationary state. As regards numerals, Irish does have the standard decimal system, but in common with other West-European languages it also has a system of counting in 20s, which is robustly alive and well in its regional dialects. Furthermore, Irish has a strong tendency to lexically mark the dual nature of eyes, ears and limbs, e.g. *mo dhá shúil* 'my two eyes' and *ar leathshúil* 'one-eyed' [lit. 'on a half eye']. As is well-known, the distribution of colour-names within the spectrum is by no means the same for Irish and English and the range of applications of the various colours can be quite different (for a general contrastive survey of Irish and English, see Mac Mathúna, 1990).

Conclusions

The somewhat artificial and repetitious nature of classroom learning in any subject can become monotonous for teaching and taught alike. In the particular circumstances of the Irish language, developing and maintaining freshness and success over 13-odd years can sap the motivational resources of many. But a judicious admixture of language awareness and cultural awareness modules might well be just the shot in the arm required to jab the Irish language class into life. Within the programme for Irish itself they can provide suitable objects of enquiry and focuses for learning. In turn, they should act as motivators, facilitating links with English and the modern continental languages and ultimately embracing geography, history, and the entire curriculum. It would be idle to claim that either cultural or language awareness elements can be a panacea which dispenses with the hard work of teaching and learning, but they can contribute to rewarding and effective renewal in Irish-language teaching programmes. The more that the Irish-language classroom can be permeated by the sense of an intriguing language delivering a vibrant cultural message, the more meaningful the learning enterprise will become.

References

An Roinn Oideachais (n.d.a.) *Siollabas don Teastas Sóisearach: Gaeilge*. Baile Átha Cliath: An Roinn Oideachais.
— (n.d.b.) *Gaeilge don Teastas Sóisearach: Treoirlínte do Mhúinteoirí*. Baile Átha Cliath: An Chomhairle Náisiúnta Curaclaim agus Measúnachta.
Blanche, P. (1992) Bilingual crosscultural education in Western Europe: An overview. *RELC Journal* 23, 81–104.
Central Statistics Office (1993) *Census 86. Imleabhar 5. An Ghaeilge/Vol. 5. Irish Language*. Baile Átha Cliath/Dublin: Oifig an tSoláthair/Stationery Office.
de hÓir, É. (1975) Sracfhéachaint ar logainmneacha Bhaile Átha Cliath. *Studia Hibernica* 15, 128–42.
Fairclough, N. (ed.) (1992) *Critical Language Awareness*. London and New York: Longman.
Farren, S. (1992) Knowledge about language: An old controversy in new programmes. *Language, Culture and Curriculum* 5, 185–97.
Gardner, R.C., MacIntyre, P.D. and Lysynchuk, L.M. (1990) Affective dimension in second language programme evaluation. *Language, Culture and Curriculum* 3, 39–64.
Hawkins, E. (1984) *Awareness of Language: An Introduction*. Cambridge: Cambridge University Press.
— (1992) Awareness of language/knowledge about language in the curriculum in England and Wales: An historical note on 20 years of curricular debate. *Language Awareness* 1, 5–17.
Little, D., Singleton, D. and Silvius, W. (1984) *Learning Second Languages in Ireland: Experience, Attitudes and Needs*. Dublin: Centre for Language and Communication Studies.
Mac Mathúna, L. (1990) Contrastive aspects of English and Irish. In B. Bramsbäck (ed.) *Homage to Ireland. Aspects of Culture, Literature and Language* (pp. 81–98). Uppsala: Almqvist & Wiksell International.
— (1992) Logainmneacha Gaeilge Bhaile Átha Cliath. *Féile Zozimus* 1, 67–84.
Murphy, E. (1988) The cultural dimension in foreign language teaching: Four models. *Language, Culture and Curriculum* 1, 147–63.
Neubert, A. (1984) Translation across languages or across cultures? In L. Mac Mathúna and D. Singleton (eds) *Language Across Cultures. Proceedings of a Symposium held at St Patrick's College, Drumcondra, Dublin, 8–9 July 1983* (pp. 21–9). Dublin: Irish Association for Applied Linguistics/Cumann na Teangeolaíochta Feidhmí.
Ó Riagáin, P. and Ó Gliasáin, M. (1994) *National Survey on Languages 1993: Preliminary Report*. Baile Átha Cliath: Institiúid Teangeolaíochta Éireann.

Report of the Review Body on the Primary Curriculum/Tuarascáil na Comhairle Athbhreithnithe don Churaclam Bunscoile (1990). Dublin: National Council for Curriculum and Assessment and Department of Education.
Singleton, D. (1992) Education towards language awareness in Ireland. *Language Awareness* 1, 47–57.
Whorf, B.L. (1956) *Language, Thought, and Reality*. Cambridge, MA: The MIT Press.

20 The Intercultural made Explicit in the Teaching of Cultural Content in a Bilingual, Multicultural Society

PETER J. HEFFERNAN

Introduction

This short article is based on a study (Heffernan, 1995) recently completed in French on 'Les contenus culturels dans l'enseignement des langues dans les cours de langue seconde et maternelle destinés aux élèves anglophones et francophones canadiens'. I have been motivated throughout my nearly quarter-century career in second language teaching by a concern for how language programmes can serve to broaden students' cultural as well as their linguistic horizons. This centering is inspired by something many researchers have come to view as both disconcerting and problematic: monolithic trends towards uniformity which particularly characterize North American society – such things as fitting the mould, one-size-fits-all, assimilative pressures which are condescending, degrading and demeaning, if not downright oppressive.

In the Francophone literature on cross-cultural and intercultural relations and education in Canada, there exist numerous examples of works depicting French-Canadians' preoccupation with how to counteract pressures to bring about Anglo-centric conformity (Ravault, 1983a; McMahon & Levasseur-Ouimet, 1987; Laforge, 1993; Mahé, 1993; Martel, 1993). Working closely with Francophone groups (particularly from 1975–77, as president of a provincial Francophone federation) has sensitised me to this issue.

French immersion programmes in both Atlantic and Prairie Canada have now become a regular feature in Canadian education, and initially seemed to offer a wealth of opportunity for Anglophone youngsters enrolled therein to come to understand and appreciate divergent cultural perspectives and to become fuller participants in genuine dialogue between and within Canada's two major linguistic-cultural communities. After all, children enrolled in French immersion programmes are exposed to a whole range of subject-matter (from Language Arts and Mathematics to Art and History) in French, their second language. If language and culture are inextricably linked, it seemed nearly impossible that anyone graduating from such a programme would not have broader outlooks, identify somewhat more with Francophone perspectives on issues and engage more in French-language activities either vicariously (e.g. radio, television) or in the presence of Francophones than their unilingually-educated Anglophone peers.

Indeed, since French-immersion appeared on the Canadian educational stage, there has been a great deal of well-intentioned generalising in both educational and political circles about the cross-cultural benefits accruing to individual programme registrants and the future well-being of a more unified nation. On the other hand, several well-researched studies have come up with contrary findings.

Carey (1984), for example, in a meta-analysis of Canadian French immersion research, arrived at the conclusion that this programme, while reasonably strong in its language goals, is relatively weak in terms of its contributions to students' cultural broadening. This observation is based on his analysis of the work of researchers such as Genesee (1978) and Cleghorn (1981), both of whom found, for example, that immersion youngsters do not listen to more French radio, watch more French television, read more French magazines, newspapers and books or get together informally more frequently with Francophones than their predominantly English-educated peers. This pattern of separation holds true also for English- and French-language teachers working in immersion settings. In fact, most of immersion youngsters' interaction in French, it appears, goes on in the classroom only. There, they are exposed to the native or native-like French model of their teachers, but even more so to the evolving French of their peers. As a result of their constrained French-language exposure, as documented by a number of researchers who have investigated this phenomenon (Pawley, 1985; Pellerin & Hammerly, 1986; Lyster, 1987; *inter alios*), most immersion youngsters lack precision in natural expression in French and, particularly, sociolinguistic sophistication. Bibeau (1991), accordingly, has referred to their French as an approximative interlanguage.

Calvé (1991) nuances the on-going debate in Canadian immersion research by suggesting that the programme has its strengths and weaknesses. Optimists concentrate on the positive outcomes; detractors on the negative. He argues then for a more balanced perspective and set of expectations relative to this bilingual education programme phenomenon.

The Study

With these considerations in mind, I set out to determine from curricular and instructional points of view, what cultural inputs immersion students are exposed to in the classroom, which might differentiate their experience from that of their English-educated peers.

In keeping with more general observations on educational systems made elsewhere by sociologists of education, such as Apple (1990), Bernstein (1975), Bourdieu & Passeron (1970), and Contenta (1993), I have observed that immersion also officially propagates mainstream, Anglo-conformist perspectives. Canale & Swain's (1980: 5) seminal article on the communicative approach, for example, implies conformity and sameness: 'One can develop a level of sociolinguistic and sociocultural competence in Canadian French just by having developed such a competence in English'. Swain & Lapkin (1982: 4) reinforce this position: 'Immersion students' education should be the same as that of students in regular English programmes offered in any given school system, with the only major difference being the language through which the teacher and students communicate in the classroom'. For all intents and purposes, the underlying curricular assumption is one of immersion-language programming being culturally neutral and free of ideology. In fact this premise is itself ideologically-loaded, rallying the legions to the apparently good-natured view: 'We're all really just the same, aren't we?'

The findings of my research into the cultural inputs to which immersion students are exposed in the classroom mainly refute these assumptions. This study focused on collective memory or historico-cultural inputs mediated in students' interactions with Canadian history texts and their teachers in their history lessons. Immersion students, it is acknowledged, are engaged in language learning across the curriculum. History offered terrain rich in cultural material. In order to compare historico-cultural inputs to which Anglophone immersion students are exposed in French with those of other groups, four comparison groups were selected:

(A) Anglophones studying Canadian history in English in Alberta;
(B) Anglophone youngsters in French immersion studying Canadian history in French in Alberta;
(C) Franco-Albertan (minority) youngsters studying Canadian history in French; and

(D) Québécois youngsters studying Canadian and Québec history in French.

All groups were of the same school grade: Alberta grade 10 and Québec secondaire iv. The period of Canadian history studied at this level and compared was Canada since Confederation (1867 to the present).

This research involved primarily two activities:

(1) content analyses (quantitative and qualitative) of the authorised and most used Canadian history texts of each of the four comparison groups; and

(2) a validation of these findings in a series of face-to-face interviews conducted with a sample of teachers from each of the four comparison groups (located throughout Alberta and in the Québec City and Lac St.-Jean areas of Québec).

The content analyses and interviews were organised around 12 key questions (which served as my hypothetical categories for content analysis):

(1) What relative importance is given to Alberta/the Prairies or Québec and to Canada as a whole?

(2) What frequency of references is made to the French-Canadian diaspora (French Canada outside Québec)?

(3) What relative importance is given to demographic, economic, political or religious questions?

(4) What interest is shown towards the historical contributions of Anglophones and of Francophones?

(5) What Canadian and what Francophone institutions in particular are focused on?

(6) What relative interest is shown in great persons and events (traditional history) or in 'ordinary people' and their lives ('nouvelle histoire')?

(7) What frequencies are there of references to great Canadian historical figures?

(8) What Anglophone and Francophone historical figures are named?

(9) What relative weighting is attached to crisis or key events in Canadian history?

(10) What variety of allusions is made to Québec (in terms of how it is named or characterised)?

(11) What indicators, if any, does one find of Québec as a 'distinct' society?

(12) What valuing is there of Québec as a 'distinct' society? What value is placed on fostering difference/distinction in society as a whole?

Analysis of Results

A summary overview of the findings relative to each of these questions just outlined is provided below. By way of preamble, though, it should be stressed that the content analyses of the Canadian history texts used and teachers' perceptions of what they emphasised in their classroom teaching did not always match. In particular, the official cursus and authorised texts tend to expose Anglophones in French immersion and minority Franco-Albertan students to similar historico-cultural content to that of Anglophones in Alberta studying Canadian history in English. (It is important to note that, while using different texts, both Albertan Anglophones and Albertans studying Canadian history in French use texts originally published in English.) On the other hand, the historico-cultural content interpreted by French immersion teachers and teachers working in Franco-Albertan school settings tends to provide students with more divergent perspectives as regards both weighting and valuing. In terms of both the content of texts and teachers' interpretation of the Canadian history represented therein, the two groups furthest apart in their exposure to Canadian historico-cultural content are Anglophones studying in English in Alberta and Francophones studying in French in Québec.

Turning now to the responses to the questions raised, it is clear that Albertans, whether studying Canadian history in English or in French, centre significantly more on Canada as a whole than on the Province of Alberta or the Prairie region. Québécois texts and teachers are significantly more pre-occupied with Québec than with Canada as a whole. The ratio in each case was in an approximate proportion of 4:1.

The French-Canadian diaspora, to which Ravault (1983b) has referred as 'la francophonie clandestine', is given the greatest weighting in the Albertan English text and the least in the Québécois French text. However, in the interview situation, it was quite clear that most Albertan Anglophone teachers know very little about French Canadians outside Québec, and deal little with them in their teaching. Québécois teachers also largely ignore them, though several expressed some regret about this and suggested more atten-tion ought to be paid to their contributions. Both French immersion and Franco-Albertan teachers indicated they heavily weighted the historical significance of French Canada outside Québec, backing up their observation with numerous examples.

Little difference was found among the teacher groups and texts in terms of the relative importance of demographic, economic, political and religious questions. All attributed greater importance to economic and political issues. French-Canadians outside Quebec and Québécois, who are often characterised as being consumed by demographic concerns, do not appear, on the basis of these findings, to be more preoccupied than Anglophones with demography. Religion got the shortest shrift, though its historical significance was recognised, particularly by Francophone respondents.

Among major contributions to the progress of Québec and of Canada were mentioned, for example, Confederation (1867), the First and Second World Wars, the Canadian and Québécois welfare state, the franchise to women, the Quiet Revolution and so forth. Wide differences in the texts showed up between Alberta and Québec in terms of the historical contributions remembered or forgotten. The Albertan texts, whether English or French, tended to remember similarly. However, in the interviews, it was clear that Albertan teachers working in French immersion and Franco-Albertan settings made up for a number of textual lacunae relative to French historical contributions and their remembering is quite different from that of their Anglo-Albertan and Québécois peers. French immersion students, it was noted too, have the most balanced presentation of all the groups in this area.

In identifying Canadian and Francophone institutions in particular, it is quite clear that Canadians have few common institutions that all readily identify, especially beyond the governmental and political. In fact, Anglophones and Francophones appear mainly to remember different institutions or else the same institutions differently. The translated text used in French immersion and Franco-Albertan settings would appear to be a source of anomie and/or neglect for students interested in identifying with Canada's French fact, because it consistently identified English-language newspapers, broadcasts, films and magazines, neglecting the French. French immersion and Franco-Albertan teachers interviewed indicated again, by their responses, that they compensated for these lacunae. Quite remarkably, several Albertan Anglophone interview respondents paused and hesitated and were virtually unable to identify any Francophone institution. Similarly, several Québécois respondents suggested they were unable to identify or identified little with any Canadian institution.

As for their focus on traditional history as opposed to 'nouvelle histoire', all texts and teacher groups appear to be moving more in the direction of the history of 'ordinary people' and their lives, though this tendency is more pronounced in French than in English. This is accounted for perhaps by a persistent French-Canadian effort to de-emphasise yesteryear's historical mythologising, while bringing more to the fore the contributions to French linguistic and cultural survival of traditionally lesser known individuals in the Francophone communities of Canada.

In terms of historical persons and events remembered, Anglophones proportionately (in a ratio of 3:1) remember Anglophones more, and Francophones (in a ratio of 4:1) remember their own more. Even when the same historical figures and events are recalled, they are also frequently valued very differently. The English texts and teachers, for instance, remember the great wars in a quite different manner from the French. French texts and teachers remember French suffragettes, while failing to mention their more numerous, more active and, in relative terms, more successful Anglophone sisters. The list of such examples goes on, and is quite extensive.

The remembering of Québec is generally very positive in both English and French, though the Francophone response is more nuanced. Generally, there is wide acceptance of the 'two founding peoples' principle as well, though the specific treatment of Québec as a 'distinct society' is rejected by some in all quarters. French texts and teacher groups, particularly in the French immersion and Franco-Albertan minority settings, appear to value fostering societal difference more than their English counterparts.

Conclusions

In the end, these findings mainly refute the generally-accepted notion in English Canada that English- and French-Canadians are sociolinguistically and socioculturally undifferentiated. In addition, while the official cursus and texts for French immersion appear to try to propagate cultural uniformity, in particular Anglo-centric conformity, the 'hidden curriculum' (what actually occurs in the classroom) has as its general effect sensitising Anglophone youngsters enrolled therein to alternative perspectives on a number of historico-cultural content variables studied in this research.

It is recognised that efforts can and should be made to mitigate highly charged divisions (and this could begin by having teams of Canadian history authors comprised of mixed groups of Anglophones and Francophones, which in general, does not appear to be the case at present). However, I have also found that efforts to stifle legitimate and recognisable differences and alternative perspectives in French immersion (and minority Francophone) curricula only force committed teachers working in these school settings to go 'underground' and effect remedial treatment, in the classroom, of the official cursus. My contention is that making intercultural (and frequently divergent) perspectives explicit in both these and majority language school settings is a more realistic means of developing in class the long-term internal peace in a bilingual, multicultural country.

References

Apple, M.W. (1990) *Ideology and Curriculum.* London: Routledge.

Bernstein, B. (1975) *Towards a Theory of Educational Transmissions: Class, Codes and Control.* London: Routledge and Kegan Paul.

Bibeau, G. (1991) L'immersion: de la coupe aux lèvres. *Études de Linguistique Appliquée* 82, 127–38.

Bourdieu, P. and Passeron, J.-C. (1970) *La Reproduction: Éléments pour une Théorie du Système d'Enseignement.* Paris: Éditions de Minuit.

Calvé, P. (1991) Vingt-cinq ans d'immersion au Canada: 1965–1990. *Études de Linguistique Appliquée* 82, 7–21.

Canale, M. and Swain, M. (1980) Theoretical bases of communicative approaches to second language teaching and testing. *Applied Linguistics* 1(1), 1–47.

Carey, S. (1984) Reflections on a decade of French immersion. *Canadian Modern Language Review* 41(2), 246–59.

Cleghorn, A. (1981) Patterns of teacher interaction in an immersion school in Montréal. PhD thesis, McGill University, Montréal.

Contenta, S. (1993) *Rituals of Failure: What Schools Really Teach.* Toronto: Between the lines.

Genesee, F. (1978) Second language learning and language attitudes. *Working Papers on Bilingualism* 16, 19–42.

Heffernan, P.-J. (1995) Les contenus culturels dans l'enseignement des langues dans les cours de français langue seconde et maternelle destinés aux éleves anglophones et francophones canadiens. PhD thesis, Université Laval, Québec.

Laforge, L. (1993) L'enseignement de la culture 'maternelle' en milieu minoritaire. *Canadian Modern Language Review* 49(4), 815–31.

Lyster, R. (1987) Speaking immersion. *Canadian Modern Language Review* 43(4), 701–17.

Mahé, Y. (1993) L'idéologie, le curriculum et les enseignants des écoles bilingues de l'Alberta, 1892–1992. *Canadian Modern Language Review* 49(4), 687–703.

Martel, A. (1993) Compétitions idéologiques et les droits scolaires francophones en milieu minoritaire au Canada. *Canadian Modern Language Review* 49(4), 734–59.

McMahon, F. and Levasseur-Ouimet, F. (1987) S'approprier ses réalités culturelles. Presentation made at Conference of the Association Canadienne des Professeurs de Formation des Maîtres, Fredericton, New Brunswick, May.

Pawley, C. (1985) How bilingual are French immersion students? *Canadian Modern Language Review* 41(5), 865–76.

Pellerin, M. and Hammerly, H. (1986) L'expression orale après treize ans de l'immersion française. *Canadian Modern Language Review* 42(3), 592–606.

Ravault, R.-J. (1983a) *Perceptions de Deux Solitudes: Étude sur les Relations entre Deux Communautés de Langues Officielles du Nouveau-Brunswick.* Québec: Université Laval/Centre International de Recherche sur le Bilinguisme.

— (1983b) *La Francophonie Clandestine.* Ottawa: Institut des communications sociales.

Swain, M. and Lapkin, S. (1982) *Evaluating Bilingual Education: A Canadian Case Study.* Clevedon, Avon: Multilingual Matters.

21 How Immersed are Students in Immersion Programmes?[1]

ANDREW D. COHEN

Introduction

Language immersion programmes in Canada and the United States usually assume that second language acquisition occurs most readily in the target language environment. Immersion programmes attempt to simulate native-like learning conditions by maximising learners' exposure to the target language and to the target-language culture. Findings from research on second language immersion programmes have shown that students who become bilingual through such programmes make normal or better than normal progress in content subjects which are taught primarily in the second language (Cohen & Swain, 1979; Genesee, 1987). Such results have led to claims that immersion pupils gain an ability to 'think in the foreign language'. By implication, the more adept they are at thinking in that language, the quicker they can process input and output and further enhance their acquisition of the language.

Nonetheless, there is a realisation that gaps exist in foreign-language proficiency, especially in speaking and writing skills. First, there are signs that pupils sometimes use English-language structures to construct their target-language utterances, a process referred to as relexification. Second, pupils also insert native-language words into their utterances – especially adverbs and interjections – a sign that they may be thinking in English and performing on-line translation. Finally, the language produced in immersion programmes may feature reduced vocabulary and structure (e.g. little or no use of complex verb tenses such as the conditional or the subjunctive).

In French immersion programmes, for example, students who have had several years of comprehensible input still speak and write with numerous morphological, syntactic, and lexical deviations from native-speaker norms (Lapkin, Swain & Shapson, 1990; Genesee, 1987). In addition, students may have relatively little opportunity for the use of extended discourse in class. One study of more than ten 6th grade French immersion classes found that only 14% of the occasions on which students spoke in teacher-fronted activities were their utterances longer than a single clause (Swain, 1988; Harley, Allen, Cummins & Swain, 1990).[2]

For these reasons, Canadian immersion education experts have recently begun to explore alternatives for increasing learners' conscious attention to the grammatical features of output (Swain, 1992). Without such measures, language ability tends to fossilise at a level which is adequate for the immersion classroom but not native-like.

Full language immersion programmes in the US usually discourage speaking in all but the second language. However, second-graders in the first US immersion programme in Culver City, California, reported using English in class about half the time (Cohen & Lebach, 1974), despite the teacher's scrupulous adherence to their target-language guise. The amount of English use during immersion language classes could easily hinder the productive skills of immersion pupils.

Yet another potential source for gaps between comprehension and production may be a systematic reluctance or inability of immersion pupils to perform cognitive operations in the target language, whether in or out of class. In essence, the students may not be as immersed as teachers and administrators think they are. There appears to be little research on this phenomenon. It might be hypothesised that a foreign-language content programme would have the potential to stimulate the performance of cognitive operations largely through that language during both processing of academic tasks (academic language proficiency) and interacting socially (conversational language proficiency) (Cummins, 1991).

Many cognitive operations are verbal, whether in the form of inner, private speech or in the form of social or public speech. *Inner speech* is abrupt, governed by predicates, and often unintelligible because referents are unclear – 'speech almost without words' (Vygotsky, 1961: 529). 'One word in inner speech is saturated with sense to such an extent that it would require many words in external speech to explain it' (Vygotsky, 1961: 531).[3] The more external or public private speech becomes, the more fully structured it is.

In recent work concerning cognitive processes and second language acquisition, Cohen & Olshtain (1993) provide detailed descriptions of the students' introspective language use in both their native and target languages while planning and executing utterances in the target language alone. The extent to which learners operate mentally in their native language during comprehension and production may shed light on the acquisition process, since it gives an indication of actual thinking in the target language.

Primary school full immersion programmes may provide a rich context for SLA research on the extent of target language use in performing cognitive operations. Thus, the following study was designed to examine the internal language environment in grade-school learners *vis-à-vis* the external language environment established in immersion classrooms. Using the learner as the locus of reference, we define *external language environment* as all language-related influences that are outside the learner: curriculum goals, classroom policies and procedures, classroom materials and activities, and communicative exchanges between students, teachers, and administrators. *Internal language environment* refers to how learners process language in their minds: the roles of native- and second-language systems in performing the cognitive tasks for which the second language is a vehicle.

The larger study investigated the selection and use of languages across subject matters – social studies, composition writing, science, and math. However, this paper will report only on language issues associated with the processing of numerical and word problems in math. Studies of native English-speaking elementary school pupils have found that difficulty with word problems was largely due to difficulty in comprehending abstract or ambiguous language (Cummins, Kintsch, Reusser & Weimer, 1988). Mestre (1988) notes the challenges that the student faces in attempting to solve math word problems in a second language. First, it is important to understand the written text in order to grasp the problem. Second, pupils may need proficiency in the relevant technical language. Third, students must distinguish between mathematical and non-mathematical word use. Finally, proficiency is needed in the symbolic language of the domain.[4]

These are the specific research questions that were asked:

- To what extent do learners use their native language and the foreign language when performing the cognitive operations involved in math problems?
- When might a language switch take place, if at all?

Design of the Study

Sample

32 pupils from a full Spanish language immersion school in St. Paul, (six at grade 3, seven at grade 4, nine at grade 5, and 10 at grade 6) participated

in the overall study. Sampling started at the grade 3 level because prior research found that, by this grade level, children could provide verbal reports of their language-using strategies (Garner, 1987; Cohen, 1987, 1991). Teachers selected pupils from their respective classrooms to represent three levels (high, medium and low) of Spanish language proficiency and academic skills. Participation was voluntary. Spanish proficiency ratings were based on *La Prueba Riverside de Realización en Español* (Riverside Publishing Company, 1964)[5] and on the teachers' rating. Academic skills were rated on the *SRA Survey of Basic Skills* (Science Research Associates, 1985)[6] and teachers' assessments. Data were available on the processing of math problems for 15 of the 32 subjects – all 10 of the sixth graders and five of the fifth graders – and these constituted the sample for the current paper. Both teachers were native English speakers fluent in Spanish.

In this full immersion programme, grades 2 to 4 had only one hour per day of English instruction in English language arts. In fifth grade, slightly more time was devoted to both English reading and social studies. In sixth grade, two hours of English instruction in all subjects prepared the students for junior high school. Instruction used co-operative learning theory and emphasised the whole-language approach to reading and language arts (cf. Shrum & Glisan, 1994: 63, 93–4). Content textbooks were written in Spanish, but based on the US curriculum; they occasionally read like literal translations of English-language textbooks into Spanish.[7] Further, the texts lacked the rich cultural dimensions present in textbooks developed in Hispanic regions.

Instrumentation

Verbal report

As the main purpose of the study was to describe the use of native versus foreign language in math problem-solving, the primary means of data collection was *verbal report* (Cohen, 1987; 1991), or, more precisely, *think aloud* (externalising verbalised thoughts without analysis or reflection), *self-observation* (introspecting about current thoughts and/or retrospecting about specific prior thoughts,), and *self-report* (indicating intentions, without referring to any specific cognitive activity).[8]

Questionnaire-based interview

Questions were designed for immersion pupils to answer about their abilities, attitudes, and preferences with regard to thinking in Spanish and using Spanish as a vehicle for communication with peers and with adults.

Classroom observation

Classroom observation was used to obtain data regarding language use patterns in whole-class, group, and paired interaction – that is, who said what to whom, in what language, and under what circumstances.

Background information

Archival data from the school files provided (1) Spanish language proficiency scores on *La Prueba Riverside de Realización en Español*, (2) scores for academic skills performance from the *SRA Survey of Basic Skills*, and learners' school grades.

Data Collection Procedures

A team of five native English-speaking research assistants from the University of Minnesota (four undergraduates and one postgraduate) collected the data over a five-month period during repeated interactions with each pupil so as to increase the reliability of the findings. The research assistants worked with the same group of pupils to establish rapport.

The fifth and sixth-grade data used here were collected by a fluent non-native Spanish speaker and by a limited speaker of Spanish.[9] The pupils were encouraged to provide their verbal reports in whatever language with which they felt more comfortable. The investigators tape-recorded the sessions so as to allow the pupils to report verbally in Spanish whenever they wanted, even though one investigator did not understand. On occasion, teacher-fronted classroom sessions were also audio-recorded for analysis.

Generally, students were not pulled out of their classrooms nor were they assigned any additional tasks for the study. Consequently, the linguistic complexity of the math word problems on which the pupils provided verbal report was not systematically varied. The students were studied unobtrusively during normal classroom activities, except that a researcher prompted them to think aloud about their activities. At times, students spontaneously talked aloud during tasks. Sometimes pupils and researchers interacted in the corridor so as not to disturb the class.

In the interactions, learners were asked (1) to indicate how they used their languages in solving the math problems, (2) to identify areas in which they had difficulty in understanding the teachers' instructions and content in the textbooks and worksheets, and (3) to indicate where they got stuck while speaking in Spanish. Particular attention was given to math problems on quizzes or tests, but problems from worksheets also served as a means of assessing math ability. From time to time, questions about pupils' ability, attitudes, and preferences were interspersed into these sessions.

Results

The data from 15 pupils gave a relatively clear picture of the extent to which learners used their respective languages to perform the cognitive operations involved in math problems, including trigger language switching. For these immersion students, English seemed at times to predominate in their internal language environment. In responding to word problems in math, the fifth and sixth graders in the study reported favouring English in their cognitive processing, which matched observations. They read problems in Spanish but would shift to English immediately or as soon as they had some conceptual difficulty.

Let us look at data from four pupils, starting with two pupils who had medium Spanish language proficiency and medium academic skills: Ana, a sixth grader, and Peter, a fifth grader. The next two examples are two sixth grade pupils, Karen and Donna, who had scored high in language proficiency and in academic skills.

Ana used an English translation if the word problem was hard:

Researcher: What language do you do math problems in?
Ana: Usually, probably in Spanish. But if it's like a hard word problem, then I have to translate it . . . Well, I know the words in Spanish. It's just that you want to . . . you sorta like want to go back to the language you know, like, more of . . .

Here, she read a math problem and solved it in Spanish. In another case, she read the word problem in Spanish and then translated it into English.

R: Why the translation?
A: Because sometimes English is easier than Spanish.
R: Are there words in the problem you do not understand?
A: [Indicates *ahorras*, 'you save', a crucial word for understanding and solving the problem.] ... so you gotta have a dictionary with you when you're doing math sometimes. [But she did not use it.] Well, I just took out the little clues, and said like, 'How much money would . . .' I was just sort of guessing what it meant . . . if you bought something . . . it's like, you add something together and then you come up with the answer and then you minus what you save, and then you come up with the answer.

She then started giving an example of thinking a problem through in Spanish if it was not too hard, but then she switched to English:

A: It's minus. So it's like take away this from this . . .

It appeared to be a problem of the number of cognitive operations involved:

A: It's hard for me to remember what number is up here [refers to top integer and fraction in subtraction] and what number is down here [bottom integer and fraction], in Spanish, so I have to translate to English; and then since you can't take away 8 through 9, then I get even more confused . . . It gets really nuts.

Peter reported using English to understand instructions better. He was just finishing a math test when the researcher arrived. On problems #28 and #29, he seemed to think in English, while on #30 he read the problem aloud, thought in Spanish and later switched to English:

> [Problem 30. *Teri usó la computadora 3 veces más minutos que Sue. ¿Cuánto tiempo trabajó Teri con la computadora?* (Teri used the computer three times more minutes than Sue. How long did Teri work with the computer?)]

R: When you read these instructions do you understand right away what it says in Spanish or when you read them do you think words in English?

Peter: I try and get them into English, so I can understand them a little bit better. OK. Now I think this one might be plus. [He reads the problem aloud in Spanish, then continues.] *Sue está aquí, cinquenta y quatro, uno, dos, tres . . . cinquenta . . . OK. ¿Cuánto tiempo . . .?* [Sue is here, 54, 1, 2, 3 . . . 50 . . . OK. How long?] How many minutes? Three times many minutes than Sue . . . whoa. OK. 54 times 3.

He then set up the problem like this:

$$\begin{array}{r} 54 \\ \times\,3 \\ \hline 162 \end{array}$$

R: What were you thinking before you went 'OK'?

P: I was thinking that Sue, right there, 54; it says three times more . . . than Sue. So, three times four, twelve. Three times five, fifteen six. A hundred and sixty-two.

In this problem, Peter began solving the problem in Spanish, but ran into a problem and then switched to English.

Karen reported using English according to the difficulty of the vocabulary, the time of day, and peer group language use at the moment. She was an example of a learner who switched freely, but still preferred to use English:

R: Do you do math in Spanish or English?

Karen: The teacher talks to us all the time in Spanish and we have to answer her in Spanish, but usually when I'm just doing it, I'll just speak in English . . . usually . . . It depends upon the time of day, and what the people around me are thinking, because I have them [words] all memorised in both languages. If, like, the environment around me is speaking Spanish, then it'll just happen in Spanish . . .

K: [Going over a math worksheet] I am doing it in English because the math is kind of hard . . . Also, I've been speaking English most of the day so it just goes along with that. But when I read the directions, it just came in Spanish . . . Sometimes I know words about math in Spanish that I don't know in English . . . it feels kind of weird to know a word in Spanish but not in English.

Karen discovered these gaps in her technical English vocabulary when trying to explain something to her parents at home. Again, on a worksheet converting from decimals to fractions, she appeared to be performing the cognitive operations in English. At one point she explained a math problem to a peer in Spanish, but mostly they interacted with each other in English, even regarding task-related activities.

R: What language do you do this word problem in?

K: . . . since it's a word problem in Spanish, I would translate it. And maybe do the numbers in Spanish . . . [With reference to some math problems from the day before that she thought were kind of hard:] Well, this one I do . . . actually I usually do these hard ones in English, because they're really difficult. [With respect to an easy problem:] This one I did in Spanish, because it was really simple, and there was no vocabulary at all, hardly.

R: [With regard to a geometry worksheet:] What language do you do this in?

K: Ah, that's hard. I usually go to English. It's not that the vocabulary's hard to understand – but the whole project . . . it's kind of easier to think in English because it comes easier – say, GD [line segment].

Donna read the word problem in Spanish and then reported thinking through the problem in English, as did other pupils. What she added was a sociolinguistic justification for reverting to English – the fact that English is the language of wider communication in the community at large:

R: Do you know the words for subtract and divide in Spanish?

Donna: . . . it's like a whole 'nother language, the math is. I usually use English vocabulary words. Sometimes I'll use Spanish ones . . . I mean, sure I've been in a Spanish school, and all, but, you just, the environment I live in, it's not like we speak Spanish there. So, I'm adapted to English more, than in Spanish, so it's easier just to switch to English.

Discussion

The qualitative findings indicated that the full immersion students used their native language more than the target language in solving math problems, especially word problems. In their self-reports and their introspective and retrospective verbal reports, processing in Spanish began by their reading a word problem silently or out loud, followed by either (1) on-line translation to English before solving the problem, or (2) continuation in Spanish until or unless a conceptual problem was encountered. Whereas it might seem obvious that the learners had to read the problem in Spanish in order to access the task, alternatives did exist, such as asking the teacher or another student to explain it in English. However, it appears that the pupils did need to have fairly good Spanish reading skills in order to gain access to the task. In some cases (especially with multiple-choice items), the context may have cued how the numbers were to be manipulated, but such shortcuts did not reveal themselves in these data.[10]

These results lend some support to the popular belief that people think in their native language when they do math, regardless of communicative require-ments. But this popular belief is at best simplistic when dealing with non-native subjects who are nonetheless taught math in the foreign language from an early age. Thus, the subjects needed to have fairly good Spanish reading skills. On the other hand, a major advantage of a full immersion programme is that the students learn to perform rapid, on-line translation so that they can think through in English a word problem written in the target language. The data indicate that this pattern of translation is quite common. One reason why partial immersion pupils have been found to be less successful at math than full immersion pupils (see Swain, 1984: 91) may be that they translate math concepts into the native language with less success.

Studies in natural translation (i.e. translation by untrained bilingual children) have suggested what characteristics make a fourth- or fifth-grade bilingual youngster a good translator (Malakoff, 1992). Malakoff purposely assigned pupils translation tasks involving ambiguity and word/sentence segmentation where the native- and foreign-language patterns were at odds.

The main factor contributing to successful translation appeared to be that of metalinguistic awareness – the ability to step back from the comprehension or production of an utterance in order to consider the linguistic form and structure underlying the meaning. Thus, the less facility a young bilingual has with the target language, the more unnatural their translating will be.

Some comments about the present research methodology are in order. The main source of data came from verbal report protocols. Since the research assistants were all native English speakers, it would be beneficial to replicate the study using either all native Spanish speakers or a combination of native English and native Spanish speakers. Thus, it would be possible to determine the effect of the researchers on the results.

Also with regard to cognitive processing, this paper assumes that if a pupil used Spanish or English in think-aloud or introspective data, cognitive operations were going on in the same language. Lantolf (personal communication, 13 May, 1994) points out that this may not be the case. In other words, the verbal report may take place in Spanish while the cognitive operation is actually in English. In this study, the subjects could choose whether to report in Spanish, given that only one of the two researchers spoke competent Spanish. Still, it was possible that respondents' self-reports did not match what they were actually doing.

On the other hand, the most convincing data are the self-reports regarding what the respondents 'tend to do'. Repeatedly, they reported tending to use English for a variety of school tasks, especially for cognitive processing of math. If accurate, this may help to explain why full immersion pupils in the Twin Cities (and elsewhere) continue to have gaps in oral and written production in the foreign language, even after as long as seven years.

Thus, the internal language environment of the pupils is not as intensively foreign-language oriented as an observer might think. Most research conclusions are based largely on observational investigation of the *external* language environment, which seems impressively filled with the foreign language discourse of teachers and pupils. Yet an accurate picture may be more consistent with the findings from this study – that there is an underground of English-language use, out of earshot of the teacher, in pupil working groups, and most importantly, in the pupils' minds, where teachers and course materials do not tread. As one fourth-grade student, Bill, put it:

> You usually think that in an immersion school, it's totally in Spanish. If you get caught speaking English, you'll like be in trouble, but that's not really what it is. I mean, you're always thinking in English. I mean they can't really stop you from thinking in English. You can think Spanish, you can act Spanish, you can doing everything in Spanish, but you're really not a Mexican.

This resistance to being *too* immersed may be a sociolinguistic inevitability, especially for immersion programmes where potential contact with native speakers of the immersion language is limited. However, there may be ways to enhance the role of the foreign language in the internal language environment. For example, it may be possible for teachers to think out loud as they do math problems, as if they were fifth or sixth graders and not speedy adults. Perhaps the pupils need to hear and internalise more of the carrier language of cognitive processing in the foreign language. With regard to the solving of math word problems in the native language, for example, Wheatley (1991) makes the point that learners need to learn how to carry on a scientific discussion internally with class discussion as a starting point: 'It is through class discussions that students learn to conduct this internal dialogue. By continuing the conversation within ourselves we begin to act mathematically' (Wheatley, 1991: 19). The same principle could apply to solving math problems in a second or foreign language. Just as a profile of problem areas in the specialised register of mathematics (at the lexical, structural and discourse levels) has been developed for ESL students (Spanos, Rhodes, Dale & Crandall, 1988), so it would be possible to do the same for Spanish and for other languages.

Restructuring the immersion programme somewhat may put a higher premium on thinking in the foreign language. At present, for example, the same Twin Cities teacher who teaches in the foreign language must drop that guise and teach English and other subjects in English as of grade 2. A structural change would place teachers in *either* the English or Spanish portions of the curriculum. One important purpose of the kind of research that is reported here is to gain insights for coaching both learners and teachers, and for providing insights for administrators about the functioning of the programme.

All of these measures presuppose that more native-like language production skills are desirable for speaking and writing in the foreign language. One argument for this is that these skills enhance the language ability of learners in the job market. Another perspective considers children's maintenance of native-language abilities and native-language access to content subjects during later transitions. The present study may help to suggest why it is that immersion children do not seem to fall behind children in the regular school curriculum.

Notes

1. Paper prepared for presentation at the Irish Association for Applied Linguistics Conference, Dublin, 24–25 June, 1994.

Acknowledgements go to the former Principal of the Adams School, Dr Luz María Serrano, for consenting to the study, as well as to the teachers, Jane Berg, Lori Dragert, Rafael Manrique, Elizabeth Tabbot and Concha Fernández, and to the pupils for their extensive cooperation. Without the efforts of the research assistants – Jim Parker, Shirley Heitzman, Karen Moline, Amy Fjerstad and Lisa Babbs – the research would have been impossible. The verbal report protocols collected by Parker and Heitzman formed the data base for this paper. Thanks also to those colleagues who constructively commented on earlier versions: Jim Lantolf, Elaine Tarone, Dick Tucker, Merrill Swain and Wally Lambert. Finally, thanks to Lee Searles who edited the paper for this volume.

2. Furthermore, feedback to learners in the form of implicit or explicit correction of their deviant utterances was observed to be inconsistent and infrequent (Swain & Carroll, 1987; Swain, 1988).
3. Actually, the verbal component of thinking can be either silent, subvocal, or aloud, with regard to either inner or social speech. Inner speech tends not to be externalised, although it may sometimes be prompted. In other words, when asked to think aloud, learners may have inner speech as part of their data – i.e. verbalised thoughts not intended for others.
4. Mestre notes that target language proficiency may mediate the learning not just of technical language but also symbolic language (e.g. knowing that '$2 > x > 8$' is not grammatical).
5. Subtests included: reading (reading comprehension, vocabulary, study skills), language (grammar, capitalisation, spelling, punctuation) and mathematics (math computation, math problem solving).
6. Subtests included: vocabulary, reading comprehension, mechanics, usage, spelling, mathematics (computation, concepts, problem solving), reference materials, social studies and science.
7. For example, the following phrase from math problem #30 is an example of literal translation from English. The sentence, *Teri usó la computadora 3 veces más minutos que Sue*, is a literal translation from English, 'Terry used the computer three times more minutes than Sue'. *En minutos, Teri usó la computadora 3 veces más que Sue* [In minutes . . .] would reflect a more Spanish-like phrasing and word order.
8. Note that a usual verbal report contains elements of all three approaches, but that respondents were encouraged to do less self-report and more relating to specific thoughts about tasks currently being or just recently executed.
9. She had studied Spanish during her 10th-grade year in high school.
10. Test-wise respondents on the SATs and other standardised tests for older students have indicated that they will avoid reading through all the verbiage in a word problem if they perceive relationships between numbers in the problem that match up with some multiple-choice alternative.

References

Cohen, A.D. (1987) Using verbal reports in research on language learning. In C. Faerch and G. Kasper (eds) *Introspection in Second Language Research* (pp. 82–95). Clevedon, England: Multilingual Matters.

— (1991) Feedback on writing: The use of verbal report. *Studies in Second Language Acquisition* 13(2), 133–59.

Cohen, A.D. and Lebach, S. (1974) A language experiment in California: Student, teacher, parent, and community reactions after three years. *Workpapers in Teaching English as a Second Language* (pp. 33–46). Los Angeles: University of California at Los Angeles.

Cohen, A.D. and Swain, M. (1979) Bilingual education: The 'immersion' model in the North American context. In J.B. Pride (ed.) *Sociolinguistic Aspects of Language Learning and Teaching* (pp. 144–51). Oxford: Oxford University Press.

Cohen, A.D. and Olshtain, E. (1993) The production of speech acts by EFL learners. *TESOL Quarterly* 27(1), 33–56.

Cummins, D.D., Kintsch, W., Reusser, K. and Weimer, R. (1988) The role of understanding in solving word problems. *Cognitive Psychology* 20, 405–38.

Cummins, J. (1991) Conversational and academic language proficiency in bilingual contexts. *AILA Review* 8, 75–89.

Garner, R. (1987) *Metacognition and Reading Comprehension*. Norwood, NJ: Ablex.

Genesee, F. (1987) *Learning through Two Languages*. Rowley, MA: Newbury House.

Harley, B., Allen, P., Cummins, J. and Swain, M. (1990) *The Development of Second Language Proficiency*. Cambridge: Cambridge University Press.

Lapkin, S., Swain, M. and Shapson, S. (1990) French immersion research agenda for the 90s. *The Canadian Modern Language Review* 46(4), 636–74.

Malakoff, M.E. (1992) Translation ability: A natural bilingual and metalinguistic skill. In R.J. Harris (ed.) *Cognitive Processing in Bilinguals* (pp. 515–29). Amsterdam: North-Holland.

Mestre, J.P. (1988) The role of language comprehension in mathematics and problem solving. In R.R. Cocking and J.P. Mestre (eds) *Linguistic and Cultural Influences on Learning Mathematics* (pp. 201–20). Hillsdale, NJ: Lawrence Erlbaum.

Riverside Publ. Co. (1964) *La Prueba Riverside de Realización en Español*. Circle Pines, MN: RPC.

Science Research Associates (1985) *SRA Survey of Basic Skills*. Chicago: SRA.

Shrum, J.L. and Glisan, E.W. (1994) *Teacher's Handbook: Contextualised Language*. Boston: Heinle & Heinle.

Spanos, G., Rhodes, N., Dale, T.C. and Crandall, J.A. (1988) Linguistic features of mathematical problem solving: Insights and applications. In R.R. Cocking and J.P. Mestre (eds) *Linguistic and Cultural Influences on Learning Mathematics*. Hillsdale, NJ: Lawrence Erlbaum.

Swain, M. (1984) A review of immersion education in Canada: Research and evaluation studies. In California State Department of Education, *Studies on Immersion Education* (pp. 87–112). Sacramento, CA: Office of Bilingual Bicultural Education, California State Department of Education.

— (1988) Manipulating and complementing content teaching to maximise second language learning. *TESL Canada Journal* 6, 68–83.

— (1992) The output hypothesis: A search for empirical evidence in a classroom second language acquisition context. *Description of Research Program submitted to the Canadian Government and Funded*. Toronto: Modern Language Centre, OISE.

Swain, M. and Carroll, S. (1987) The immersion observation study. In B. Harley, P. Allen, J. Cummins and M. Swain (eds) *The Development of Bilingual Proficiency: Final Report, Vol. II* (pp. 190–263). Toronto: Modern Language Centre, OISE.

Vygotsky, L.S. (1961) Thought and speech. In S. Saporta (ed.) *Psycholinguistics* (pp. 509–37). NY: Holt, Rinehart & Winston.

Wheatley, G.H. (1991) Constructivist perspectives on science and mathematics learning. *Science Education* 75(1), 9–21.

22 Topic and Language Activity in Teaching Irish at Sixth Grade in Primary School: A Classroom Observation Study

JOHN HARRIS and LELIA MURTAGH

Introduction

National surveys of achievement in spoken Irish conducted by ITÉ (Institiúid Teangeolaíochta Éireann/Linguistics Institute of Ireland) and the Curriculum Unit of the Department of Education over the last decade and a half have established the extent to which the objectives of the curriculum in Irish are being attained in ordinary primary schools (Harris, 1984; Harris & Murtagh, 1988). Because surveys require the sampling and testing of large numbers of pupils, however, they have to be confined to relatively narrow aspects of pupil performance. In addition, they tend to be limited to questionnaire-type data on teaching processes and practices. In order to overcome some of the problems associated with the survey approach, therefore, we decided to carry out a more focused study (Harris & Murtagh, 1991, 1995). This involved selecting a relatively small number of diverse classes to represent the broad range of linguistic, social and educational conditions under which spoken Irish is taught at present. A series of new instruments were then developed to measure a number of aspects of the teaching and learning of Irish which had hitherto been overlooked.

One of these is a classroom observation instrument, the Irish Lesson Analysis System (ILAS). In the present paper we present data from ILAS relating to topic and language activity in Irish language lessons at sixth grade in primary school. We also report a preliminary comparison of the Irish results with the results of a Scottish study of French language teaching at first year post-primary – the 'Stirling Study' (Mitchell, Parkinson & Johnstone, 1981).

It will be useful to begin with a sketch of the teaching of Irish. Excluding 'all-Irish' (immersion) and *Gaeltacht* (Irish speaking area) schools, all other children study Irish (in the vast majority of cases their second language) as a subject from the beginning of primary school, at approximately four years of age. Thus, by sixth grade (at approximately 12 years of age), they have had eight years of exposure to Irish as a school subject. The mainly audio-visual *Nuachúrsaí* or 'New Courses' (Ireland: Department of Education, 1978) provide the basis for the teaching of spoken Irish in the vast majority of these 'ordinary' primary schools. In recent years, courses developed by commercial publishers and others have become more common. Most estimates suggest that about an hour a day is spent teaching Irish – including speaking, reading and writing (Harris & Murtagh, 1988). Questionnaire data indicate that Irish is widely used as a means of routine classroom communication and, in addition, that about one fifth of classes in ordinary schools are taught some other aspect of the curriculum, such as music or physical education, through Irish (Harris & Murtagh, 1988).

In contrast to this language-learning situation, the Stirling Study involved post-primary students who presumably had only recently begun to study French as a foreign language. In addition, all students in the Stirling Study had followed a particular audio-visual course, while the children in the various Irish classes in the present study were taught using a range of courses.

Sample

The intention was to select 20 sixth-grade primary school classes that would represent the full range of social, educational and linguistic conditions under which Irish is taught at present. Among those selected were schools in disadvantaged areas; schools in areas with a predominantly urban working class population; schools using different methods and courses (audio-visual *Nuachúrsaí*; more communicatively oriented courses; and traditional aural/oral 'ABC' methods); schools in which there is a substantial amount of Irish-medium teaching or classroom communication in Irish; schools where there is a particularly high level of involvement or interest on the part of the parents in the teaching of Irish or in the school generally. Apart from these requirements, we also sought a geographical spread of classes, covering the major regions of the country, and including both urban and rural locations. Ideally, we hoped the characteristics of the 20 classes selected (n = 533 pupils) would not depart too radically from the picture nationally in terms of important variables such as achievement in spoken Irish, pupil general ability and social-class composition. In the event, the achievement in spoken Irish of the pupils as a whole, based on the results of an objective test, turned out to be only marginally lower than the national average (Harris & Murtagh, 1991).

Instrument

The ILAS is an adaptation of the Stirling System developed by Mitchell *et al.* (1981). Central to the Stirling System and to the ILAS adaptation of it is the notion of a lesson segment. Most teachers conceptualise the language class as being composed of distinctive teaching units or events (such as 'drilling', 'repetition', etc.). The segment is designed to correspond to these 'naturalistic' teaching units. In formal terms, it is defined as a stretch of lesson discourse, having a particular topic, and involving the participants (teacher and pupils) in a distinctive configuration of roles, linguistic and organisational (Mitchell *et al.*, 1981; Mitchell, 1988). Each segment lasts for a minimum of 30 seconds and typically for between one and 10 minutes. Segment boundaries will often be indicated by 'framing' moves, for example where the teacher uses markers such as 'Right', '*Anois*' (now), '*Ciúnas*' (quiet), etc. and 'focusing' moves, e.g. 'Put away your books, please', '*Tá go maith*' (all right), etc. (Sinclair & Coulthard, 1975).

In practice, segments are defined in terms of five main dimensions of analysis: *Topic, Language activity, Pupil behaviour, Teacher mode of involvement* and *Classroom organisation*. For each of these five dimensions, the Stirling System defines a set of categories. In the case of *Language activity*, for example, there are categories such as 'Translation', 'Imitation', 'Drills'. Each segment identified in the lesson discourse is allocated to one or more category on each of the five dimensions. Whenever a change of categorisation occurs on any dimension, a new segment is considered to have begun. We leave aside for the purposes of the present paper a number of other dimensions coded in ILAS (e.g. class attention) which have no equivalent in the Stirling System (see Harris & Murtagh, 1995).

Two Irish lessons were observed in each school. The observation covered all aspects of the Irish lesson – oral/conversational Irish, Irish reading and Irish writing. The work was carried out by primary school inspectors of the Department of Education. As the lesson progressed, the Observer identified the main segments of classroom activity (or of the lesson), recording the real starting time of each segment and then coding each segment on the eight dimensions using a short form of ILAS. The Observer also made an audio tape-recording of each of the lessons.

The present authors subsequently used these tapes to recode the lessons based on a more detailed version of ILAS. Our recoding, however, relied in important ways on the in-class work done by the Observers. We were able to relate the Observers' notes, record of segment starting times, and ratings of attention and interest to our own segmentation based on the tapes. The recodings were carried out a number of times, with the authors working first jointly, then independently, until no disagreements regarding segmentation and assignation to categories remained. The data which are presented here are all based on our recoding of 39 of the 40 lessons – the recording failed in the case of one lesson. Full details are provided in Harris & Murtagh (1995).

In the present paper, we can only provide a very brief description of the Stirling System itself and of our modifications to it. In the case of the two dimensions on which we focus, 'topic' and 'language activity', we provide a short summary of the main ILAS categories, indicating with an * which categories depart from the Stirling System. It should be noted that some of the category descriptions in ILAS run to nearly a page, if examples are included. A number of categories which apply to very small proportions of segments are listed only as titles due to lack of space. It scarcely needs to be said that no assessment of the original Stirling System should be made on the basis of the summary description of ILAS categories here – the Mitchell *et al.* (1981) report should be consulted.

Topic

The topic categories of ILAS describe 'what is being talked about' and range over situations deriving from different course books, as well as aspects of lesson content which research suggests are important, e.g. topics related to pupil/teacher real life, Irish life, culture and music, the linguistics/structure of Irish itself, and routine class management. The topic dimension in ILAS was divided into eight categories, compared to twelve in the Stirling System. Thus, the single category 'Linguistic notions/grammar of Irish' in ILAS spans three corresponding narrower categories in the Stirling System: 'General linguistic notions', 'Language points (course)' and 'Language points (other)'. In the rest of the paper we follow Mitchell *et al.*'s (1981) practice of using the term 'Metalinguistic' to refer to the latter three topic categories combined.

- *Situation: Nuachúrsaí*:* The discourse directly concerns a situation narrated or presented in Step A (Bunchomhrá) of the audio-visual *Nuachúrsaí* handbooks.
- *Situation: Other than Nuachúrsaí*:* The discourse concerns specific third party situations and stories from sources other than that defined in the immediately preceding category – e.g. from other course books, or from the teacher herself/himself.

- *Situation: pupil/teacher real life:* The discourse concerns aspects of the pupils' and teacher's life and interests, including home and school life, and including narrative material which directly relates to the personal experiences of the participants in the discourse.
- *Fragmented/non-contextualised*:* The discourse is incoherent, consisting of a series of propositions with no obvious situational relationship between them. The unity and coherence of the discourse does not rest in the content but in formal aspects of the language being practised.
- *Routine management/organisation:* The discourse concerns classroom management and organisation (e.g. discipline; setting homework).
- *Linguistic notions/grammar of Irish*:* The discourse concerns the nature of language in general, possible ways of analysing it, explicit analytical discussion of particular grammatical structures or semantic notions.

The two remaining categories are *Feedback/discussing pupils' performance* and *Irish life, culture and music*.*

Language activity

The *language-activity* dimension was designed to investigate the range of language activities planned and directed by the teacher (including pupil demonstrations where control temporarily passes to a pupil or group of pupils). The categories were designed to capture some of the different kinds of linguistic and communicative experience which, on the basis of current theoretical understanding, appear to be particularly important for learning Irish or any second language.

A major distinction within the categories of *Language Activity* relates to language practice versus communication. Language-practice categories involve the use of Irish primarily to give learners training in the manipulation of the language – the transmission of messages is incidental. In the case of real communication, in contrast, the focus of attention is on meaning and on the message being transmitted. Simulated communication might be thought of as intermediate between language practice and real communication.

- *Comprehension*:* This category includes all Irish language practice discourse realised in a single code, which originates from a non-pupil speaker, and to which no pupil contribution (apart from responses to comprehension checks) is expected.
- *Imitation:* Irish practice discourse where pupils' utterances imitative of previously-provided Irish models are expected. The focus of attention is on Irish phonological or orthographic form.
- *Transposition:* Irish practice discourse where utterances are simultaneously realised in both written and spoken codes, and where the focus of attention is on the relationship between them (includes reading aloud, and dictation).

- *Contextualisation exercise*:* Irish practice discourse with an expected component of pupil utterances, where the focus is on the appropriacy of utterances to their discourse context. The information being transmitted is typically known, and there may therefore be non-structural constraints on pupil utterances (e.g. getting the story line right). Discourse in this category will not exhibit the systematic structural regularities which are typical of drills.
- *Drills: Structural/vocabulary/pronunciation/spelling*:* Irish practice discourse in one code which has an expected component of pupil utterances, and which is structurally constrained beyond the rules of normal discourse. The focus of attention is primarily on syntactic form. Non-imitative vocabulary, pronunciation and spelling tasks are also included.
- *Simulated communication in Irish (No direct equivalent in the Stirling System)*:* Irish discourse which has the outer form of real communication but where the underlying concern is with contextualised realistic language practice rather than with the message for its own sake. The discourse superficially adheres to the rules of normal discourse (oral or written) but may not be truly open ended, and the pupil may not speak from a really 'personal' self. Unlike real communication, where the emphasis is on pupils conveying a message as clearly and accurately as possible within the limits of their linguistic ability, pupils engaged in 'simulated communication' may alter the 'story line' or the intended content of their utterances in order to accommodate the strengths and weaknesses in their own knowledge of the language. At the same time, 'simulated communication' does imply that the pupil makes some creative contribution and that some element of meaning negotiation is involved.
- *Real communication in Irish (at least 80% of discourse is in Irish)*:* Irish discourse in which messages are being transmitted and in which the focus of attention is on the meaning of what is being said.
- *Compound:* This category covers all discourse in which distinct exchanges relating to more than one of the other eleven language activity categories, but each shorter than 30 seconds, occur in complex sequences.

The remaining categories are *Translation, Real communication in English (L1), Bilingual real communication*, Bilingual simulated communication** and *Irish song/poem*.*

Results and Discussion

The 39 Irish lessons observed here amounted to over 42 hours of teaching time (excluding breaks etc.) and contained 828 segments. The mean duration of segments was three minutes and three seconds, a little shorter than reported by Mitchell *et al*. (1981) in their observational study of French foreign language lessons (three minutes, 12 seconds). Durations ranged from 30 seconds up to four minutes for about 75% of the segments in the Irish lessons.

Topic

Table 22.1 shows the percentage of segments in each category of the Topic dimension over all lessons. More than half of all 828 lesson segments (51.1%) were classified as 'Situation: other than *Nuachúrsaí*'. This is more than six times that in the nearest corresponding category ('Situation: other course') in the Stirling Study (7.7% of all segments). The fact that 'Situation: other than *Nuachúrsaí*' should account for so many segments in the Irish study, however, indicates the need for more differentiated categories in this dimension, e.g. at the very least topics from 'other' coursebooks/workbooks should be in a separate category from situations described or set up by the teachers themselves. It is possible that some of this difference in topic emphasis between the two studies can be accounted for in terms of the fact that classes in the Stirling Study followed a specific audio-visual course whereas the Irish classes used a wider variety of courses. Table 22.1 shows that only one tenth of all lesson segments in the Irish study have topics associated with the *Nuachúrsaí* audio-visual course ('Situation: *Nuachúrsaí*': 10.9%). Mitchell reports, in contrast, that the proportion of lesson segments which had topics deriving from the recommended audio-visual French course approached one-third (31.9%).

Table 22.1 Percentage distribution of lesson segments and mean segment duration by topic

Topic	Total:	*Percentage of segments* *(n = 828)*	*Mean segment duration (mins:secs)* *(3:03)*
Situation: Other than *Nuachúrsaí*		51.1	3:08
Fragmented/non contextualised		19.8	3:01
Situation: *Nuachúrsaí*		10.9	4:04
Pupil/teacher real life situations		8.7	3:15
Routine management/organisation		6.2	1:04
Linguistics/grammar of Irish		2.2	1:48
Irish life/culture/music		0.6	1:33
Feedback/discussing pupil performance		0.6	2:28
	Total:	100%	—

More importantly the data relating to these two categories in Table 22.1 indicate that while primarily course-related topics ('Situation: Other than *Nuachúrsaí* or 'Situation: *Nuachúrsaí*') account for almost two-thirds of all segments in the Irish lessons, equivalent topic categories account for only two-fifths of all segments in the French lessons. The difference is made up in the Stirling Study by higher proportions of segments being devoted to three topic categories: 'Routine procedures', 'Metalinguistic' and 'Civilisation'. While these three topic categories account for 26.5% of French lesson segments, data in Table 22.1 show that in all only 9% of Irish lesson segments are assigned to equivalent topic categories ('Routine management/organisation' – 6.2%; 'Linguistics/grammar of Irish' – 2.2%; and 'Irish life/culture/music' – 0.6%).

An additional point here is that in the Stirling Study, the French lesson segments associated with the three topic categories just mentioned overwhelmingly involved the use of the student's native language, English. While lower proportions of segments are associated with the equivalent topic categories in the Irish study, crosstabulations with language activity data (not shown here) reveal that the discourse involved is in Irish rather than in the children's native language, English. The greatest difference between the two studies in these three topic categories relates to 'Linguistics/grammar of Irish' (2.2%) and the corresponding 'Metalinguistic' topic category (12.3%) in the Stirling study. There are a number of factors which could account for this difference. One possibility is that because pupils in the Irish study begin instruction in Irish at a young age and continue the learning/acquisition process over a relatively long period, it is possible to transmit metalinguistic concepts and distinctions in a more gradual and indirect way – by illustration and by informally drawing attention to significant linguistic patterns in the context of drills etc. If this assumption is correct, it means that direct discussion and explanation of metalinguistic issues, either in Irish or English, is rarely necessary. In contrast, because the students in the Stirling Study presumably began French instruction only on entry to post-primary school, direct explanation and discussion of certain metalinguistic issues may have been judged to be a faster and more efficient route to competence in the language than a more distributed process of illustration and attention-focusing. Needless to say our results here do not allow us either to assess the merits of the two strategies, or to say whether these hypothesised strategies have any basis in fact.

There was a closer degree of correspondence between the present Irish study and the Stirling Study in the proportion of segments allocated to the three remaining topic categories: 'Fragmented/non contextualised', 'Pupil/teacher real life' and 'Feedback/discussing pupil performance'. A fifth of all

Irish lesson discourse had no coherent topic ('Fragmented/non-contextualised': 19.8%), slightly lower than the proportion in the Stirling Study (22.5%). Topics relating to 'Pupil/teacher real life' situations account for 8.7% of the discourse in the case of the Irish lessons compared to 9.4% in the Stirling Study. 'Feedback/discussing pupil performance' accounts for less than 2% of segments in both the Irish and Stirling studies.

Language activity

Table 22.2 shows the proportion of Irish lesson segments associated with each of the language activity categories of ILAS. Before discussing these data in detail it may be useful to note that the Irish lessons had higher proportions of segments associated with each of the first five language activity categories than had the Stirling Study (i.e. 'Contextualisation exercises' through 'Simulated communication in Irish'). Compensating for this, higher proportions of segments in the Stirling Study compared to the Irish study are associated with each of the remaining language activity categories ('Imitation' through 'Translation'). We leave aside for purposes of the present discussion the three small categories at the bottom of Table 22.2 which have no direct equivalent in the Stirling Study.

Table 22.2 Percentage distribution of lesson segments and mean segment duration by language activity

Language activity	Total:	Percentage of segments (n = 828)	Mean segment duration (mins:secs) (3:03)
Contextualisation exercises		32.7	3:31
Drills		15.2	3:39
Real communication in Irish		12.6	1:40
Transposition (read aloud/dictation)		12.1	2:41
Simulated communication in Irish†		9.3	4:40
Imitation (repeat/copy write)		5.8	2:33
Comprehension		4.7	1:55
Compound (regular cycles of activities)		1.9	2:41
Real communication in English (L1)		1.6	1:35
Translation		0.8	1:27
Irish song/poem†		1.9	1:07
Bilingual real communication†		1.2	1:23
Bilingual simulated communication†		0.1	8:10
	Total:	100%	—

† No direct equivalent in the Stirling system

The first five language activity categories listed in Table 22.2 account for 81.9% of the Irish lesson segments, while equivalent categories account for not much more than half that proportion of segments in the French lessons (43.8%). Looking at the first two rows in Table 22.2, it may be seen that 32.7% of the Irish lesson segments involve 'Contextualisation exercises' and 15.2% involve 'Drills' – making 47.9% in all. In the Stirling Study only 34% of segments were assigned to the corresponding language activity 'Drill/ exercise' (a broader category which approximates our 'Drills' and 'Contextualisation exercises' combined).

'Simulated Communication in Irish' accounts for 9.3% of segments. It will be recalled that there was no category directly corresponding to this one in the Stirling System. In the Stirling System, discourse of this type might have been included in the 'exercise' component of the 'Drill/exercise' category, or perhaps even in the 'Real FL', though this is really no more than supposition. It may also be noted in Table 22.2 that 'Simulated communication' segments tend to be rather long in duration, running to over four and a half minutes on average.

The data for 'Real communication in Irish' (12.6%) indicate a much greater emphasis in the Irish study than in the Stirling study (only 1.8% of segments) on using the target language for communicating messages. Data on mean segment duration in the second column of Table 22.2 show, in addition, that 'Real communication in Irish' segments are shorter than segments associated with the other language activity categories. Looking back to Table 22.1 for a moment, it can be seen that, of all the topic categories, 'Routine management/organisation' is the one associated with the shortest segments. Cross-tabulations reveal that 'Real communication in Irish' is the language activity involved in four-fifths of the segments in this relatively small topic category. 'Real communication' in this context usually means the teacher giving brief instructions in Irish in the course of organising the class for the next activity – e.g. instructing pupils to take out a specific book and to open it a specific page. 'Real communication' is also the language activity involved in about one-quarter of the segments falling into the somewhat larger 'Pupil/teacher real life' topic category.

Mitchell et al. (1981) likewise report a tendency for 'Real FL' segments in their study to be associated with these same two topic categories and, again, to be relatively short in duration – though, as we noted above, the proportion of such 'Real FL' segments is quite low in the Stirling Study. If we add the proportion of segments devoted to 'Simulated communication in Irish' and 'Real communication in Irish', we can estimate that about one-fifth of all Irish lesson segments involve some kind of communication broadly defined.

'Transposition' activities accounted for 12.1% of all segments in the Irish study compared to 7.4% in the Stirling study. Crosstabulations reveal that practically all 'transposition' activities in the Irish lessons involve 'reading aloud'.

We turn now to the five remaining language activity categories which have direct equivalents in the Irish and Stirling Studies: 'Imitation', 'Comprehension', 'Compound' 'Real communication in English' and 'Translation'. These categories account for only 14.8% of segments altogether in the Irish study, compared to more than half of all the French lesson segments (56.2%) in the Stirling Study. 'Real communication in English' is involved in only 1.6% of segments in the Irish study, in marked contrast to the Stirling Study where over one-fifth (21.3%) of all segments involve English. 'Translation' features hardly at all in the Irish lessons (less than 1% of segments) whereas it occurs in 10.6% of the French lesson segments. And 'Imitation', an important component of audio-visual lessons, only accounts for 5.8% of segments in Irish, just half the proportion for the same category in the Stirling Study (12.3%). This latter difference reflects presumably the greater emphasis on the audio-visual approach in the French lessons. The other two language activity categories 'Comprehension' (4.7%) and 'Compound' (1.9%) are each a few percentage points lower in the Irish study than in the Stirling Study.

Conclusion

An important advantage of lesson analysis systems based on segments is that teachers and others involved in language teaching appear to use such units themselves in conceptualising the process. As language teaching practices change in response to new research findings and theoretical developments, therefore, it seems only sensible that one goal of classroom second language acquisition research should be to document the impact of such changes at the level of lesson segments. In the present study, we have shown how the descriptive categories applied to segments can be revised in order to take account of new theoretical insights and teaching approaches (e.g. the creation of the new category 'simulated communication in Irish'). We have also shown how such systems might be used to identify pedagogic similarities and differences between second and foreign language programmes.

Acknowledgements

We are greatly indebted to the teachers and pupils who participated in this study. The ILAS was adapted from the Stirling System by kind permission of Rosamond Mitchell and her co-authors.

References

Harris, J. (1984) *Spoken Irish in Primary Schools.* Dublin: Institiúid Teangeolaíochta Éireann.
Harris, J. and Murtagh, L. (1988) National assessment of Irish language speaking and listening skills in primary-school children: Research issues in the evaluation of school-based heritage language programmes. *Language, Culture and Curriculum* 1(2), 85–130.
— (1991) Scéim Phíolótach i dteagasc na Gaeilge sa Bhunscoil. Report: Part 1. The contribution of pupils and parents to achievement in spoken Irish. Unpublished report submitted to the Department of Education, April 1991.
— (1995) An observational study of the Irish language classroom in primary school. (Provisional title. In preparation.)
Ireland: Department of Education (1978) *Lá Faoin Tuath/Sean Neidí: Cúrsa Comhrá Gaeilge le hAghaidh Ranganna Sinsearacha.* Dublin: Oifig an tSoláthair.
Mitchell, R., Parkinson, B. and Johnstone, R. (1981) *The Foreign Language Classroom: An Observational Study.* Stirling Educational Monographs No. 9. Department of Education, University of Stirling.
Mitchell, R. (1988) *Communicative Language Teaching in Practice.* London: Centre for Information on Language Teaching and Research.
Sinclair, J.McH. and Coulthard, R.M. (1975) *Towards an Analysis of Discourse.* London: Oxford University Press.

23 Databases – a Useful Tool for Language Teachers to Better Meet the Diverse Needs of Modern Learners

EDITH BUCHHOLZ and ANTJE DÜSTERHÖFT

Introduction

Computerised information retrieval systems can aid teachers and learners in selecting the best learning material for specific learner needs within seconds. Databases are a rapidly growing computer tool that is spreading to ever more common spheres of application. There is an increasing demand for them in almost all professions. Scientists of all sorts, general practitioners, dentists, supermarkets, storehouses, shops, not to mention industries of all kinds control their goods and processes by means of databases.

The amount of information which is still stored on cards, in card indexes, catalogues, bibliographies, thesauri, lists, etc. will, in the not too distant future, be stored in and handled by computers in database management systems. Database management systems, mostly called databases for short, form an ever-increasing part of software and are an area where the PC may in future be largely employed.

Schools will not only have databases of rooms, teachers, subjects, time-tables in order to create the curricula and timetables for each teacher, room, class, and for the whole school two or three times per term or year, but teachers will also want to find, or to store themselves, information on their teaching material, their teaching goals and how to achieve them, they will want to have a database of additional material for the eager student or just for themselves.

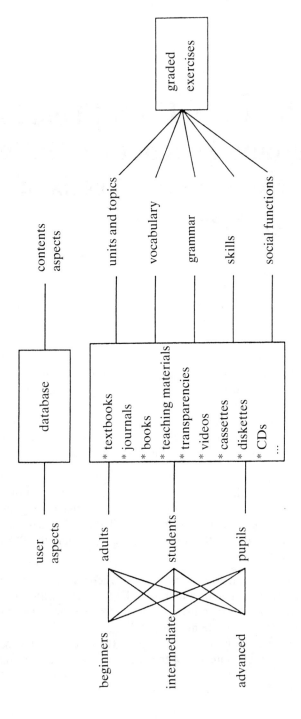

Figure 23.1 Databases for teachers

Databases of this type are emerging increasingly. To mention just a few examples:

- Datenbank DaF (German as a Foreign Language), developed by the Goethe-Institute to supply teachers of the German language abroad with materials and information on a large number of German institutions.
- SODIS, a German software documentation and information package for teachers of all school subjects informing them about the software available for their subject and their pupils.

Some of the better-equipped schools, e.g. the Eurocentres, have started to build up so-called textbases of their teaching materials and other texts needed in the running of the schools (certificates, lending protocols, etc.) (Arnold, 1994).

Knowledge-Base Great Britain

The Knowledge-Base Great Britain presented here is a concept for an innovative combination of a textbase with a system of CALLware exercises. This system will allow teachers and other users to enter data from the database/textbase part into CALL programmes without having to rewrite or scan the text files first. Out of a number of different authoring packages they can select the exercise that will be suited to their needs and their teaching goals.

The database is designed to comprise the following parts:

(a) Documentary Part (I): compilation of materials (texts, abstracts of short stories; newspaper cuttings, articles from journals; songs and poems and other language learning materials).
(b) Language training Part (II): computer-assisted exercises of different types based on the material included in Part I.
(c) Reference Part (III): information about textbooks chosen, their authors and publishers, about newspapers, journals, additional reading materials, etc. including electronic information and how to get access to it.

In order to obtain an overview of the demand for such a database and of the amount and type of materials we would have to include, we began to gather information from teachers in different types of German schools. For this purpose a questionnaire was sent out to the teachers. A computer-aided evaluation of the first 100 questionnaires returned is described below.

All of the teachers who responded regard the database as a useful supplement to the process of language learning and teaching. A great majority of them believe that the database is most appropriate for use at university level and for the further improvement and intensification of individual language knowledge and skills. When asked to give us their opinion about the way the

four countries of the United Kingdom should be represented in the database
the teachers made the recommendations summarised in Table 23.1.

Table 23.1 Representation of the countries of the UK

	Recommendable	Very recommendable	Not recommendable
Each country will be represented in great detail	27	54	19
UK will be represented as a political unit of the countries	30	20	50
Only one country in great detail, the others represented in general	3	3	94

We offered a list of different topics and asked the teachers to decide which
topics should be included and to what extent.

Table 23.2 Teachers' recommendations regarding topics represented in the database

Topics	In great detail	In detail	Briefly	Very briefly
Geography/population	20	22	32	21
Historical facts	16	42	38	4
Government	11	37	39	12
Legal system	4	6	36	53
Role of churches	2	16	45	37
Aspects of education	42	36	16	6
Economy	6	18	42	33
Languages	20	32	36	10
Modern literature	58	24	14	2
Traditions, habits	29	38	27	4
Monarchy	5	19	45	28
Cultural life	19	34	40	4
Political/social life	36	40	17	4
Britain: multi-racial society	44	38	16	2
London – the capital	25	31	32	12

When designing the database we paid great attention to a clear and easily understandable layout of the user interface. To achieve this, a WINDOWS environment was selected for the implementation of the database. The main menu offers information on the contents in a well-structured form. The items of the menu can be activated either by mouse or cursor keys. This design makes the database easy to operate even for computer beginners, as can be demonstrated by the following example:

A teacher wants to obtain some additional information and background knowledge on the topic 'Welsh people'. The teacher also wants to introduce some additional exercises into class to teach the grammar and vocabulary relevant to this topic. To do so, the teacher makes use of the database. In the main menu the item 'United Kingdom' is selected, which calls up a submenu (Figure 23.2).

Out of these submenus the teacher selects the item 'People', a new sub-menu pops up and in it the line 'Welsh people'. Pressing the ENTER-key, a window appears on the screen containing information on the Welsh people. The user can scroll forward and backward within this window. Pressing a certain key the teacher can activate a printer to print out this information. Pressing another key will give the teacher the option to transform the file information into a CALL exercise. The teacher can select the most suitable CALL exercise from a number of programmes offered.

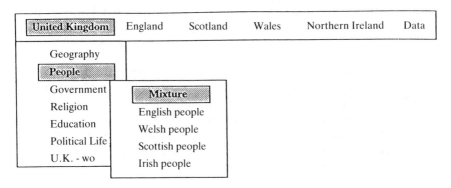

Figure 23.2 The UK as a mixture of people

Inserting the file text into the CALL programme does not require any specific computing or programming knowledge. The screen will tell the teacher what to do step by step. If the teacher wants to read more on this subject, it is simple to go back to the main menu and select Part III of the database (Reference) where bibliographical data of further literature for additional reading is found. For more details see Baumann *et al.* (1993).

Depending on further support we plan to add a number of features that will contribute to the usefulness of the database in language teaching and learning. Such a useful addition will be recordings of the files (on tape or CD) so that users who have audiocards integrated into their computers can add listening comprehension exercises (including folk-songs and other music) to the scope of the exercises on offer. This will support independent autonomous learning, a requirement of modern learning especially for adults on continuation courses. Pictures and video clips may form another useful addition as visual images are known to con-tribute greatly to the learning process as well as to the acquisition of inter-cultural knowledge.

Natural Language Access and Design

One of the disadvantages of present databases for linguists and language teachers is that access to them is limited and established by keywords or search words only. A wider acceptance and a more widespread use of data-bases can be achieved by a natural language access, i.e. by formulating applications and queries in a natural way instead of resorting to long lists of keywords before starting the search process. Computational linguistics is putting tremendous effort into natural language retrieval systems. Retrieval is not, however, the first stage in a database system. If databases are to fit the most individual needs, then some thought will first have to go into their design.

Databases are not easy to design. The bottleneck during the design process is the high degree of abstraction and the abstract language that has tradition-ally been used for this purpose. There are not many users who can learn the database design formalisms easily, but most potential users are able to describe in their native language the entities that will form the basic elements of the prospective database, how to administer them and the processes they will have to undergo.

There is a growing demand for a natural language tool that will allow the user to present his informal knowledge about a domain of a database to be designed in a natural language. The natural language tool we are at present developing is a dialogue tool consisting of a syntactics analyser, a semantic roles analyser and a pragmatics interpreter.

Let us consider a person who has used a library at least once in their life. To this person the sentence:

Der Benutzer entleiht ein Buch mit Leihschein
(The user borrows a book with a borrowing slip)

automatically conveys a large amount of information. Because of linguistic as well as world knowledge the person knows that:

(1) user and book are two partners in an act;

(2) a certain relationship exists between these two, expressed by the verb;

(3) the relationship is the change of possession;

(4) the change of 'ownership' is only temporarily (in contrast to buying or presenting);

(5) the user is not a specific one, in fact it can be any person that fulfils the conditions going along with this business;

(6) *a* book does not mean one book, it can be two or three and more books;

(7) a book does not necessarily have to be a book, it can be a picturebook, a journal, a magazine, an atlas;

(8) in 'book with a borrowing-slip', 'with' does not express possession or part of like in 'a book with pictures', it expresses instrumentality (by means of);

(9) 'borrowing-slip' is not just a slip of paper but has the function of a contract;

(10) borrowing means that the book will have to be returned;

(11) a book is borrowed at some place (library);

(12) this sentence does not include details about user or book, it describes a general lending process.

This complex information and the associations made by a person reading the sentence will be elicited by the Dialogue Tool in various steps. These steps have to comprise:

(1) a linguistic analysis of the structure of natural sentences for syntax and semantics;

(2) a set of transformation rules for extracting the database structure;

(3) rules and heuristics for handling world knowledge;

(4) classification rules for modelling the behaviour of the database.

The syntax analyser (a GPSG parser) will yield the following syntax trees when analysing our sentence (Figure 23.3):

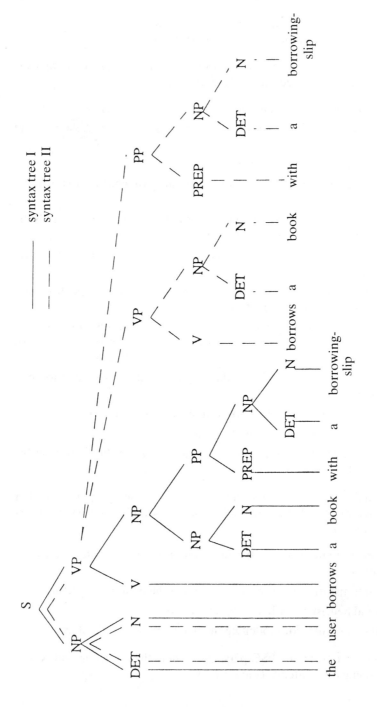

Figure 23.3 Syntax trees of the sentences *Der Benutzer entleiht ein Buch mit einem Leihschein* (The user borrows a book with a borrowing-slip)

The correct sentence is to be found out by means of the semantics analyser, i.e. the ambiguity produced by the parser will be eliminated. Verbs form a central part in defining the meaning of sentences and the relationships between parts of sentences. Basically they describe actions, processes and states. We have tried to find a classification of verb semantics that can be applied to all verbs in the German language. Our aim was to keep the number of classes small and fairly general but large enough to identify their function in a sentence correctly. This classification is, at this stage, independent of the domain to be analysed (Figure 23.4).

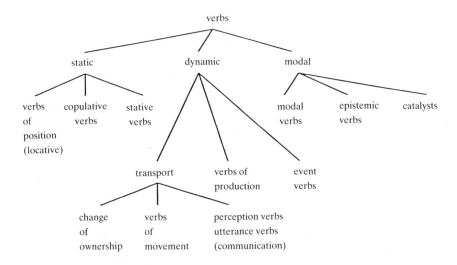

Figure 23.4 Verb classification

For more details about the classification see Buchholz *et al.* (1994).

The pragmatic interpretation is the next part of the Dialogue Tool. The aim of the pragmatic interpretation is the mapping of the natural language input onto a database design model using the results of the syntactic and semantic analyses. A basic feature of the pragmatics is the domain model which defines a frame for every specific application in order to support the acquisition of semantics and behaviour of the prospective database.

Buchholz & Düsterhöft (1994) show how common rules are used for making general assumptions about how information gained from natural sentences is related to entities, relationships, sets, keys and other database design structures.

Conclusions

Our society has to handle vast amounts of information. The individual member is submerged in a flood of input from all sorts of media which constantly has to be filtered for its information value, i.e. whether it is meaningful or meaningless for the receiver. Teachers are confronted with a plethora of textbooks, all of which claim to have the very best material for her or his needs. Many a teacher would like to use a number of textbooks and take the best or most fitting parts out of each of them. But consulting these books, finding and selecting suitable parts and copying them for the learners, takes up a considerable amount of time which, in most cases, simply is not available to the teacher.

A database containing the complete material of several textbooks plus information on additional reading material is an effective way of solving this problem. Within seconds it will display whatever material it offers in answering the query of the user. It is this capacity of almost instantaneous presentation of the information needed that has made databases an increasingly used tool in many applications. In the database the teacher can select the appropriate learning material out of a large number of different texts and exercises from a number of publishers.

The knowledge base proposed here will take the user one step further and offer possibilities beyond the ones mentioned. We suggest a textbase combined with a number of CALL authoring frames. Any text in the database can easily be exported into a CALL programme and become a CALL exercise. This can then either be printed out for use in the classroom or may directly be solved by the learner at the PC. As most learners have a PC at home now, the teacher can thus assign more individual homework.

In future, databases will form the backbone of most language data processing applications. In many cases they will have to suit the needs of individual users. This places a new focus on the design of databases. At present computational linguistics is involved in developing natural language interfaces that will allow the users to design their own databases according to their personal needs. Other interfaces will help to retrieve information from international databases via a natural – e.g. the native – language.

One day teachers will join the people on the 'Data Highway', but even there they will have to find suitable teaching material for their learners – that is, they will access databases.

Acknowledgement

This research was promoted by DFG project TH 456/2-2.

References

Arnold, J.W. and Weiland, K. (1994) Eurocentres: erste Erfahrungen mit einem Volltextdatenbanksystem – 'database' versus 'textbase'. Computer und Fremdsprachen. *Beiträge des Innovations- und Bildungszentrums Hohen Luckow e.V.* 2, 1, 36–9.

Baumann, K., Buchholz, E., Düsterhöft, A. and Pudschun, M. (1993) An ELT database for teachers and learners: A cross-cultural perspective. *Literary and Linguistic Computing* Vol. 8, No. 3, 153–9.

Buchholz, E., Cyriaks, H., Mehlan, H. and Düsterhft, A. (1994) Zur natürlichsprachigen Unterstützung im Datenbankentwurfssystem RAD. *Rostocker Informatik-Berichte* 15, 41–60.

Buchholz, E. and Düsterhöft, A. (1994) Using natural language for database design. Proceedings of *Deutsche Jahrestagung für Künstliche Intelligenz.* Workshop: Reasoning about structured objects: Knowledge representation meets databases. 18–23 September.

24 LSP Theory and Second Language Acquisition

ANGELA CHAMBERS

Introduction

Since the early 1960s LSP research has been dominated by English for Special Purposes, as the increasing importance of English as an international language led to rapid growth in the demand for higher education through English, both at undergraduate and postgraduate level. This in turn created a huge international market for English language courses designed to prepare students to follow degree programmes, mostly in science and technology. The research produced in language teaching and learning for special purposes which resulted from this activity is in many ways ahead of research relating to the teaching of other languages to students or specialists in areas such as business, science and technology. In these circumstances it is natural that teachers and researchers in other languages should consult published ESP research with a view to applying it to their own activity. It is the aim of this study to investigate to what extent the research which has been carried out in ESP can be applied to the teaching of other languages for special purposes.

After a brief initial survey of the development of ESP research in the last three decades, the paper will compare the situation of ESP learners and students of other languages, particularly French and German, who are also following a language course intended to be relevant to their specialist studies. This will enable us to assess to what extent the large body of published ESP research can inform the work of those designing courses in other languages for special purposes. Clearly, in a brief study such as this, it is not possible to provide an exhaustive analysis of this important issue. The aim is rather to initiate debate on the subject, at a time when researchers in French and German are increasingly devoting attention to the use of the language by specialists in various fields.

232

The Development of ESP

Over 30 years ago, when researchers first began a systematic study of the type of language which scientists and students of science would require, quantitative lexicostatistical studies (Barber, 1962; Halliday, McIntosh & Strevens, 1964) not only provided information on specialist terminology but also indicated which syntactic structures occurred most frequently in scientific prose. This type of (English) research informed the design of ESP courses, but later researchers observed the limited relevance of such studies. For example, the discovery that the passive voice occurs much more frequently than the active in written scientific English does not mean that a course can omit the active voice, or that a non-native speaker can communicate effectively as a scientist without ever using it (Hutchinson & Waters, 1987: 31). Moreover, the use of authentic scientific prose in the ESP class could pose a major problem for the teacher or student who is not a specialist in the relevant discipline. Later studies question the need for advanced scientific texts to be included in the language course, stressing the usefulness of semi-technical texts on everyday technological products (Hutchinson & Waters, 1988: 181).

Alongside studies of the desirability of incorporating scientific texts in language classes, there is a significant body of research attempting to define the term 'Language for Special Purposes'. Some researchers in linguistics still maintain that there is no such thing as LSP, as it cannot be easily defined according to the criteria normally used to define a language. However, Sager, Dungworth & McDonald's (1980: 68) definition of LSP as 'specialist-to-specialist communication' is now generally accepted, although it is not always directly applicable to the situation of the language learner. Moreover, it has been pointed out that different levels of specialisation exist (Balboni, 1986: 6; Varantola, 1986: 11). The view that special language can exist at any stage from popularisation level to the highest level of knowledge of the subject is particularly relevant to the situation of language learners, who may initially be non-specialists both in the language and in the subject which they are studying. The practical application of this research is evident in the use of popularised texts on scientific subjects in many LSP courses. While the teachers may choose the texts intuitively rather than as a result of having read the relevant published work, they are nevertheless making available to learners texts which are pertinent to the subject which they are studying or intend to study.

However, the use of popularised texts such as journal articles is unlikely to provide students with examples of language use appropriate to their needs. Indeed the major influence on theory and practice in LSP has been the development of the communicative approach to language learning which, together with developments in research in discourse analysis, has moved the focus of LSP courses away from written language to include spoken language as well, and, more particularly, has established the fundamental importance of the communicative character (Widdowson, 1979: 56) or the communicative purpose (Swales, 1990: 10) of what is said or written. Particularly relevant in this context is the definition of LSP as the language used by a particular discourse community, which Swales defines as a group of people with expertise in an area of activity, who share 'a broadly agreed set of common public goals, a specific lexis and accepted communicative practices or genres' (1990: 24). This concept provides a framework for the design and content of LSP courses, as well as mapping out a path for research in specialist language use. If the language teacher's role is to prepare learners for membership of a discourse community, then one of the researcher's functions is to identify the relevant discourse community and analyse its use of language.

It is at this point that it becomes evident how difficult it is to apply ESP research to the teaching of languages other than English to students of business, science and technology. For example, the recent expansion of such courses in French and German in British and Irish institutions of further and higher education is producing several categories of students who cannot easily be compared to the case studies used by researchers such as Sager *et al.*, Swales, Johns and Dudley-Evans, and many others. Firstly, ESP researchers have long enjoyed the benefit of huge numbers of learners whose needs can be precisely defined. A course may be designed to prepare prospective students for studies in medicine or plant biology, or to ensure that doctors who are non-native speakers of English can communicate effectively with patients. The prospective student, for example, clearly requires a course which will prepare him or her to understand lectures, read literature in the subject, write essays, communicate in tutorials, etc. In his highly regarded work on genre analysis and the discourse community, Swales (1990) provides a detailed study of the research article in English, and the relevance of this is obvious for the very large number of researchers who are non-native speakers of English and whose career advancement depends to a large extent on their ability to publish in English language journals. Clearly the increasing dominance of English as the international language of academic research makes it easy to understand why ESP research is characterised to a large extent by its focus on the use of scientific language in an academic setting.

LSP for English-speaking Students

In general the English-speaking student of science or business who chooses a programme including language study to degree level has needs which are much more difficult to determine than those of the learners of English who have been the inspiration for the research which has been considered so far. Where the English courses were clearly a market-led development from the start, the inspiration for degree programmes combining the study of business or science with French and German came initially from groups of academics who decided that students in these disciplines should be offered the possibility of studying a language. The reasons which tend to be given in course documentation stress the importance of preparing the student to work abroad, to liaise with speakers of the language or to read research in the subject. The combinations of language and specialism which are chosen reflect economic or academic perceptions of the importance of a particular language for a particular economic benefit or area of study. For example, chemistry may be combined with German, reflecting the important position occupied by German research in that subject. Until very recently the only way to study Japanese throughout an undergraduate degree in Ireland was as a component of a degree programme in Business Studies or International Marketing, thus reflecting Ireland's interest in the Japanese economy as a destination for exports and a source of inward investment. In both these examples the language may be studied from beginning level, which limits the amount of time which can be devoted to meeting the perceived specialist needs of the students. Furthermore, individual students may have perceptions of their needs which do not conform strictly to the justification for the study of the language put forward by the course design team. They may be motivated by a desire to provide themselves with a professional qualification and at the same time to study the language of a country which they find interesting. In short, course designers cannot define student needs as easily as their counterparts in ESP, nor can they identify with certainty a discourse community in which their students will participate in the future.

As a result of this, LSP course design does not have the uniformity which one can observe in courses in English for Special Purposes or English for Academic Purposes. Without the studies of the precise needs of specific groups of learners which have appeared in ESP, courses tend to be an eclectic mix of the planner's or teacher's perception of what is required. At the less advanced levels of language learning, where a trainee may be prepared for work as a waiter or for communicating by telephone in a specific situation, it is clearly possible to identify the needs of a specific group and to design a course accordingly. Many such courses, certified by national and private organisations, exist already, and the momentum is growing to create a common European framework for language teaching and learning (Fitzpatrick, 1994). To meet the needs of these learners, published coursebooks in language for business or technology are increasing in number and in quality. These vocationally oriented courses will no doubt provide useful language training for those requiring to work abroad or to communicate in other languages in a work-related context. However, they do not provide a framework for planning the language programme of students who wish to study language to a high level but whose precise needs, even if they could be established, would vary enormously.

Conclusion: Trends in ESP and LSP Research

This is not to say that the communicative purpose of the language learning cannot be determined at all in the specialised context of such programmes, or that the concept of the discourse community is totally irrelevant in this context. Students of electronic engineering and German, for example, may be studying the language for a number of reasons, which might include the knowledge that previous students in the subject have found employment in Germany or that German-owned companies in their own environment offer the possibility of employment. Moreover, it is not unlikely that such students will be given the possibility to study in Germany for a semester or a year. Two discourse communities can already be distinguished, namely that of students of electronic engineering and employees in electronic engineering companies. Both of these discourse communities can be seen as subdivisions of larger groups, namely students and companies. Thus the possible needs of the students can be divided into several categories: firstly, knowledge of student life in general in Germany and the ability to use the appropriate language; secondly, the specific language activities necessary to succeed in the study of the discipline; thirdly, language use in business generally; and finally the specific language likely to be used in the context of an electronic engineering company. It is clear from this example that the needs of the learners are less easily determined and less homogenous than those of non-English speakers who wish to follow a particular course of study or to communicate appropriately in a well defined discourse community. However, the model devised in the context of English language acquisition can still be applied with a high expectation that the broader focus of the course will be relevant to the future situations of the learners.

The example of the student of electronic engineering and German highlights another important and related area where ESP diverges significantly from other languages, namely in the treatment of the cultural component. Learners preparing for study in London or New York may well find that their course contains an element of British or American Studies. Increasingly however, ESP courses present English as an international language, as learners may have needs which do not involve communicating with English or

American people, or indeed with any native speakers of the language. The same is seldom true of LSP courses in other languages. The second largest French-speaking city in the world is Montréal, and the language is spoken in more than 40 countries, but the LSP course in a European context still focuses almost entirely on France, with perhaps a token gesture towards Belgium, Switzerland and other Francophone countries throughout the world. At present this seems to correspond to the needs of most learners, rather than representing a refusal to accept the reality of a post colonial world. In this case the situation noted earlier when comparing ESP with French and German for Special Purposes is reversed, in that the needs of learners of languages other than English can be more specifically defined as a preparation for intercultural communication.

It is interesting to note how, in the areas of research and course design, English and other languages, both influenced by an increasing awareness of the importance of needs analysis and of designing the course to meet the learners' needs, have moved in opposite directions. On the one hand English language courses have moved away from being essentially a preparation for life in an idealised England or America, as researchers and teachers discover the increasing irrelevance of such a focus. Many articles on the subject have a negative focus, stressing the need to avoid the temptation to use the language class as a means of producing stereotypical Americans or Southern English clones (Alptekin, 1993). Researchers are, of course, aware that all language teaching and learning is culture bound, even if a cultural element is not explicitly included in the syllabus. Moreover, it has been pointed out that even the teaching of scientific writing and methods of study and research to learners from radically different cultures is imposing cultural norms (Valdes, 1990: 26). However the removal of explicit cultural references from ESP course materials leads to the conclusion that the emphasis is on the international rather than the culturally specific dimension.

In the European languages, on the other hand, the developing focus on the specific needs of the learners, far from excluding an explicit cultural dimension, tends to emphasise its importance. Students of electronic engineering going to Germany are already members of the international category of students and as such will have much in common with German students. However, as language learners they will have special communicative needs of a sociocultural nature which are peculiar to the German context. Moreover, the vast majority of those learning German will be doing so in order to communicate with native speakers of the language, almost certainly of European origin. The importance of including a specific cultural component in LSP courses in European Languages thus presents a challenge of a totally different nature to the increasing internationalisation of English. The specialist component must be included alongside the intercultural, as both are necessary if the learner is to fulfil the communicative purpose of the course. The definition of this explicit cultural component and its relationship to LSP are areas of research where the paths of research and teaching in English and other European languages are likely to diverge, and where, despite the increasing cultural relativism of language learning materials in languages other than English, cultural preparation for membership of a discourse community is likely to retain its importance. In this, as in the other points of comparison and contrast which have been observed, researchers in ESP and in other Languages for Special Purposes can benefit from each other's experience.

References

Alptekin, C. (1993) Target language culture in EFL materials. *ELT Journal* 47 (2), 136–43.

Balboni, P. (1986) LGP versus LSP: Which way to the razor's edge? *UNESCO ALSED-LSP Newsletter* 9 (1), 22, May, 2–8.

Barber, C.L. (1962) Some measurable characteristics of modern scientific prose. *Contributions to English Syntax and Phonology* (pp. 1–23). Stockholm: Almquist and Wiksell.

Fitzpatrick, A. (1994) *Language Learning for European Citizenship: A Common European Framework for Language Teaching and Learning*. Strasbourg: Council of Europe.

Halliday, M.A.K., McIntosh, A. and Strevens, P.D. (1964) *The Linguistic Sciences and Language Teaching*. London: Longman.

Hutchinson, T. and Waters, A. (1987) *English for Special Purposes: A Learning-centred Approach*. Cambridge: Cambridge University Press.

— (1988) ESP at the crossroads. In J. Swales (ed.) *Episodes in ESP* (pp. 177–85). London: Prentice Hall.

Johns, T.F. and Dudley-Evans, A. (1985) An experiment in team-teaching of overseas postgraduate students of transportation and plant biology. In J. Swales (ed.) *Episodes in ESP* (pp. 140–53). London: Prentice Hall.

Sager, J.C., Dungworth, D. and McDonald, P.M. (1980) *English Special Languages: Principles and Practice in Science and Technology*. Wiesbaden: Athenaion.

Swales, J.M. (1990) *Genre Analysis: English in Academic and Research Settings*. Cambridge: Cambridge University Press.

Valdes, J. (1990) The inevitability of teaching and learning culture in a foreign language course. In B. Harrison (ed.) *Culture and the Language Classroom* (pp. 20–30). London: Modern English Publications and the British Council.

Varantola, K. (1986) Special language and general language: Linguistic and didactic aspects. *UNESCO ALSED-LSP Newsletter* 9 (2) 23, Dec., 10–9.

Widdowson, H.G. (1979) *Explorations in Applied Linguistics*. Oxford: Oxford University Press.

25 Developing a Dynamic Concept of L2 Motivation

EMA USHIODA

Introduction

In Second Language Acquisition (SLA) research, motivation has traditionally been conceptualised as either a cause or a product of second language learning success. Recent SLA theory, however, underlines the dynamic nature of motivation, in the shape of reciprocal causation between motivation and achievement (Gardner & MacIntyre, 1992, 1993).

This paper sets out to explore further the notion of L2 motivation as a dynamic phenomenon. First, the dynamic concept of L2 motivation offered by Gardner & MacIntyre will be examined, and I will argue that its theoretical development requires a more qualitative type of research approach. Next, the context and methodology of an empirical study currently being conducted at Trinity College Dublin will be described briefly. Finally some of the findings which have emerged will be discussed. These findings suggest that important developments in language learning motivation are not always perceived simply in terms of cumulative loss or growth, since patterns of change and stability are felt by learners to evolve differently for different aspects of L2 motivation. Moreover, the relevant interacting factors derive not always from the L2-related context but also from other personal circumstances.

The Social-Psychological Research Tradition

L2 motivation and L2 achievement: A dynamic chain of causation

The study of L2 motivation has long been dominated by the social-psychological research tradition, under the influence especially of the work of Gardner and his associates. In a recent reformulation of their model of second language acquisition, Gardner & MacIntyre (1992, 1993) give particular emphasis to its dynamic nature, in the shape of reciprocal causation between linguistic outcomes and attitudinal-motivational variables. This emphasis reflects a notable change from the theoretical position supported by Gardner and his associates over the years, which has been a fairly rigid adherence to the hypothesis that strong motivation is a cause rather than a result of L2 learning achievement. Other researchers have offered the counter-hypothesis that success in language learning promotes better motivation and attitudes (e.g. Burstall *et al.*, 1974; Hermann, 1980).

Gardner & MacIntyre's recent model thus encompasses both causal perspectives in a cyclical relationship, underlining the dynamic processes involved in second language acquisition:

> Thus the model is dynamic, with cognitive and affective variables influencing the individual's level of achievement in the language. In turn, the student's level of achievement and experiences are seen as having an influence on the individual primarily on affective attributes [. . .]. (Gardner & MacIntyre, 1992: 213)

Moreover, it is not only the relationship between motivation and achievement which is perceived as dynamic, but also the motivational construct itself, since motivation is subject to change through 'reinforcement associated with the act of learning' (Gardner & MacIntyre, 1993: 4). This development in L2 motivational theory is made explicit:

> The important point is that motivation itself is dynamic. The old characterization of motivation in terms of integrative vs. instrumental orientations is too static and restricted. (1993: 4)

Limitations of the traditional research approach

The new theoretical focus on dynamic motivational phenomena is certainly to be welcomed. After all, within the context of institutionalised learning especially, the common experience would seem to be motivational flux rather than stability, with high and low points represented perhaps by the kind of motivation graph that Ellis & Sinclair (1989) advocate for learner training purposes. Graphs, however, record changes in *levels* of motivation only. Similarly, in SLA research on motivation the traditional methodology, based on obtaining composite indices of amount of motivation, is limited in scope to the investigation of causal and resultative changes in global *levels* of motivation and achievement.

Yet the potential for developing a dynamic theory of L2 motivation would seem to extend beyond the phenomenon of motivational loss or growth alone. In this respect, a more introspective type of research approach is needed to explore qualitative developments in motivational experience over time, as well as to identify the contextual factors perceived to be in dynamic interplay with motivation. Such an approach underpins the empirical investigation to be reported here.

The Study: An Introspective Approach

Context and methodology

This study is a small-scale exploration of learner perceptions of L2 motivation currently in progress at Trinity College Dublin, in conjunction with the college's Modern Languages Research Project (Singleton, 1990). With its qualitative approach focusing on the role of motivational thinking in L2 learning, the study is designed to complement the quantitative research tradition which has dominated the investigation of L2 motivation since the early 1960s. The subjects are 20 undergraduate students learning French as a second language.

Earlier reports on the study (Ushioda, 1993, 1994) have discussed aspects of L2 motivational theory in relation to initial findings. These findings emerged from content analysis of data elicited by means of open-ended interview in December 1991, when subjects were simply prompted to explain their motivation for learning French.

The findings to be reported here derive from the second stage of data elicitation in March to April 1993, some 16 months later. Fourteen subjects were recalled for follow-up interviews. The remaining subjects were unavailable because they were abroad in France or had withdrawn from their course of study. The follow-up interviews adopted a slightly more structured format, comprising nine questions relating to dynamic aspects of language learning motivation. These questions were, however, couched in open-ended terms, allowing subjects freedom to describe relevant processes and experiences from their point of view. Each interview lasted 15–20 minutes and was tape-recorded.

The findings to be discussed here will be confined to those arising from subjects' responses to the first three interview questions, which probe developments in motivational experience since the first stage interviews:

- How would you describe your present state of motivation for learning French, and have you experienced any motivational changes over the past year?
- Have you any further ideas or experienced any changes in your ideas about future career plans? If so, do you think these have had any impact on the way you feel about studying French?

- Has anything happened in your personal life that has influenced the way you feel about your studies?

Data analysis

Subjects' responses to these three questions were collectively analysed. The aim of the content analysis was firstly to identify elements of motivation perceived to have changed or to have remained stable, and secondly to classify these elements according to common features.

Initially a two-fold classification was attempted. This was done to explore the descriptive adequacy of a dynamic concept of L2 motivation defined in terms of global positive or negative changes. However, it readily became apparent that only a small number of the motivational changes identified could be classified as global growth or loss attributed to L2 experience or L2 achievement. The data clearly yielded other more differentiated patterns of change. These patterns were provisionally classified as follows:

- *Qualitative developments*
- *Overriding short-term incentives*
- *Clearer definition of L2-related personal goals*
- *Other priorities now affecting L2 motivation*
- *Personal crises which have affected L2 motivation*
- *Stable motivational elements*

Patterns of motivational change: L2 context and experience

Classified among these differentiated patterns of change are a number of perceived modulations in certain aspects of motivation, rather than in strength of motivation as a whole – development of intrinsic motivation, instrumental motivation, positive or negative feelings about France or French people, interest in language teaching, pride, exam motivation. These are attributed to a variety of factors, some arising from L2 experience over the segment of time evaluated, and others relating to future concerns (career goals, examination pressures). They can be detailed as follows:

Qualitative developments
- development of intrinsic motivation through positive L2 experience in France
- positive feelings about France from personal experience
- appreciation of instrumental value of L2 skill through work experience
- interest in language pedagogy with definition of career goal
- pride from association with well-respected academic staff

- dominance of exam-oriented motivation at expense of intrinsic motivation
- negative feelings about French people from personal experience

Overriding short-term incentives
- high motivation from immediate exam pressure
- high motivation to pass exams for reward of spending year in France

Clearer definition of L2-related personal goals
- pursue postgraduate studies in L2
- enter teaching profession
- integrate L2 into professional career

Motivational patterns are thus determined not only by the reinforcing or negative effects of L2 learning and L2-related experience, but also by the clarification or growth in importance of particular goals and incentives which qualitatively modify the learner's original motivation.

An important implication is that goal-orientation may be more appropriately conceived as a potential *evolving* aspect of language learning motivation, rather than as its basic defining attribute as conceptualised in the social-psychological research tradition (e.g. Clément & Kruidenier, 1983; Gardner, 1985: 50–6). It seems that for different learners, personal goals may crystallise, strengthen or change at different stages of the learning time span. Intrinsically motivated learners may also develop an instrumental motivation, or lose some of their intrinsic motivation in the face of exam-oriented motivation. Some may find their motivation focusing on overriding short-term incentives, such as passing exams or spending the following year in France. Others may gain a clearer perception of more long-term goals such as the pursuit of postgraduate studies or of particular L2-related careers.

Patterns of L2 motivational change: Factors outside L2 context

On the other hand, L2 motivation may also be affected by aspects of individual experience which are not related to the L2 learning context, but which also compete for attention and priority within the individual's overall hierarchy of personal needs and motives. Research on L2 motivation has traditionally emphasised the social-psychological implications of learning a second language which distinguish this type of motivation from other types of learning motivation. As a result studies have inevitably tended to focus on L2 motivation in isolation, rather than in the context of individuals' learning motivation and personal experience as a whole. The findings here however suggest that this relative perspective is important. Two clear patterns of non-L2-related motivational change emerge in this study: competing study priorities and personal emotional crises.

Competing study priorities now affecting L2 motivation
- development of stronger motivation for other subject
- motivated by career prospects in other subject
- motivated by better academic success potential in other subject
- L2 motivation restrained by immediate study pressures of other subject

Personal crises which have affected L2 motivation
- temporary loss of motivation during period of depression
- temporary loss of motivation following parental bereavement
- disruption of motivation with parental separation
- disruption of motivation with family emigration to US

With regard to the former, changes in L2 motivation evolve in reaction to the competing priorities of students' other subjects of study, rather than because of factors inherent in the L2 experience itself. Greater motivation for the other subject may result in less motivation for French. Alternatively, the pressure of other study commitments may restrain the motivation to spend time studying French.

Similarly, the impact of personal emotional crises (such as depression or bereavement) is perceived as a temporary but salient feature of learners' motivational experience. Moreover, such emotional events may entail complex motivational repercussions. One student for example reports that his motivation to pursue further study in France partly derives from a desire to take control of his life, in reaction against his parents' decision to emigrate to the United States. Another student finds that after serious motivational loss following the death of her mother, L2 motivation itself develops a new dimension when the determination to pursue and prioritise her studies becomes a therapeutic means of coping with the emotional trauma in her personal life.

L2 motivation: Stability over time

Equally relevant to a study of motivational evolution are those enduring aspects of L2 motivation which are perceived not to change, despite experiences which might be expected to have motivational repercussions. They can be categorised as follows:

Stable motivational elements
- intrinsic L2 motivation constant
- little perceived change overall in L2 motivation

In this regard *intrinsic L2 motivation* (expressed as love of French or love of studying French) appears to have particularly enduring qualities. Two learners affirm this unchanging aspect of their motivation, despite a decision to major in the other subject of study in the fourth year, or the motivational restraint imposed by the study pressures of the other subject. For another learner, negative experiences in France over the summer intensify her dislike of French people but do little to diminish her original intrinsic L2 motivation. In contrast another learner feels little perceived change overall in her motivation ('I'm no more motivated than I was last year'), despite positive experiences in France over the summer.

Conclusion

I began by discussing Gardner & MacIntyre's dynamic concept of L2 motivation, and argued that its development required a more qualitative research approach. The introspective findings reported from my own study suggest that global changes in strength of motivation relating to L2 achievement and L2 experience account for only a small part of learners' motivational experience over time. Patterns of change and stability are perceived to evolve differently for different aspects of motivation. Moreover, the relevant interacting factors derive from outside as well as within the L2 context. There is clearly much potential in the theoretical development of a dynamic concept of L2 motivation. The concept of motivational change after all brings with it the notion of motivational control, or self-motivation. In this respect, a qualitative approach may be the most fruitful means of exploring the role of motivational thought processes over the language learning time span.

References

Burstall, C., Jamieson, M., Cohen, S. and Hargreaves, M. (1974) *Primary French in the Balance*. NFER Publishing Co.

Clément, R. and Kruidenier, B. (1983) Orientations in second language acquisition: I. The effects of ethnicity, milieu and target language on their emergence. *Language Learning* 33, 273–91.

Ellis, G. and Sinclair, B. (1989) *Learning to Learn English: A Course in Learner Training. Teacher's Book*. Cambridge: Cambridge University Press.

Gardner, R. (1985) *Social Psychology and Second Language Learning: The Role of Attitudes and Motivation*. London: Edward Arnold.

Gardner, R. and MacIntyre, P. (1992) A student's contributions to second-language learning. Part I: Cognitive variables. *Language Teaching* 25, 211–20.

— (1993) A student's contributions to second-language learning. Part II: Affective variables. *Language Teaching* 26, 1–11.

Hermann, G. (1980) Attitudes and success in children's learning of English as a second language: The motivational vs. the resultative hypothesis. *English Language Teaching Journal* 34, 247–54.

Singleton, D. (1990) *The TCD Modern Languages Research Project: Objectives, Instruments and Preliminary Results*. Dublin: Trinity College (CLCS Occasional paper No. 26).

Ushioda, E. (1993) Redefining motivation from the L2 learner's point of view. *Teanga* 13, 1–12.

— (1994) L2 motivation as a qualitative construct. *Teanga* 14, 76–84.

26 Crosslinguistic Lexical Operations and the L2 Mental Lexicon

DAVID SINGLETON

Introduction

This paper examines the question of the separation/integration of the mental lexica associated with different languages at an individual's disposal in the light of previous research and also data from the Trinity College Dublin Modern Languages Research Project (henceforth TCD MLRP). It argues for a position which steers a *via media* between the postulation of, at one extreme, total separation and, at the other, total integration of the L1 and L2 lexica.

Separation or Integration? A *tour d'horizon* of Previous Research

One version of the separatist view of the L1/L2 mental lexica derives from the modular model of mind (see, e.g. Fodor, 1983), which claims that language is sealed off from other cognitive subsystems. Modularists differ about what precisely falls within the domain of the language module (cf. Singleton, 1993). At least some, however, hold that a substantial part of the functioning of the L1 mental lexicon is intramodular (see, e.g. Emmorey & Fromkin, 1988) and there is also a view abroad that any L2 competence acquired after puberty is extramodular (see, e.g. Bley-Vroman, 1989). Taken together, these two positions imply that, in the case of post-pubertal L2 learners, L1 and L2 lexical operations are insulated from each other.

Other lines of argument have less extreme implications but nevertheless suggest some degree of separation. Thus, for example, recent research indicates that the common phonological composition of particular sets of lexical items induces analogising tactics for morphologising uncommon or nonce words (see Bybee, 1988; Stemberger & MacWhinney, 1988), and that these 'gang effects' are based on a search through the store of already accumulated lexis for relevant phonological groupings. Since languages diverge radically in terms of their phonology, the phonological search on which gang effects depend must, it seems, run through the lexicon of each language separately. Another indication of inter-lexical separateness comes from cases of language loss due to brain damage where one language is recovered before another. Grosjean, for instance, writes (1982: 260) of a native speaker of Swiss German who first recovered French, a language he had learned imperfectly as an adult, who then recovered High German, but who failed to recover his L1, Swiss German. Similarly Whitaker (1978: 27) reports the case of an English Classics scholar who recovered Ancient Greek, Latin, French and English in that order.

Integrationist arguments are not difficult to find either. Cook (1992, 1993), arguing for a general 'multicompetence' position, cites lexical evidence such as the following:

reaction time to a word in one language is related to the frequency of its cognate in another known language (Caramazza & Brones, 1979);

morphemic similarities between two known languages influence translation performance (Cristoffanini, Kirsner & Milech, 1986);

when processing an interlingual homograph (such as French/English *coin*) bilinguals access its meanings in both their languages rather than just the meaning specific to the language being used (Beauvillain & Grainger, 1987);

bilinguals consult the lexical stores associated with both their languages when taking vocabulary tests in one of their languages (Hamers & Lambert, 1972).

Further evidence in favour of L1–L2 lexical integration comes from, for example, Kirsner, Smith, Lockhart & King's (1984) finding that the presentation of a stimulus in one of a bilingual subject's languages primes his/her response to a corresponding stimulus in his/her other language and Green's (1986) finding that when a person has a reasonable command of two languages, lexical items are subconsciously activated in both languages, those in the language not required being subsequently suppressed.

Evidence from the TCD MLRP

The TCD MLRP gathers data from undergraduates taking degree courses in French, German, Italian or Spanish. 'Level I' of the project has involved (from 1990) seeking from the entire yearly intake of such students (via questionnaire) information about their general educational and language learning experience and tracking respondents' progress by reference to annual university language examination results. 'Level II' of the project elicits actual L2 data and related introspections from relatively small subsamples of subjects recruited from among students of French and of German. In the case of the students of French, all subjects are advanced learners, having already studied French for at least five years at school. In the case of the students of German, these include both advanced and *ab initio* groups, which since the end of the pilot phase of the project in 1990 have been treated as separate subsamples. The instruments employed for 'Level II' data collection include C-tests (with associated introspection), word-association tests, story-tell tasks and translation tasks (with associated introspection).

A general problem confronting researchers interested in crosslinguistic lexical phenomena is the 'attribution problem' (cf. e.g. Singleton, 1987a), which consists in the fact that a given L2 error is often attributable either to crosslinguistic influence or to overgeneralisation of an L2 rule (or indeed to both). The attribution problem looms less large in the case of L2 lexical innovations – lexical forms that would not be recognised by native speakers as actually existing in their language. L2 coinages tend of their very nature to be formally idiosyncratic, and their formal idiosyncrasies frequently point quite transparently to crosslinguistic origins. The following selection of innovations, taken from the TCD MLRP French C-test, word-association and translation data, illustrates the above point very well. It would be difficult to explain such coinages without referring to the crosslinguistic factor, and such items clearly indicate the existence of at least an interface between L1 and L2 lexical operations.

volcanos   (C-test stimulus *vol-*, required word *volcans*, cf. English *volcanoes*)

excludait   (C-test stimulus *excl-*, required word *excluait*, cf. English *excluded*)

fathome   (word-association test stimulus *mer*, cf. English *fathom*)

lionesse   (word-association test stimulus *lion*, cf. English *lioness*)

harnesses de siège (expression to be translated *seat belts*, cf. English *harness*)

affairs personales (expression to be translated *personal belongings*, cf. English *affair, personal*)

The TCD MLRP introspective data also provide evidence – in this case rather direct evidence – of cross-consultation between the L1 and L2 mental lexica, as the following French C-test-related examples show:

I chose an English word beginning with 'col' that sounded right for the context and translated it into French (stimulus *col-*, required word *colline*, solution offered *colonie*)

better solution -mises. I suddenly remembered the English word 'transmit' when I was re-reading the text (stimulus *trans-*, required word *transmises*, solution offered *transposées*)

I keep thinking of chairman but I can't think of a French word for what I want to say. It must mean chief or operator but I don't know a word for it (stimulus *cha-*, required word *chargé*, no solution offered)

Evidence of crosslinguistic lexical operations is not confined to our French data. For instance, in one of the German C-tests the string *Iro-* was completed by an *ab initio* learner as *Irony* rather than the required word *Ironie* – which in one fell swoop indicates both that the subject concerned was on exactly the right track semantically and that she was referring to her L1 lexical knowledge while operating in German. Some further examples of English-German coinages – taken from the TCD MLRP German translation data produced by *ab initio* learners – follow:

Perfumer (expression to be translated *perfumes*)
Razoren (expression to be translated *razors*)
Packete (expression to be translated *packet*)

It must be admitted, however, that 'creations' of the above kind crop up less often in our German data than in our French data. The precise difference between the two data-sets in this regard has yet to be quantified in global terms, but in an earlier study based on pilot MLRP C-test data, Singleton & Little (1991) found English-French coinages to be roughly 10 times more frequent than English-German coinages (relative to all lexical innovations produced), a fact which they explain in terms of perceived language distance (cf. e.g. Kellerman, 1977; 1979; Ringbom, 1987: *passim*; Odlin, 1989: 140ff):

. . . the English-speaking learner of French quickly realises that there are large numbers of English words that, after being subjected to a fairly simple phonological 'conversion' process, will do very good service in French. English-German conversions . . . are less straightforward. Leaving aside loanwords and a handful of cases where German and English share virtually identical descendants of Proto-Germanic, 'converting' English words into their German cognates requires one, at the very least, to put into reverse the Great English Vowel Shift and then to re-run the Second German Sound Shift. (Singleton & Little, 1991: 75f)

In the above case, the quantification relates to a mixture of advanced and *ab initio* learners of German. In a more recent study (Ridley & Singleton, forthcoming) a comparison was made strictly between the advanced learners of German and the advanced learners of French recruited to the second level of the TCD MLRP in 1990–91 with regard to frequency of recourse to L1 knowledge in response to lexical problems in a translation task. It was found that the learners of French borrowed from English nearly twice as often as the learners of German. This finding, though perhaps less dramatic than the one cited above, clearly points in the same direction and is amenable to the same kind of explanation.

Interesting recent developments of the theme of language distance in relation to bilingual lexical organisation are De Groot's (1993) suggestion that concrete words in the two languages and words perceived as cognates across the two languages are stored in a 'compound' manner, whereas abstract non-cognates in the respective languages are stored in a 'co-ordinate' manner, and Kirsner, Lalor & Hird's suggestion that on the basis of morphological relatedness 'some fraction of the second language vocabulary is stored as variants of the first language vocabulary' (1993: 228). If there is any truth in Singleton & Little's comments about Anglophones' perceptions of French versus German vocabulary, De Groot's and Kirsner *et al.*'s proposals – which, incidentally, bear comparison with Singleton's (1987b) notion of 'assimilative encoding' – imply a higher degree of integration between the L1 and the L2 lexicon in the case of an Anglophone learner of French than in that of an Anglophone learner of German. Such a view would go some way towards explaining the greater abundance of evidence of inter-lexical interaction in the MLRP French data than in the German data.

It should perhaps be added that, even in the French data, evidence of reference to L1 lexical knowledge is not hugely prominent. Again, global quantification has yet to be completed, but present indications are that inter-lingual coinages account for less than 10% of solutions offered in the various tasks, and, likewise, that introspections with a crosslinguistic dimension account for less than 10% of the comments elicited by the introspective dimensions of the C-tests and the translation tasks. Such figures, self-evidently, do not represent the full extent of crosslinguistic influence; nevertheless, they do suggest that even in the case of the processing of two languages with a large number of obvious cognates, the extent of interaction between the L1 and the L2 lexicon is not such as to deprive the latter of a high degree of autonomy *vis-à-vis* the former.

Conclusion

The message which appears to emerge from the foregoing is that neither a strict separatist nor a strict integrationist model of bilingual lexical organisation is supported by the available evidence. It is clear that the L1 and the L2 lexicon do interact, but it also appears that much of the functioning of each of the two lexica proceeds with little or no reference to the other. One possibility that suggests itself is that of separate storage with interconnections between the storage systems – whether direct or via a common conceptual store. Another (not incompatible) possibility is that some portions of the L2 lexicon are very closely assimilated to parts of the L1 lexicon, while others are more separately organised.

References

Beauvillain, C. and Grainger, J. (1987) Accessing interlexical homographs: Some limitations of a language-selective access. *Journal of Memory and Language* 26, 658–72.

Bley-Vroman, R. (1989) What is the logical nature of foreign language learning? In S. Gass and J. Schachter (eds) *Linguistic Perspectives on Second Language Acquisition* (pp. 41–68). Cambridge: Cambridge University Press.

Bybee, J. (1988) Morphology as lexical organisation. In M. Hammond and M. Noonan (eds) *Theoretical Morphology* (pp. 119–41). London: Academic Press.

Caramazza, A. and Brones, I. (1979) Lexical access in bilinguals. *Bulletin of the Psychonomic Society* 13, 212–14.

Cook, V. (1992) Evidence for multicompetence. *Language Learning* 42, 557–91.

— (1993) Wholistic multicompetence – jeu d'esprit or paradigm shift. In B. Kettemann and W. Wieden (eds) *Current Issues in European Second Language Acquisition Research* (pp. 3–8). Tübingen: Narr.

Cristoffanini, P., Kirsner, K. and Milech, D. (1986) Bilingual lexical representation: The status of Spanish-English cognates. *Quarterly Journal of Experimental Psychology* 38A, 367–93.

De Groot, A. (1993) Word-type effects in bilingual processing tasks: Support for a mixed representational system. In R. Schreuder and B. Weltens (eds) *The Bilingual Lexicon* (pp. 27–51). Amsterdam: Benjamins.

Emmorey, K. and Fromkin, V. (1988) The mental lexicon. In F. Newmeyer (ed.) *Linguistics: The Cambridge Survey. III Language: Psychological and Biological Aspects* (pp. 124–49). Cambridge: Cambridge University Press.

Fodor, J. (1983) *The Modularity of Mind: An Essay on Faculty Psychology*. Cambridge, MA: MIT Press.

Green, D. (1986) Control, activation, and resource: A framework and a model for the control of speech in bilinguals. *Brain and Language* 27, 210–23.

Grosjean, F. (1982) *Life with Two Languages: An Introduction to Bilingualism*. Cambridge, MA: Harvard University Press.

Hamers, J. and Lambert, W. (1972) Bilingual interdependence in auditory perception. *Journal of Verbal Learning and Verbal Behavior* 11, 303–10.

Kellerman, E. (1977) Towards a characterization of the strategy of transfer in second language learning. *Interlanguage Studies Bulletin* 2, 58–145.

— (1979) Transfer and non-transfer – where are we now? *Studies in Second Language Acquisition* 2, 37–57.

Kirsner, K., Lalor, E. and Hird, K. (1993) The bilingual lexicon: Exercise, meaning and morphology. In R. Schreuder and B. Weltens (eds) *The Bilingual Lexicon* (pp. 215–48). Amsterdam: Benjamins.

Kirsner, K., Smith, M., Lockhart, R. and King, M. (1984) The bilingual lexicon: Language-specific units in an integrated network. *Journal of Verbal Learning and Verbal Behavior* 23, 519–39.

Odlin, T. (1989) *Language Transfer*. Cambridge: Cambridge University Press.

Ridley, J. and Singleton, D. (forthcoming) Contrastivity and individual learner contrasts. *Fremdsprachen Lehren und Lehren* 24.

Ringbom. H. (1987) *The Role of the First Language in Foreign Language Learning*. Clevedon: Multilingual Matters.

Singleton, D. (1987a) The fall and rise of language transfer. In J. Coleman and R. Towell (eds) *The Advanced Language Learner* (pp. 27–53). London: CILT.

— (1987b) Mother and other tongue influence on learner French. *Studies in Second Language Acquisition* 9, 327–46.

— (1993) Modularity and lexical processing: An L2 perspective. In B. Kettemann and W. Wieden (eds) *Current Issues in European Second Language Acquisition Research* (pp. 253–62). Tübingen: Narr.

Singleton, D. and Little, D. (1991) The second language lexicon: Some evidence from university-level learners of French and German. *Second Language Research* 7.1, 61–82.

Stemberger, J. and MacWhinney, B. (1988) Are inflected forms stored in the lexicon? In M. Hammond and M. Noonan (eds) *Theoretical Morphology* (pp. 101–16). London: Academic Press.

Whitaker, H. (1978) Bilingualism: A neurolinguistics perspective. In W. Ritchie (ed.) *Second Language Acquisition Research: Issues and Implications* (pp. 21–32). New York: Academic Press.

27 Helping L2 Readers To See

BRIAN TOMLINSON

Introduction

Until the late nineteenth century, books and articles on reading seemed to take it for granted that readers converted words on the page into pictures in the mind (Paivio, 1979). Then the powerful insistence of Ebbinghaus on rote learning in the 1880s and Watson's influential theories of behaviourism at the beginning of the twentieth century made reading researchers sceptical about the psychological reality of visualisation as a feature of the reading process. For example, Stout in the chapter on 'Implicit Apprehension' in his 'Analytical Psychology' was certain that the part that images played in consciousness had been over-estimated and dismissed imagery in reading as neither useful nor essential (Stout, 1896). This dismissal of visualisation has persisted among reading researchers throughout this century. This has been in part because visualisation has been considered as a 'mentalistic' concept on which it is very difficult to access rigorous scientific data and partly because it has been dismissed as an epiphenomenon (see, for example, Pylyshyn, 1973). Even with the demise of the belief that behaviour consists only of reflexes, innate or conditioned, there has still been little research on visualisation in reading. There is no reference, for example, to visualisation in any of the major models of the reading process put forward in the last 30 years.[1]

This paper sets out to examine the role of visualisation in first language reading and from there it will explore the significance of visualisation for second language readers.

Do L1 Readers Visualise?

Surveys of introspective reports of visualisation among 80 L1 teachers of English at seminars in England, Japan and Spain (Tomlinson, 1995) revealed that 95% of them saw images in their minds (varying in detail and vividness) when reading texts such as the following:

River Station Plaza

Out the stopped train
window the station plaza
glistens, empty but for one
car, one woman in it
waiting under bluegray
clouds – dark regattas
running heeled over
in a glitter of wind off
the river.

Her car
faces me. Yellow
light moves about
the square, enters
the car, lights on
yellow hair, a hand's
edge the shape of
patience curved to
a leaning cheek.

No one
gets off.
She shakes
her hair, scattering
light.

Our eyes
I think meet,
then tack
away as
the river rolls past
stilting herons;
rolls its
deep stones beneath
barges, sloops, duck
flotillas,
mute
bowing swans,
to the mouth of
the sea

Sheldon Flory (1990)

Stevick also reports 95% visualisers in his experiments with L1 listeners and readers and says that 'words that have come into our heads from reading or listening commonly leave us with pictures, sounds and feelings in our minds' (Stevick, 1986: 3). It seems that not all visualisers achieve the same vividness and effect; they can be placed on a cline from very low imagers to very high imagers (see Ernest, 1977; Denis, 1982).

Strangely, many books on the reading process and the teaching of reading make little or no mention of the fact that L1 readers typically visualise before, whilst and after reading (see, for example, Nuttall, 1995; Barnett, 1989; Carr & Levy, 1990).

Is L1 Visualisation Functional?

Eysenk & Keane (1990) ask whether visual imagery has 'functional signifi-cance' or whether it is a 'mere epiphenomenon'. Studies of visualisation such as those cited in this paper, and personal introspection, lead me to agree with Esrock when she asserts that, 'the reader's visual imagery can have unique cognitive and affective consequences that heighten the reader's experience' (Esrock, 1994: vii). It is also my contention that visualisation plays a major role in helping most L1 readers to achieve involvement, com-prehension, retention and recall.

Among the many functional roles claimed for visualisation in L1 reading it is argued that it can help:

- whilst-reading retention of concepts and propositions originally repre-sented by words (see Tomlinson, 1993);
- post-reading retention of the content of a text (see Kulhavy & Swenson, 1975);
- to increase comprehension of a text (Anderson & Kulhavy, 1972; Knight, Padron & Waxman, 1985);
- to achieve affective impact (Esrock, 1994);
- to personalise a text and make it relevant to the reader (Tomlinson, 1993).

Do L2 Readers Visualise?

There appears to have been very little research seeking to determine whether L2 readers typically visualise while reading. Knight, Padron & Waxman (1985) investigated the reading strategies reported by ESL and by monolingual students. They found that imaging was significant for L1 readers but was not mentioned at all by the L2 readers, whose primary concern was with low level decoding skills (1985: 789). Barnett (1989) devised a questionnaire, 'What Do You Do When You Read?', which she administered to L2 readers.

However, her report makes no reference at all to visualisation as a strategy used by anybody in her sample. Tomlinson (1993) also found that the L2 readers studied did not seem to visualise very much whilst reading. These subjects were 476 students from universities in Kobe and a further 86 students from Nagoya Women's University. They had a mean age of 20 and they were all L2 readers of English. Subjects were studied in classes ranging from 20 to 60 in size. Most had studied English for seven years and their general level of competence ranged from lower intermediate to upper intermediate. Most of the subjects made no reference to visualisation when asked to reflect on how they had read a text. For example, in one experiment only seven out of 41 students reported any visualisation when they were asked to say what they had done in order to try to understand and remember a poem, on which they knew they would have to answer comprehension questions later. The main strategies reported by the non-visualisers were 'looking up difficult words', 'trying to translate the poem', 'reading the poem over and over again', 'trying to memorise the poem', and 'giving up',

Likewise out of 19 students who were asked to read the poem *River Station Plaza* (Flory, 1990) and then to reflect on the process of reading it only four reported visualising. What is most interesting is that these four students performed better than the others when asked after an interval to recall words from the poem and to write a summary of it. In fact in all my experiments the few students who reported visualising tended to achieve greater comprehension and recall than those who did not. This was also the case when Padron & Waxman (1988) administered a Reading Strategy Questionnaire to 82 Hispanic ESL students and found that one of the most frequently cited strategies by the successful students was 'imaging or picturing the story in your mind' (1988: 147).

What are the Characteristics of L2 Visualisation?

Anderson & Pearson (1984) say that younger children are not predisposed to draw inferences spontaneously and the example is given of five year olds being less able to infer the instrument than eight year olds when reading the sentence 'the man dug a hole'. From my studies of L2 learners it appears that when they do visualise they are less likely to make default inferences than L1 readers are and that, like the young L1 child, they depend on the writer to provide most of the information to be visualised. For example, when asked to visualise the poem *River Station Plaza* my Japanese subjects recalled that a yellow light is described as shining on the plaza but, unlike the L1 readers, they did not visualise its undescribed source.

However, this childlike state seems to be typical rather than inevitable. Groups of L2 readers taught to visualise while engaged in L2 reading, as part of the study outlined above (Tomlinson, 1995) were easily capable of seeing what is not actually described. In another study (also described in Tomlinson, 1995) a multinational L2 class taught to visualise at the University of Luton cited 'the sun', 'a car headlight' and 'a shop window' as the source of light in *River Station Plaza*. These experiments, in which I have encouraged L2 learners to visualise, have revealed that there are invariably gaps in the mental pictures they create. Thus, when drawing what they saw whilst reading the first two pages of *Brazzaville Beach* (Boyd, 1990), the Japanese students did not draw the topless sunbathers mentioned, nor the working fishermen (sights not common on Japanese beaches) nor did they draw the itinerants and scavengers (words they did not know); but most of them did draw the volleyball players (beach volleyball is very popular on Japanese television). Some of the students just left gaps in their pictures where they knew other activities should go, others compensated by seeing the volleyball game in vivid detail and many others compensated by imaging details not described in the text at all (e.g. birds in the sky and boats at sea). The L2 readers who are content to leave many gaps in their mental images of what a text represents seem to be those who achieve the least understanding of the text, whereas those who try to fill in the picture by, for example, compensating from their visual schemata, seem to understand more.

Another typical characteristic of L2 visualisers in this sample was the tendency to see only prototypical or stereotypical images suggested by key words and not to develop them into instantiated images on the strength of further evidence in the text. The 'debilitating effect of' this 'premature commitment to a particular schema' (Rumelhart 1980: 47) was most evident in an activity in which I asked students at Kobe University to draw the party which was about to happen in Harold Pinter's *Birthday Party*. All the students drew young boys drinking soft drinks (the stereotypical image of a birthday party in a country where adults do not normally have birthday parties) even though the text made it clear that the characters were adults and the party was going to be a 'booze up'. In the same way, another class at Kobe University when asked to read an extract from *Brazzaville Beach* and then 'draw Clovis' all drew a small boy. When asked twice to read on and draw Clovis again they all continued to draw a boy even though by now the text had made it clear that Clovis is a monkey of some sort who swings away through the trees. Native speakers drew boys and men for the first two extracts but all of them changed Clovis to a monkey after reading the third extract.

Can L2 Readers be Helped to Improve their Visualisation?

Overall, the studies outlined above, in which L2 readers were taught or encouraged to visualise, led to improvement in their reading competence and confidence. This was evidenced by increased comprehension scores, by improved attendance and by a greater willingness to tackle apparently difficult texts. These reading courses included the following activities designed to help readers to use visualisation effectively:

(1) Students were told before reading a text not to study it or to translate it but to imagine pictures as they read it and then to change these pictures as they found further information in the text.
(2) They were also sometimes told to focus their images initially on what was familiar in the text and then to use these images to help them work out what was unfamiliar in the text.
(3) Another frequently given instruction was to picture a summary of each section of the text immediately after reading it and also to attempt a pictorial summary immediately after finishing the text.
(4) Students were sometimes given reading texts which contained explicit visualisation instructions either just before the text or in the margins within the text. Often these were instructions designed to help them achieve interactive imaging which would facilitate interpretative connections between different parts of the text.

Visualisation Activities

I found overt Visualisation instruction to have beneficial effects in aiding comprehension but agreed with Van Dijk & Kintsch that 'a comprehension strategy which must be applied consciously . . . is of limited usefulness' (1983: 335). I therefore also devised visualisation activities designed to induce visualisation sub-consciously with the intention of establishing visualisation as something the students do habitually when reading narrative and descriptive texts. These activities included:

(1) Drawing

Pre-reading drawing activities appeared to help the students to achieve relevant images in their minds when they started to read the text. These images are activations of their schemata. They enable them to read interactively straight away rather than being initially reliant on text data and running the risk of word dependence. These activities often involve drawing predictions of the characters, the setting or the narrative from a rapid sampling of the book or from the title, the blurb, the front cover or the introduction to the book. Alternatively, they might involve drawing scenes from the student's own lives connected to the title or front cover of a book.

Whilst-reading drawing activities also appeared to facilitate interactive reading and thus help readers to relate data from the text to their knowledge of their world.

Post-reading drawings helped students to read visually and interactively, provided that they were told what they were going to be asked to draw prior to reading the text. Thus, being told they were going to be asked to draw a picture to show what they understood of *First Day at School* by Roger McGough helped students to gain access to the following poem through focusing on what they could understand and see.

> *First Day At School*
>
> A million billionwillion miles from home
> Waiting for the bell to go. (To go where?)
> Why are they all so big, other children?
> So noisy? So much at home they
> must have been born in uniform
> Lived all their lives in playgrounds
> Spent the years inventing games
> that don't let me in. Games
> that are rough, that swallow you up.
>
> And the railings.
> All around, the railings.
> Are they to keep out wolves and monsters?
> Things that carry off and eat children?
> Things you don't take sweets from?
> Perhaps they're to stop us getting our
> Running away from the lessins. Lessin.
> What does a lessin look like?
> Sounds small and slimy.
> They keep them in glassrooms.
> Whole rooms made out of glass. Imagine.
>
> I wish I could remember my name
> Mummy said it would come in useful.
> Like wellies. When there's puddles.
> Lellowwellies. I wish she was here.
> I think my name is sewn on somewhere.
> Perhaps the teacher will read it for me.
> Tea-cher. The one who makes the tea.
>
> *McGough* (1979)

Calling up pictures in their mind also helped them to re-read the poem with greater understanding. Thus, for example, none of the students initially understood the word 'railings' on lines 10 and 11, but when they visualised what could be all around a school they all began to draw railings.

(2) Illustrations

Illustrations of texts often inhibit active visualisation because they impose a visual interpretation of the texts. However, I found that involving the students in relating illustrations to their own visualisation of the text can facilitate interactive reading. Examples of such activities include the students:

- selecting from a number of possible illustrations;
- completing partial illustrations by relating them to the text;
- re-drawing an illustration to fit the reader's interpretation.

(3) Miming

Miming also seems to be an effective way of inducing visualisation. I have often mimed extracts from texts before asking students to read them so that they start reading with images to which they can relate the text. Other methods which proved successful include having students read a story in order to be able to mime it to another group, having students mime a story or poem as I read it aloud to them and then to read it silently, or having students mime a text as they are reading it.

Conclusions

L2 readers appear typically not to use the strategy of visualisation commonly found in L1 readers, but they can be encouraged to visualise in order to improve their reading comprehension. The visualisation activities outlined above (see also Tomlinson, 1994; Tomlinson & Masuhara, 1994) have helped many of these L2 students to understand and enjoy texts normally considered beyond their linguistic level. This has been achieved by encouraging an appropriate balance between concept driven and data driven processing which has enabled them to personalise, interpret and retain.

Note

1. See Goodman, 1967, 1985; Smith, 1971; LaBerge & Samuels, 1974; Rumelhart, 1977; Kintsch & Van Dijk, 1978; Just & Carpenter, 1980; Stanovich, 1980; Anderson & Pearson, 1984; Gough, 1985; Rumelhart & McClelland, 1981; Nuttall, 1995.

References

Anderson, R.C. and Kulhavy, R.W. (1972) Imagery and prose learning. *Journal of Educational Psychology* 63/3, 242–3.

Anderson, R.C. and Pearson, P.D. (1984) A schema-theoretic view of basic processes in reading comprehension. In P.D. Pearson (ed.) *A Handbook of Reading Research*. New York: Longman.

Barnett, M. (1989) *More Than Meets the Eye: Foreign Language Reading*. Englewood Cliffs, NJ: Prentice Hall Regents.

Boyd, W. (1990) *Brazzaville Beach*. London: Penguin.

Carr, T. and Levy, B. (eds) (1990) *Reading and Its Developments: Component Skills Approaches*. San Diego: Academic Press.

Denis, M. (1982) Imaging whilst reading text: A study of individual differences. *Memory and Cognition* 10/6, 540–5.

Ernest, C.H. (1977) Imagery ability and cognition: A critical review. *Journal of Mental Imagery* 2, 181–216.

Esrock, E. (1994) *The Reader's Eye*. Baltimore: The John Hopkins University Press.

Eysenk, N.W. and Keane, M.T. (1990) *Cognitive Psychology. A Student's Handbook*. Hillsdale, NJ: Lawrence Erlbaum Associates.

Flory, S. (1990) *River Station Plaza*. London: *The Observer*.

Goodman, K. (1967) Reading: A psycholinguistic guessing game. *Journal of the Reading Specialist* 6, 126–35.

— (1985) Unity in reading. In H. Singer and R. Ruddell (eds) *Theoretical Models and Processes of Reading* (pp. 813–40). 3rd Edition. Newark, D.E.: International Reading Association.

Gough, P. (1985) One second of reading: postscript. In H. Singer and R. Ruddell (eds) *Theoretical Models and Processes of Reading* (pp. 687–8). 3rd Edition. Newark, D.E.: International Reading Association.

Just, M. and Carpenter, P. (1980) A theory of reading: From eye fixations to comprehension. *Psychological Review* 4, 329–54.

Kintsch, W. and Van Dijk, T. (1978) Toward a model of discourse comprehension and production. *Psychological Review* 85, 163–82.

Knight, S.L., Padron, Y.N and Waxman, H.C. (1985) The cognitive strategies of ESL students. *TESOL Quarterly* 19, 789–92.

Kulhavey, R.W. and Swenson, I. (1975) Imagery instructions and the comprehension of text. *British Journal of Educational Psychology* 45, 47–51.

La Berge, D. and Samuels, S.J. (1974) Towards a theory of automatic information processing in reading. *Cognitive Psychology* 6, 293–323.

McGough, R. (1979) First day at school. In R. McGough and M. Rosen (eds) *You Tell Me*. London: Kestrel.

Nuttall, C. (1995) *Teaching Reading Skills in a Foreign Language* (new edition). London: Heinemann.

Padron, Y.N. and Waxman, H.C. (1988) The effect of ESL students' perceptions of their cognitive strategies on reading achievement. *TESOL Quarterly* 22, 146–50.

Paivio, A. (1979) *Imagery and Verbal Processes*. Hillsdale, NJ: Lawrence Erlbaum.

Pylyshyn, Z.W. (1973) What the mind's eye tells the mind's brain: A critique of mental imagery. *Psychological Bulletin* 80, 1–24.

Rumelhart, D.E. (1977) Towards an interactive model of reading. In S. Dornie (ed.) *Attention and Performance 6* (pp. 573–603). Hillsdale, NJ: Lawrence Erlbaum Associates.

— (1980) Schemata: The building blocks of cognition. In R.J. Spiro, B.C. Bruce and W.F. Brewes (eds) *Theoretical Issues in Reading Comprehension*. Hillsdale, NJ: Lawrence Erlbaum Associates.

Rumelhart, D.E. and McClelland, J.L. (1981) Interactive processing through spreading activation. In A.M. Lesgold and C.A. Perfetti (eds) *Interactive Processes in Reading* (pp. 37–60). Hillsdale, NJ: Lawrence Erlbaum Associates.

Singer, H. and Ruddell, R. (1985) *Theoretical Models and Processes of Reading*. 3rd Edition. Newark, D.E.: International Reading Association.

Smith, F. (1971) *Understanding Reading*. New York: Holt, Rinehart and Winston.

Stanovich, K. (1980) Toward an interactive-compensatory model of individual differences in the development of reading fluency. *Reading Research Quarterly* 16, 32–71.

Stevick, E. (1986) *Images and Option in the Language Classroom*. Cambridge: Cambridge University Press.

Stout, G. (1896) *Analytical Psychology*, Vols 1–2. London: MacMillan.

Tomlinson, B. (1993) Do we see what they mean? Unpublished PhD paper, University of Nottingham.

— (1994) *Openings*. London: Penguin.

— (1995) The role of visualisation in reading literature in a foreign language. Unpublished PhD thesis, University of Nottingham.

Tomlinson, B. and Masuhara, H. (1994) *Use Your English*. Tokyo: Asahi Press.

Van Dijk, T. and Kintsch, W. (1983) *Strategies of Discourse Comprehension*. New York: Academic Press.

28 Strategy Training or/and Extensive Reading?

HITOMI MASUHARA, TAKASHI KIMURA, ATSUSHI FUKADA
and MASAO TAKEUCHI

Introduction

The advancement of reading research in the last two decades has resulted in our greater awareness of the complex and interactive nature of L1/L2 reading processes involving readers' variables as well as those belonging to text itself. This development has stimulated the quest for alternative approaches to teaching reading other than the Grammar-Translation Method, which still seems to prevail in ELT programmes in many parts of the world (e.g. Japan). This paper will consider two potential approaches (i.e. extensive reading and strategy training) in detail and examine their efficacy.

Extensive Reading Approach

How do we develop reading ability in L2? 'We learn to read by reading' asserts Krashen (1988), quoting Smith (1976). His argument is based on the remarkably positive result gained in his extensive review of a total of 62 studies in secondary level L1 reading, investigating a relationship between the amount of pleasure reading done and reading ability. He found that 'the amount of free reading consistently correlates with performance on reading comprehension tests' (1988: 291). According to Krashen (1991: 409) reading is another source of comprehensible input which stimulates language acquisition. He argues against scholars who assume that skills must first be taught directly and are made 'automatic' by reading (e.g. Mork, 1972: 441; Sadoski, 1980 reported in Krashen, 1988: 286–7). He claims that genuine reading for meaning is far more valuable than workbook exercises and that 'it is the source of "skills"' (1988: 286–7).

There are very few empirical studies in L2 extensive reading available. In fact articles on L2 extensive reading itself are rare. Susser & Robb (1990) report that they could only find three articles on L2 extensive reading after a vigorous search. A literature search done by the authors in 1994 confirmed this lack of research in L2 extensive reading, apart from general work on graded readers, book selection and course administration such as Nuttall (1982/95) and Hedge (1985).

The authors could only find five research-based studies relevant to this present article: Elley & Mangubhai (1983); Mason (1987); Hafiz & Tudor (1989); Robb & Susser (1989) and Kanatani et al. (1994). Their experimental design was longitudinal with an aim to measure the effect of extensive reading treatment by comparing comprehension test scores, pre- and post-test. Except for Mason, experiments reported a significant positive effect for the extensive reading procedure. However, the authors recognised various methodological weaknesses (Lysynchuk et al., 1989) in all the studies which undermine their research findings (some of the limitations are quite rightly acknowledged by the authors themselves in their papers). For example, in Hafiz & Tudor (1989), the sampling of the subjects was not random, the comparability of the control and experimental groups was not established, and the possibility of influence outside the treatment was not tested.

What seems more disconcerting to the authors is the lack of theoretical framework underlying the extensive reading approach. What was available in the literature search of extensive reading disclosed that we do not seem to: (a) have a clear definition of what extensive reading is (e.g. Munby, 1979: 143 treats extensive reading as one of the skills in his list); (b) know the optimum amount of input and duration of extensive reading; or (c) be sure what the teachers' roles are. For example, Susser & Robb (1990) collected 17 variations as to what it means to be 'extensive' in reading. They concluded that the 'variety suggests that quantity of reading is not an absolute number of hours or pages but depends on teacher and student perception of how extensive reading differs from other reading classes' (1990: 166). The working definition of extensive reading as a language teaching/learning procedure in this paper is that it involves: reading of fairly large quantities of material (authentic or graded); for pleasure; in an individualised manner with students having full control over the selection and fulfilment of the reading and the pace of reading; the learners will not be required to prove their understanding after the reading and the teacher's role is to provide help if necessary. Therefore the authors of this article have decided to call their version of extensive reading treatment the Reading Experience. Their treatment generally incorporated aspects of extensive reading but involved a certain amount of control in using a reading laboratory kit, having the subjects keep reading records, and in including short content comprehension questions to be self-marked.

Strategy Training

Remarkable progress has been made in the 80s in literacy research in L1 and also increasingly in L2 reading supported by developments in related areas such as cognitive psychology and information processing. The current conceptions of reading research portray readers as active agents who direct their own cognitive resources in reading. Learners' cognitive resources include knowledge of the reading process and use of a variety of reading strategies, i.e. conscious or unconscious procedures used in reading as a way of achieving a goal (e.g. scanning a text for specific information).

Both descriptive and empirical research of readers' strategy use seem to suggest that successful readers are those who are aware of the kinds of texts and the kinds of suitable strategies, and who can monitor and control their own strategy use according to the particular purpose of reading. In L1 reading research younger and less proficient readers are reported to use fewer strategies in a less effective manner and are less effective at monitoring properly (extensive reviews in Garner, 1988). Similarly in the L2 context, the successful readers are shown to be better and comparatively conscious strategy users, with somewhat more contradictory data indicating the complexity of the issue which involves unsolved research topics such as reading ability transfer from L1 to L2, and how the learners' language ability affects their reading ability in L2 (Alderson, 1984; Bossers, 1991; Carrell, 1991).

These findings have inspired strategy training experiments in which direct explicit instruction of reading strategies is given to the learners for a certain period of time and its effect is then measured. In L1, consistent positive results have been reported. (Winograd & Hare, 1988; reviews in Garner, 1988) In the context of L2, some empirical studies measuring longitudinal training effects with pre- and post tests have proved strategy instruction to be relatively effective (Carrell, Pharis, & Liberto, 1989; Barnett, 1988; Kern, 1989). The results of these studies showed that there seems to be a positive relationship among reading comprehension, strategy use and strategy awareness. The implication of these studies is that L2 reading pedagogy, at least at university level, would benefit from employing comprehension-fostering strategy training. However, the research on strategy training seems to be very much in the developing stage, considering the scarcity of L2 strategy studies and their limitations in scope and depth. Kimura *et al.* (1993) portrayed how the results of previous strategy training research should be interpreted with caution because of its methodological weaknesses. Anderson (1991) and Pritchard (1990) depicted how the relationship between strategy use and comprehension is not simple and straightforward and warned against simplistic assumptions concerning the effect of strategy use on reading comprehension.

The Experiment

In evaluating the efficacy of these two different approaches to L2 reading, this study specifically addresses the following questions:

(1) Can strategy training and extensive reading programmes improve the learners' EFL reading ability?
(2) Which teaching procedure will bring about greater improvement?
(3) What are the major factors causing this result?

Sampling

Altogether, there were three classes in the first year of the English Department in the College of Nagoya Women's University. The two classes were chosen randomly out of the three and 91 female students aged 18 to 19 years participated in this study. Due to administrative constraints, it was not possible to make the third class as the control group. Out of 91 students, two students could not take the post-test due to sickness, which left 89 subjects for the final analyses.

Treatment

The same instructor (first author) provided the two different teaching procedures (one 90 minute class per week for eight consecutive weeks) to the Strategy Training Group (43 subjects) and to the Reading Experience Group (46 subjects) using L1 as a medium of instruction. The circumstances of the two groups were very similar. All the subjects had already had six years of previous regular EFL training in Japanese secondary schools using the Grammar-Translation Method. The courses they were taking in the college alongside the experimental treatment were almost identical: only one course was taught by different instructors for each group but the same Grammar-Translation Method was used. The details of the two experimental teaching procedures are shown in Table 28.1 on pages 268 and 269.

Measurement

The subjects' reading proficiency was examined before and after the treatment using the Vocabulary and Reading Comprehension section of two different but parallel forms of Level 2 TOEFL in ITP (Institutional Testing

Program). TOEFL is a standardised multiple-choice test which was originally developed to measure the English proficiency of non-native speakers of English wishing to study at colleges and universities in the United States. The ITP was devised to allow schools and other organisations to administer a TOEFL test at their own locations on dates convenient for them. The Level 2 TOEFL, available only through ITP, is constructed to measure the same language skills as the ordinary TOEFL but designed for testees with lower levels of English proficiency.

The characteristics of Level 2 TOEFL Vocabulary and Reading Comprehension Section are as follows (Educational Testing Service, 1991): Possible Score Range (20–50); Number of Items (40); Testing Time (31 minutes); Reliability (Standard Error of Measurement) (0.85).

The first and last class periods of the ten-week treatment were used for administering the Level 2 TOEFL, following strict administration guidelines so that the two groups would have the same conditions for the measurement. The scoring was done by the Educational Testing Service and the statistical analyses were done by the authors. The questionnaire was given at the end of the treatment period and the subjects were asked to evaluate, on a five-point scale with five as the highest, in terms of the usefulness, interest, and effect of what they had learned. The subjects were asked to add comments for each rating specifying why they chose that rating, and also to make comments on the whole course in a free composition.

Results

Testing the assumptions prior to applying the statistical tests

The degree of equivalence between the two groups was examined using the distribution of the pre-test scores. The shape of both samples was recognised as not significantly different from normal. The homogeneity of variance of the two groups was confirmed. However, the independent t-test showed a significant difference, which indicated that the Strategy Training Group belonged to a population of a higher mean than that of the Reading Experience Group.

The amount of involvement in supplemental learning (i.e. the subjects' individual involvement with English learning outside the experimental treatment) was tabulated in terms of the minutes for each activity and was included in the analysis. The analysis of two-way ANOVA confirmed that there was no interactions between the treatment and the supplemental learning and that the treatment was the reason for the improvement ($p < 0.05$).

Table 28.1 Experimental teaching procedures for Strategy Training Group and Reading Experience Group

Strategy Training Group (STG)	Reading Experience Group (REG)
Strategies taught	
(1) Scanning	None
(2) Identifying paragraph organisation	
(3) Guessing the meaning of unknown words	
(4) Recognising the referents of referring expressions	
Materials used	
Sources	*Sources*
EFL materials (e.g. Mikulecky, 1990) and some articles from English newspapers and magazines.	SRA Reading Laboratory 2b, a series of graded reader packages originally designed for mid teenage native American students. Only texts and content comprehension questions were used.
Average length of text	*Average length of text*
More than 41 texts in all, mixture of many short (50–100 words) and some long (more than 300 words) passages.	Each text of one 'Power Builder' file was usually 750–850 words long.
Estimated amount of language exposure	*Estimated amount of language exposure*
More than approx. 4,500 words excluding the long texts used for scanning in eight weeks.	More than approx. 9000–10,200 words in 8 weeks.

Classroom procedures (no dictionaries in class)

(1) A discovery task was introduced, using an example from L1 reading in order to raise awareness of the reading strategies used in L1.

(2) A reflective discussion in L1 was held, concerning strategy options suited for the reading situation.

(3) A short lecture was given on the effective use of a particular strategy.

(4) Practice using short texts and tasks.

(5) Confirmation exercises, making use of authentic texts (i.e. not written for the purpose of language teaching) and real-life-like activities.

(1) Administration of the SRA placement test.

(2) Subjects chose one Power Builder file suited to their level and read the text at their own pace.

(3) After reading the text, they answered a few comprehension questions, which they were instructed to mark themselves.

(4) Each subject kept her own progress record.

(5) When a subject achieved more than 80% of full scores of comprehension tests in six files, she was advised to go on to files belonging to the next grade.

(6) After finishing at least one Power Builder file, the subjects were encouraged to read high interest/low vocabulary original literature, English newspaper and magazines from the class library.

Comparison of the improvement within and between the two groups

The paired t-test revealed that both groups improved after treatment ($p < 0.05$). The greater improvement of the Reading Experience Group was noted.

The result of an independent t-test showed that the difference between the two groups is no longer significant in the post-test ($p < 0.05$). This indicates that the Reading Experience Group has caught up with the Strategy Training Group within a 10-week period.

Qualitative analysis of the two approaches

As a whole, their rating of both teaching approaches was high: 90% of each group rated their approaches favourably (fair to excellent) in all three criteria (usefulness, effectiveness and interest). A clear difference is observed in 'Interest'; the Reading Experience approach was rated as more interesting and engaging.

Discussion

In answer to the first research question as to the efficacy of the two teaching approaches, the result seems to suggest that both the Strategy Training and the Reading Experience do enhance L2 reading performance. The answer to the second research question as to the more effective procedure resulted in the Reading Experience. This result happens to be consonant with a similar study by Robb & Susser (1989) with the same two teaching procedures being compared on Japanese University subjects for a year. Then, if we hold to the assumption that extensive reading does improve the learners' reading performance, at least, for the Japanese college/university freshmen right after the treatment, what has caused this phenomenon? This third research question is harder to answer. What seems to emerge from these quantitative and qualitative data concerning the differences between two treatments is listed below.

Quantity of texts

Even though equal time was given to the groups during the treatment, the total quantity of text provided to the Reading Experience Group was twice as much. Is the quantity of input the influential determiner of the outcome as Krashen (1988) maintains?

Learners' attributes:

(1) Readiness

Strategy Training may require a certain level of language proficiency. In L2 reading, a reader normally has to tackle two things at a time; the language and the meaning of the content. In the Strategy Training Group the learners not only had to manage the task of processing the language in the texts freshly received from the teacher in the class but also had to struggle with the unfamiliar task of reflecting on their own metacognitive reading behaviour. Confident learners may be able to take the demand of a new text and strange task but weaker ones may find the dual tasks to be too demanding. Comments in the questionnaire seem to provide evidence for such speculation: three subjects disclosed that strategy training was demanding, three others that they felt tired and sleepy, and another three subjects commented that they *could* not do the tasks because they were concerned with the unknown words in the texts.

(2) Previous training

Extensive reading may be welcomed especially by Japanese college/university students who have had six years of formal English instruction in their secondary schools. The purpose of reading in high school English classes was almost always to learn about new vocabulary or structures through intensive translation of the textbooks. Many learners had been led to believe that reading in English means decoding accurately with heavy reliance on the grammar and the use of a bilingual dictionary. This explains why as many as 21 subjects out of 46 in the Reading Experience Group commented positively on the fact they could enjoy reading interesting stories in every class.

(3) Affective filter

In the Reading Experience Group many subjects commented how the atmosphere was relaxing – the teacher is more of a consultant and caretaker who is there to be of help when asked. In the Strategy Training Group, however, the teacher is 'the one who knows' and learners 'the ones who don't', which may remind them of their experience in traditional secondary school classroom situations and their covert or sometimes overt one-way power relationship.

Treatment:

(1) Mode

The way in which the material was presented in the Strategy Training Group may be described as deductive and discrete while in the Reading Experience Group the texts were offered to the subjects in a holistic inductive approach. It could be that the holistic inductive presentation worked just as a 'well-balanced diet of wholesome food' nourishes children better than lockstep 'single or even multiple vitamin therapy' (Krashen, 1982: 70).

(2) Duration

In strategy training research, Barnett (1988) speculated that one semester may not be enough for the effect to emerge, whereas Carrell *et al.* (1989) reported the effect after three-day intensive treatment. It is possible that the Strategy Training Group could have shown greater improvement if the duration of the training was longer or more intensive.

The data in this experiment does not give specific answers but the implication that these different aspects of the two methods should certainly have had influence in some form. Exploratory research is much needed to clarify the factors which influenced the effect of each approach.

Conclusion

Both teaching procedures of the Strategy Training and the Reading Experience applied to Japanese EFL college female English majors proved to be significantly effective, with an indication that the Reading Experience was more effective. Two approaches were compared and hypotheses about the factors that might have influenced this result were presented.

One implication of this study seems to be the necessity of considering, when employing strategy training, the learner's developmental stage, the mode of teaching, the duration of time given for each strategy, and the methodology.

So far, research in L2 strategy training has paid very little attention to learner variables. The subjects' developmental stage and the kinds of previous training they have had should have had a vital influence on the available research results. Learners' age, aptitude, learning styles and affective factors such as interest and sensitivity to teacher control should also have been significant. Furthermore, in an EFL situation, perceived need for strategy training may be lower than in an ESL context. The accumulation of research that has taken these learners' variables into account will lead to our better understanding of when and how to provide a particular group of learners with the appropriate kinds of strategy training for a suitable period of time.

The other implication would be an urgent call for research investigating why 'extensive reading' seems to work. Is it the amount of exposure? Is it the quality of reading? If so, can we predict the optimal amount, duration and quality of extensive reading exposure? It may be the methodology, stress-free environment, or holistic learning experience. If so, what would be the teacher's role? How can a teacher make sure the learners acquire reading ability? Extensive reading is usually associated with 'reading for pleasure'. Then what should be done for other kinds of reading for different purposes?

So many vital questions concerning the extensive reading approach have been left unresearched at present.

Meanwhile, the results of this present research seem to encourage our intervention with L2 readers using both approaches discussed above, with different types of learners benefitting from different orientation.

References

Alderson, J.C. (1984) Reading in a foreign language: A reading problem or a language problem? In J.C. Alderson and A.H. Urquhart (eds) *Reading in a Foreign Language*. London: Longman.

Anderson, N.J. (1991) Individual differences in strategy use in second language reading and testing. *Modern Language Journal* 75 (iv), 460–72.

Barnett, M.A. (1988) Reading through context: How real and perceived strategy use affects L2 comprehension. *Modern Language Journal* 72, 150–62.

Bossers, B. (1991) On thresholds, ceilings and short-circuits: The relation between L1 reading, L2 reading and L2 knowledge. Reading in Two Languages. *AILA Review* 8, 45–60.

Carrell, P.L. (1991) Second language reading: Reading ability or language proficiency. *Applied Linguistics* 12, 2, 159–79.

Carrell, P.L., Pharis, B.G. and Liberto, J.C. (1989) Metacognitive strategy training for ESL reading. *TESOL Quarterly* 23, 4, 647–78.

Educational Testing Service (1991) *TOEFL Institutional Testing Program* (pp. 4–7) (Japan Edition). Princeton, NJ: Educational Testing Service.

Elley, W. and Mangubhai, F. (1983) The impact of reading on second language learning. *Reading Research Quarterly* 19, 53–67.

Garner, R. (1988) *Metacognition and Reading Comprehension*. Norwood, NJ: Ablex Publishing Corporation.

Hafiz, F.M. and Tudor, I. (1989) Extensive reading and the developments of language skills. *English Language Teaching Journal* 43 (1), 4–13.

Hedge, T. (1985) *Using Readers in Language Teaching*. London: Macmillan.

Kanatani, K., Osada, M., Kimura, T. and Miyai, Y. (1994) An extensive reading program for junior high school students – its effects on motivation and reading ability. *The Bulletin of the Kanto-Koshin-Etsu English Language Education Society*, Vol. 8, 39–47.

Kern, R.G. (1989) Second language reading strategy. *Modern Language Journal* 73, 135–49.

Kimura, T., Masuhara, H., Fukada, A and Takeuchi, M. (1993) Effectiveness of reading strategy training in the comprehension of Japanese college EFL learners. *JACET Bulletin* 24, 101–20.

Krashen, S.D. (1982) *Principles and Practice in Second Language Acquisition*. Oxford: Pergamon Press.

— (1988) Do we learn to read by reading? In D. Tannen (ed.) *Linguistics in Context: Connecting Observation and Understanding* (pp. 269–98). Norwood, NJ: Ablex.

— (1991) The input hypothesis: An update. In J.E. Alatis (ed.) *Georgetown University Round Table on Languages and Linguistics 1991* (pp. 409–31). Georgetown University Press.

Lysynchuk, L.M., Pressley, M., d'Ally, H., Smith, M. and Cake, H. (1989) A metho-
    dological analysis of experimental studies of comprehension strategy instruction.
    Reading Research Quarterly XXIV Fall, 458–70.
Mason, B. (1987) Effects of a self-selecting reading program on the results of the
    TOEIC. In *The 26th JACET Annual Convention*. Kyoto, Japan.
Mikulecky, B.S. (1990) *A Short Course in Teaching Reading Skills*. Reading, MA:
    Addison-Wesley.
Munby, J. (1979) Teaching intensive reading skills. In R. Mackay, B. Barkman and
    R.R. Jordan (eds) *Reading in a Second Language* (pp. 142–58). Rowley, MA:
    Newbury House.
Nuttall, C. (1982, 1995 revised) *Teaching Reading Skills in a Foreign Language*.
    Oxford: Heinemann Educational.
Pritchard, R. (1990) The effect of cultural schemata on reading processing strategies.
    Reading Research Quarterly 25, 273–95.
Robb, T.N. and Susser, B. (1989) Extensive reading vs skills building in an EFL
    context. *Reading in a Foreign Language* 5 (2), 239–51.
Smith, F. (1976) Learning to read by reading. *Language Arts* 53, 297–99, 322.
SRA Reading Laboratory Series. Tokyo, Japan: Meynard.
Susser, B. and Robb, T. (1990) EFL extensive reading instruction: Research and
    procedure. *JALT Journal* 12, 2, 161–85.
Winograd, P. and Hare, C. (1988) Direct instruction of reading comprehension
    strategies: The nature of teacher explanation. In C.E. Weinstein, E.T. Goetz
    and P.A. Alexander (eds) *Learning and Study Strategies: Issues in Assessment,
    Instruction, and Evaluation* (pp. 121–39). San Diego: Academic Press.

29 Thinking Crazy about Mother Tongue Literacy; Acting Responsibly to Foster Appropriate Education

ROLAND WALKER

Thinking Clearly about Literacy and Development

Literacy for human development

Human development is the goal of literacy and the foundation of community and national development. I use the word literacy to mean the *use* of written language, not just the ability to read. By 'sustained literacy' I mean the ongoing practice of reading and writing to meet societal needs.

Every society in the world can benefit from literacy. However, rather than *adopt* imported versions of Western literacy and educational models, each society needs to *adapt* literacy practices to meet the community's unique needs (Street, 1984, 1993). The temptation for developing nations is to copy forms of literacy and education from more developed nations, assuming that these forms will bring about the desired development in their own country.

At AILA '93, Victor Ordoñez, Director of UNESCO's Basic Education Division, asked us to consider literacy as just one part of human resource development. It is not a panacea. Education can make people employable, but does not create employment. 'Education is the yeast, but not the dough' (Ordoñez, 1993).

Literacy can be a potent factor in human development, but does not necessarily lead to development. Only the appropriate kind of education will lead to sustained development, and only when literacy meets felt needs will literacy be sustained. 'Literacy for specific purposes', literacy adapted to local needs, is a central part of 'appropriate education'.

Appropriate education

Educators should strive to deliver education appropriate to each community's needs, education that contributes to human development. Curle (1970: xv) describes an inappropriate pattern of education observed in a number of developing nations:

> At present everyone hopes to pass his examination and so to move closer to a coveted administrative job. In fact, the work of the schools concentrates on getting students through and started on the long trek from village to town, field to office, and hoe to IBM typewriter – or more probably, to 'educated' unemployment.

According to Curle (1970: xiv),

> developing nations need an education system that not only purveys universal knowledge, but also helps people to live creatively within their own culture.

> The schools themselves must be rooted in the community, not only in the sense of community pride and participation, but in the sense that the work of the school is connected with the ecology of the community, preparing children both technically and emotionally to work within it . . .

Appropriate education, parallel to the concept of appropriate technology, uses resources of language, content, methods, and technology that are appropriate to the needs of the community. Appropriate language is the language/s the community desires to use for beginning literacy and education. Everyone has the right to learn in a language they know well, i.e. their mother tongue. Appropriate content is that which builds the community up, enabling them to enjoy a richer life. Appropriate methods are those that respect the culture and take preferred learning styles into account. Appropriate technology is that which can be used and maintained by local people using local resources over the long term.

Appropriate education integrates literacy and education with community development. It does not just teach certain development skills (e.g. better farming methods), but rather opens up new possibilities for the community by enabling them to acquire the skills and knowledge necessary to translate these possibilities into reality.

Appropriate education for many communities begins with literacy in the mother tongue. Mother tongue literacy should not be used just to preserve the language, but rather to extend its use and serve as a bridge to literacy and education in a language of wider communication (Barton, 1993).

Why Think Crazy about Literacy?

At AILA '93, Ordoñez painted a vivid picture of the growing illiteracy in the world. Quoting a participant of the Jomtien conference in 1990, Ordoñez challenged us to 'think crazy' about ways to turn the tide on this crucial element of human development. His clear message was that just doing more of what we have been doing is not going to solve the world's literacy needs.

Barriers to sustained literacy

Providing literacy opportunities for all people may seem like an over-whelming challenge. Doing it in such a way that results in sustained literacy is even more demanding. It requires innovative, 'crazy' thinking.

Ordoñez reminded us that sustained literacy is a 'demand issue' (i.e. tapping into existing motivation), not just a 'supply issue' (i.e. providing schools and teachers). Besides lack of motivation, some barriers to sustained literacy are (1) not enough reading material (of the kind the people want to read) and 2) the whole community not being involved (Ordoñez, 1993). To these, I would add (3) the difficulty of finding long-term funding from within the community.

There is a growing wave of interest in and support for mother tongue literacy. The benefits are significant, as compared to learning to read in a language one does not know well: the learning curve is not so steep, reading for meaning is enhanced, and the ability to read can be transferred to other languages. Self esteem and ethnic identity can also be bolstered for minority group members through appropriate mother tongue literacy.

Those who question the practicality of mother tongue literacy for all minority groups cite the huge cost of developing the language and producing educational materials (Fasold, 1984: 297). Without ignoring the practical problems and challenges, we must free ourselves to look for new solutions, to 'think crazy' about facilitating sustained literacy for all, and to make use of innovations that bring literacy within the reach of all who want it.

Going under the barriers

If it looks impossible to get over the barriers to sustained literacy for all, we need to look for novel, innovative solutions. 'Going under the barriers' means looking for resources to spread literacy where we expect to see only needs.

The greatest resources for spreading literacy in the communities where illiteracy is rife are the people themselves – people who long to be able to read. Outside help, in the form of facilitation, creative ideas, and appropriate technology can be the spark to set an educational fire ablaze in the community. But the members of the community are the fuel – their ambitions, abilities, and energy.

In this paper, I take up the challenge Ordoñez gave us to think crazy about literacy with specific reference to rural communities in the developing world. The specific challenges are to (1) empower people to develop themselves and their own communities, involving the entire community in the process; (2) uncover and build on existing motivation; (3) produce quantities of literature that meet felt needs; and (4) integrate literacy with other development activities, in order to provide an economic base within the community that can support ongoing literacy, education, and development.

Sustained literacy is possible only when it is creative, economical, and tailored to the community's needs. What is suggested here is a fresh approach to education and development, not just the diffusion of a new technology.

Thinking Crazy about Mother Tongue Literacy

Empowering local people to develop themselves

Illiterate people may seem to be the problem, but they are really a big part of the solution. They know their mother tongue well and often have time free from modern distractions to develop their languages. With some training, they can produce their own literature and teach others to read.

Maama was a crippled boy lying in the dust under a tree in Sudan. A literacy promoter noticed him and taught him to read his mother tongue. Being a natural teacher and having lots of time on his hands, Maama started teaching other young men to read, and it spread. Some women learned to read from the literacy promoter, too. Then they taught their friends and children.

> The children were fast learners and before long most of them were able to read better than their mothers . . . Literacy began slowly permeating the . . . community (Arensen, forthcoming: 6–7).

The Dani of Irian Jaya, Indonesia, are another example of effective each-one-teach-one literacy spread (Walker, 1987: 22).

Local people can also make excellent classroom teachers in formal programmes and take part in designing the curriculum for mother tongue schools (C. Spaulding, 1994: 14–24; P. Spaulding, 1994: 25–9). In Papua New Guinea community-based mother tongue literacy is beginning to spread like wildfire through many rural communities, often with school leavers as teachers (Stringer, 1987: 6).

With help from the Summer Institute of Linguistics, Mairasi people in Irian Jaya, Indonesia, with little formal education, helped design their own orthography, translate portions of the Bible, and input texts on the computer. All of these activities were aimed at developing their community in ways that they recognised as beneficial to themselves.

The Adivasi Oriya of India (also with assistance from SIL) have conducted extensive literacy programmes, teaching their own people to read, producing literature, and supervising the programme themselves. They have published a monthly 'Educational Newsletter' for 10 years, experimented with improved agricultural practices, and are now branching out into numerous income-generating development projects that will enable them to continue these programmes after outside resources are withdrawn (Gustafsson, 1991). It often does take substantial outside resources to get a mother tongue literacy programme started, but, with wise planning, development projects linked with literacy can help the community to be able to fund their own programme to make it ongoing.

In contrast are the many projects which outsiders (government and non-government bodies) have completed on behalf of rural communities without their involvement and ownership: literacy programmes, water wells, clinics, etc. Many of these look great at their inception, but fail shortly after outside help is withdrawn.

Only when members of a community are involved in every facet of a literacy programme can we expect to see literacy practised after outsiders leave the community. Local people are the fuel of the fire. They *can* develop their own communities, when they are motivated.

Building on existing motivation

Motivation exists in all communities. It is there below the surface, like gold waiting for a prospector to discover it. The job of the literacy/development worker is not to create motivation, but to identify felt needs and show how literacy can meet those needs. 'Felt needs are the beginning point for change' (Smith, 1984: 105) because needs are the core of motivation. (See Walker, 1993, for a model of basic needs and motivation underlying language choice.)

Literacy is not for everyone. It is only for those who see value in the written word. It is for those who can imagine how literacy will help them meet their felt needs. 'The insider obviously knows the problem best . . . but the outsider brings new possibilities' (Smith, 1984: 102). Mother tongue literacy is a new possibility for many of the world's minority language groups.

Economic advancement, safety from exploitation, and greater respect from their better educated neighbors were felt needs of the Adivasi Oriya of India. They saw mother tongue literacy as a means of meeting those needs by providing access to information for agricultural innovation and as a means to greater fluency and literacy in Telegu, the language of wider communication (Gustafsson, 1991: 92, 103–5). The Ulum of Sudan and the Dani of Indonesia were motivated to read the Christian Scriptures. Mother tongue literacy met a need of the oppressed Vagla of Ghana to bolster their ethnic identity. The Tzeltal of Mexico learned to read in order to avoid being deceived by outsiders and to study the Bible (Spaeth, 1991: 117, 125, 135).

Though it does take resources to develop an unwritten language and produce educational materials, there are several innovations (i.e. 'crazy ideas') that now make it much more feasible to provide literacy and primary education in the mother tongue for all communities who are motivated to work together for it.

Literature production within the reach of any community

Indigenous peoples are experts in their mother tongue and can author great quantities of creative literature. Wendell (1982) describes how to help the newly literate develop into effective authors to produce volumes of reading material for new readers. Stringer & Faraclas (1987: 13–22, 107–24) give detailed instructions on how to guide students into creating their own stories that become the basis for a whole-language approach to reading instruction. Their 'multi-strategy method' unleashes creative use of written language, while addressing the need to adapt reading instruction to community learning styles and to produce low cost initial reading materials.

Another innovation which facilitates the production of high quality (though less creative) books is the 'shell book' project. Pioneered in Papua New Guinea by the Summer Institute of Linguistics, the shell book is a reader with illustrations available on computer media. Once a prototypical book is developed, it can be cloned for other languages whose speakers share similar cultures (Trainum, 1989; Eliason, 1990; Cooper, 1991).

The high cost of book publication is a major hurdle in achieving universal mother tongue literacy. Two technological innovations now help to lower publishing costs. Silkscreen printers, made from locally available materials, are ideal for small publications, thus enabling people in rural communities to write and publish their own literacy materials (Stringer & Faraclas, 1987:

175–84, 199–201). Risograph technology is more suitable for larger publications. Though the initial cost of this sophisticated equipment is substantial, risograph is inexpensive and simple to operate.

Community development integrated with literacy and education

Curle (1970: iv) suggests that developing countries adopt:

> a form of education oriented, at least at primary level, to the productive life of the community. And so, in the rural areas . . . the orientation would be agricultural. This education would be complete in itself, not . . . a mere stepping-stone . . . to secondary education.

Employing mother tongue literacy to meet felt needs in the community is the goal. Pat Spaulding (1994) describes how all school subjects can be integrated around a text. This could be a traditional text or a text related to innovation (e.g. how to grow better crops). Maths, science, and reading, virtually any subject, for that matter, could be taught in the context of that text (e.g. maths related to selling produce; reading about new farming techniques). It is exciting to consider schooling in which the subject matter is integrated so closely with topics relevant to community life that students are enthusiastic about learning and can see immediate benefits.

Few children in marginalised indigenous peoples go far in school, and few who do continue their education get productive jobs. Therefore, primary education should begin in the mother tongue with a focus on acquiring practical skills to improve community life through holistic development. (Those who do go on in school, of course, will need preparation for education in the second language.)

The Adivasi Cultural Society (India) provides a good model for adult education, integrating mother tongue literacy, language of wider communication literacy, and development education. A rabbit-raising project for literate women has increased nutrition and income. A printing project publishes literacy and development materials in the mother tongue. A book on coffee growing, translated into the mother tongue, has become a popular selling item because it complements a government development project and gives new literates access to information that will increase their income (Gustafsson, 1991: 62, 117–44). Many other projects illustrating how mother tongue literacy and development have been married could be cited if space permitted.

Conclusions: Acting Responsibly to Foster Appropriate Education

Local people are successfully creating their own literature, developing their own languages, and making decisions about their own destiny in a number or countries. Papua New Guinea has recently embarked on the ambitious venture of promoting mother tongue literacy for each of its 860 languages.

> The vernacular languages are no longer perceived as backward languages which hinder the modernisation of Papua New Guinea, but are seen as essential resources in the education and mobilization of the rural masses in the process of development. (Ahai, 1991: 9)

Over the past four years, Papua New Guinea has promoted community-based vernacular education for holistic development. The National Education Department stipulates that 'all education must meet the social-cultural, spiritual, economic and political needs of the learner'. This is accomplished by combining literacy with 'lessons on health, agriculture, banking, environ-ment, conservation, etc.'. and community discussions led by 'developmental information workers' (Ahai, 1991: 9).

Hartmann argues that many students are kept in the dark without mother tongue education. The title of his paper at AILA '93 is a challenge to each of us: 'Let's open the doors to the world – The international responsibility of mother tongue education in the 21st century'. Success in this task will require much crazy thinking, the willingness to re-evaluate traditional practices, and the courage to chart new paths in language and education in our changing world.

References

Ahai, N. (1991) Literacy in an emergent society: Papua New Guinea. *Read* 26, 1, 3–13.
Arensen, J. (forthcoming) Literacy without schools. In C.H. Bradley (ed.) *Working Together for a Better World*. Dallas: International Museum of Cultures.
Barton, D. (1993) Literacy as a language issue. Paper presented at AILA 10th World Congress, Amsterdam, 1993.
Cooper, R. (1991) Learning to do linguistic quality control in the production of vernacular shell books. *Read* 26, 1, 21–6.
Curle, A. (1970) *Educational Strategy for Developing Societies*. London: Tavistock Publications.
Eliason, J. (1990) The production of literature: From A.T. to AT. *Read* 25, 2, 20–2.
Fasold, R. (1984) *The Sociolinguistics of Society*. Oxford: Blackwell.
Gustafsson, U. (1991) *Can Literacy Lead to Development?* Dallas: Summer Institute of Linguistics.
Hartmann, W. (1993) 'Let's open the doors to the world' – The international respon-sibility of mother tongue education in the 21st century. Paper presented at AILA 10th World Congress, Amsterdam.

Ordoñez, V. (1993) Literacy in developing countries after the international literacy year: New perspectives. Paper presented at AILA 10th World Congress, Amsterdam, 1993.

Smith, D.K. (1984) *Make Haste Slowly*. Portland: Institute for International Christian Communication.

Spaeth, D.H. (1991) *Development Program Planning: A Process Approach*. Dallas: International Museum of Cultures.

Spaulding, C. (1994) Community directed development through literacy: Fact or myth? *Read* 29, 1, 14–24.

Spaulding, P. (1994) Community directed curriculum development. *Read* 29, 1, 25–9.

Street, B.V. (1984) *Literacy in Theory and Practice*. Cambridge: Cambridge University Press.

— (1993) *Cross-cultural Approaches to Literacy*. Cambridge: Cambridge University Press.

Stringer, M.D. (1987) The multi-strategy method used for pre-school literacy in the Enga province. *Read* 22, 1, 3–9.

Stringer, M.D. and Faraclas, N.G. (1987) *Working Together for Literacy*. Wewak, Papua New Guinea: Christian Books Melanesia.

Trainum, M. (1989) Introduction to the shell project. *Read* 24, 2, 30–2.

Walker, R.W. (1987) Dani literacy: Explorations in the sociolinguistics of literacy. *Irian* 15, 19–34.

— (1993) Language shift in Irian Jaya, Indonesia: Toward the heart of the matter. *AILA Review* 10, 71–87.

Wendell, M. (1982) *Bootstrap Literature*. Newark, Delaware: International Reading Association.

Index